This book helps kids see themselves as characters in Jewish history. Rabbi Hantman has made American Jewish history come alive!

— *Rabbi Cherie Koller-Fox, President, NewCAJE*

Choose Your Path is a fun way to learn about American Jewish History. The idea of charting a learning journey by exercising choice will inspire readers. A fascinating book that will delight a wide range of ages and interests.

— *Rabbi Arnie Samlan, Executive Director, Orloff Central Agency for Jewish Education of Broward County, FL*

It's informative ... it's fascinating ... this book was good because I actually wanted to keep reading. I loved it!

— *The fifth-grade class, Bet Am Shalom synagogue, White Plains, NY*

CHOOSE YOUR PATH

Choose Your Path:

Adventures in American Jewish History

Shoshana Hantman

Sidney Books

NEW YORK

Copyright © 2018 by Shoshana Hantman

All rights reserved, including the right to reproduce this book or
portions thereof in any form whatsoever.
For information about permission to reproduce selections from this
book, write to Sidney Books, POB 1108, Yorktown Heights, NY 10598.

www.sidneybooks.com

To contact the author, write to RabbiHantman@sidneybooks.com

Cover design: Christina Mattison (www.christinamattison.com)
Interior typeface: Book Antiqua
Cover typefaces: Komika Title – Axis and Iowan Old Style

ISBN: 978-0-9913512-3-7

First Sidney Books trade paperback edition February 2018

10 9 8 7 6 5 4 3 2 1

This book is dedicated to my children,

Mollie Hantman-Weill

and

Isaac Hantman-Weill

Their paths lie open before them.

ACKNOWLEDGMENTS

First and foremost, I thank my husband and partner, Richard Weill. Not only did he share his encyclopedic knowledge of law, sports, politics, movies, the stage, popular history and culture, but also this entire book was his idea. *Choose Your Path* wouldn't exist without his loving support.

Many people granted me their advice and wisdom; they are listed in the introductions to the chapters.

I owe a major debt to the people's encyclopedia, Wikipedia, which alerted me to facts I never knew, reminded me of other things I'd forgotten, and pointed the way toward the interesting historical alleyways which fill my book.

Other online institutions filled with treasures are My Jewish Learning, the Jewish Virtual Library, and Tablet Magazine. Also I want to acknowledge the Jewish Women's Archive, the Forward, Jewish Currents, and YIVO. This book could never have been composed without these resources.

In the oddest way, I guess I also owe thanks to several racist, Nazi-type websites I shall not name here. They occasionally publish lists of the Jews they hate, sometimes causing me to exclaim, "Wait, *he's* Jewish?" and scramble off to add a new dimension to a story.

Once again, I owe this book's lovely cover art to the talented Christina Mattison. May her colors ever wave.

February 2018

CONTENTS

Introduction

This book seems like non-fiction, since nearly every character is, or was, a real person, and the events described really happened. The main character, however, is fictional, and that character is you. Maybe this is a sort of historical fiction.

America is a unique nation. Seen as a place of refuge and opportunity by its first European arrivals, it attracted immigrants from every country of the globe. Each arriving community influenced its character and destiny. The United States was created by the labor, ideas, values, languages, arts, folkways, humor, religions, and philosophies of its immigrants, as well as by its aboriginal population. (At the end of the book, a glossary explains foreign words you may need translated.)

If you're lucky, your grandparents, or other older folks, told you stories about what life was like in the old days. Maybe they also knew what obstacles faced their own parents and grandparents. They had a lot of challenges.

Choose Your Path is like a time machine. It allows you step back in history, to see what life was like for young Jews in America many years ago who—just like you do now—had something special they wanted to be when they grew up. So take off your shoes of today, and step into theirs of yesterday. The decisions you make along the way will determine how the story ends. Each choice could mean the difference between fulfilling your dream and having to settle for something else. And yet, the "something else" might turn into a welcome surprise.

In these pages, you are cast as a young Jew ready to offer your talents and skills to this country. Events of your time will affect your circumstances and your decisions. Neighbors, colleagues, fellow students, bosses, and even people you encounter by chance, may persuade you to leave behind your well-planned career to grab an unexpected opportunity. It's your life, your ship to sail.

1

People's lives are generally not predictable, and our life plans get changed – sometimes by our conscious choices, and sometimes by the impenetrable hand of fate. A chance meeting or a missed train may open or close doors of opportunity. We plan our careers, and sometimes they unroll as we predict; but often, something happens that brings us somewhere we never imagined.

Select a chapter that seems interesting, and its first page will tell you where you are in the United States, and when your career begins. At the bottom of that page, you're presented with several choices, and you must make a decision. When you decide, turn to the page indicated. You'll be led to the resulting situation, and asked to make another choice. After several more, you'll reach a resolution of your career path (marked with ✿). If you don't like it, go back to the beginning and make different choices. (This is not exactly like real life.)

Each chapter introduces a number of Jewish Americans who have added something unique to our nation's character. Before each chapter, they are listed by name. I hope you'll find some surprises. And I hope, too, that you'll become very proud of your people.

Shoshana Hantman

Chapter One

I Want to Be a Doctor

Jewish Americans, both native-born and immigrant, figure prominently in the field of medicine. Famously, many kids were encouraged by their parents, who wanted so badly to refer to "my son, the doctor." Medicine is a profession that assured security, if not outright prosperity. And if America ever expelled its Jews, which had happened so many times in Europe and the Middle East, a doctor's skills were useful anywhere.

And of course the prospect of relieving suffering is a motivator, too. Few careers offer such a direct experience of helping one's fellow human, preventing disease, or adding to the body of knowledge that promotes health. The practice of medicine can be an immensely fulfilling life.

As this chapter begins, you are a child in the Bronx, New York, where you were born in 1914. In your high-school Latin class, you might sit next to the boy who will grow up to create Batman. Depending on your choices, you may travel to Long Island, Illinois, Canada, Scotland, Israel, or the Pacific theater of war. Possibly you'll study at DeWitt Clinton High School or the University of Edinburgh, or work at the Hadassah Medical Center, the Walter Reed Army Medical Center, the Jewish General Hospital in Montreal, or the Chief Medical Examiner's Office of New York.

Among the Jewish medical professionals you might encounter are epidemiologists Albert Sabin and Jonas Salk, the Hadassah nurse Rae Landy, and the great Scottish pediatric surgeon Gertrude Herzfeld.

My profound appreciation to Dr. Andrew Y. Silverman and to Sandra Similes Mamis for their assistance.

It is the year 1926. You are twelve years old, and you live with your parents, two brothers and sister in a small apartment on Macombs Road in the Bronx. Your parents work hard in their grocery store, where they don't make enough money for luxuries, though your family always has food.

One morning your mother tells you that your little sister Rebecca has developed a fever overnight, and your father is going to summon a doctor. In a few hours an older gentleman carrying a black bag arrives. With this doctor is a young man who says little, but watches everything the doctor does.

You are worried about your sister, of course, but also fascinated by the doctor. He holds Rebecca's wrist for a long time, counting her heartbeats; takes her temperature with a thermometer; looks at her throat with a tiny light on a stick, and listens to her lungs with a stethoscope.

You know that only eight years before, a ravaging epidemic had terrified not only America, but the entire world, and killed over twenty million people. The doctor smiles at you as he removes the stethoscope earpieces, and you feel brave enough to ask him, "Does my sister have influenza?"

"Oh, no, no," chuckles old doctor, "Rebecca just has a little touch of sinusitis. Her nasal passages are swollen, so she's uncomfortable. It will almost certainly go away in a week or so."

You remember having sinusitis once. "So, do you think we should spray warm salt water in her nose?" you ask.

His smile grows wider. "That can be a very effective treatment. Look," he says to the man with him, "we have a young doctor here!" He tells you, "My associate is Albert Saperstein. He plans to go to the medical school at New York University. Mr. Saperstein, what do you think? Should this young person go to medical school?"

Albert answers in a strong Russian accent, "If you want very much to help people, and you love science, and are willing to work very hard, then of course you should go to medical school."

You ask Albert, "When will you have your own patients?"

He hesitates, a little amused. "In fact, I don't think I'll be treating patients at all," he tells you. "I want to find cures for disease. I'll probably spend my life in a laboratory."

That is really interesting to you! You want to ask more questions, but the doctor is standing up and Albert is helping him put on his coat. "I will leave this medicine with you, young doctor," he says. "Make sure your sister takes a teaspoonful three times a day. Keep her warm and don't let her tire herself. And that salt water spray you mentioned – I agree with your advice. It will reduce the inflammation of the sinuses, and make her feel much better."

Albert Saperstein winks at you as they leave. The door closes and your heart is pounding with excitement. Is it possible that you might really be able to become a doctor?

During junior high school you study constantly, especially math and science. When you are fourteen, you must decide which high school is best for you. You can stay in your own neighborhood, or, if you want to take the train every day, you can attend DeWitt Clinton High School in Manhattan.

If you decide to stay in the neighborhood so you can help your parents in the grocery after school, go to page 6.

If your parents convince you that commuting to such an excellent school as DeWitt Clinton is more important, turn to page 7.

It is 1929, and you begin high school taking English, German, Latin, biology, history and math. You work hard for your high grades, and you decide to enter the Science Fair.

You swab germs off surfaces around your school – doorknobs, desks, books, and even bathroom sinks – and grow cultures in Petri dishes. Examining them under a microscope, you draw color pictures of the bacteria for the Science Fair. Your classmates are fascinated – but the principal worries that people will think his school is unsanitary!

Four years later, in 1933, with the top grades in your school, you are accepted to the City College of New York. The country is deep in the Depression; money and jobs are scarce and nearly everyone is struggling. But City College charges no tuition, and you can live at home and commute to class.

At City College, you find that your father had been right when he said that you'll learn more from your fellow students than from books or professors.

One of those brilliant colleagues had entered City College when he was only fifteen. Jonas Salk is majoring in chemistry. During the summers, he's a camp counselor in the countryside fifty miles north of the New York City. "Everyone wants to send their kids out of the city in summer," he says. "Polio outbreaks are worst in warm weather, and it's more contagious in crowded areas. Those summer camps really save lives."

You graduate from City College in 1937, and must decide about medical school. Will you travel to Illinois to live with your uncle and establish residency there, so you can pay reduced tuition at the University of Illinois Medical School? Or will you apply to the prestigious, expensive Dartmouth Medical School, your old family doctor's alma mater?

If you go to Illinois, turn to page 8.

If you apply to Dartmouth Medical School, turn to page 9.

It is 1929. You have been accepted to the Dewitt Clinton High School in the West Side of Manhattan. It is a great honor and you're excited to begin, though the nickname of the neighborhood, "Hell's Kitchen," worries you a little.

You get to know your classmates, and are glad you decided to attend this high school. True, the area is a little tough – bad kids sometimes knock you down and take your money when you get off the subway – but it's great once you arrive at school. It's filled with all kinds of talented students.

Your best pal is Bobby Kahn; what an imagination he has! He creates fantastic stories with pictures. In Latin class, it's hard to pay attention because of Bobby's notebook: he's drawing heroes battling evil warlords. You are sure he's going to be a professional artist someday. You have no idea that, in ten years, with his friend Bill Finger, another Jewish student from DeWitt Clinton, Bobby Kahn is going to invent a great American superhero: Batman.

Your parents are enthusiastic about your studying to become a doctor. They believe you'll help your community, and make enough money someday to raise a family in financial security. They also want to brag about their son, the doctor.

Your grades are excellent because of your brains and hard work, and you are accepted to Columbia University. There, you work towards your Bachelor of Science in biology, and afterwards you plan to attend medical school.

You graduate Columbia with honors, the first in your family to earn a college degree. Several of your friends hope to attend the Columbia College of Physicians and Surgeons, and others think they'll apply to med school in Scotland.

To apply to a Scottish medical school, turn to page 10.

To apply to Columbia College of Physicians and Surgeons, go to page 11.

Your uncle Solomon went to Chicago after coming to the United States from Russia. His wife's brother had arranged for him to get a job in a clothing factory on Maxwell Street, and he has been working there for more than twenty years. He has invited you to come live with him so you can attend the University of Illinois School of Medicine.

Your uncle and aunt live above a street market in a poor Jewish neighborhood. It's crowded and noisy, but you feel at home because so many people speak Yiddish, just as your parents do. The smells of the neighbors' cooking – noodle pudding, gefilte fish, chicken soup and pickles – remind you of home.

The apartment is also near the medical school. Establishing Illinois residency is easy, and so the cost of your tuition is low.

Your professors are dedicated and talented, and encourage you to follow your interests. Studying epidemiology, the science of infectious diseases, you remember the stories of the 1918 influenza pandemic and begin to think about joining the fight against transmissible illness.

But it's 1941 when you graduate medical school, and you are very concerned about the Nazis in Germany who has been bombing America's close ally, Britain, and invading country after country in Europe. Maybe the right thing would be to join the U.S. military and serve in a medical unit; your country could be at war any day.

If you choose to do research at the Jewish General Hospital in Montreal, Canada, turn to page 16.

If you choose to enlist in the United States Army Medical Corps, turn to page 17.

City College of New York has prepared you well for medical school. You have earned high grades in biology, anatomy, and chemistry, and your professors assure you that your application to medical school will be a strong one.

You are shocked, however, when you're rejected by Dartmouth Medical. When you tell your high school friend Jonas Salk of this disappointment, you learn something even worse. Dartmouth's medical school, and many others, has a policy of "selective admissions." Probably because their trustees dislike Jews, they limit the number of Jewish students they accept. Jonas says, "A lot of them do this – Yale, Columbia, Cornell. At Yale they accept one out of every four white Protestant applicants, but only one out of every forty Jews. And half of the applicants are Jewish! That's why I went to New York University's med school instead."

You learn that Yale's medical school president has told his admissions office to accept no more than five Jews a year, two Italian Catholics, and no African-Americans at all.

"Nice!" you think grimly. But then you realize that, even were you accepted, the Ivy League medical schools like Dartmouth and Yale cost $2500 a year, an astronomical amount. You couldn't have attended anyway.

You could give up the idea of being a medical doctor and instead train to be an optometrist, dentist, pharmacist or other medicine-related field. You could enroll at an unapproved medical school, and take your chances on getting licensed as a doctor. Or you could attend medical school in Europe, where some countries don't have quotas for Jewish medical students. You decide to pare your choices down to two.

If you want to apply for a job in the Chief Medical Examiner's Office, turn to page 18.

If you want to attend the medical school at the University of Edinburgh, Scotland, turn to page 10.

In Scotland, the cost of medical school is much lower than in the U.S. And the University of Edinburgh welcomes your application and admits you immediately. In the summer of 1937, with money you've saved from working in a commercial chemistry lab, you book passage on a transatlantic ship. Your mother makes you promise to dress warmly in the cold Scottish winters, and to write every week.

You arrange to share a small flat near the University with three other medical students. Two of them have recently arrived from Germany, where the government of Adolf Hitler does not tolerate Jewish students in universities. These two young men, Jacob Friedburg and Werner Korn, are worried about their parents who, for now, are still in Germany.

In your first year, you take classes in physiology, pathology, chemistry and therapeutics. In the years that follow, you study child health, surgery, and infectious diseases.

Two years after you arrive, you hear terrible news. Germany has invaded Poland. Britain must act to defend her ally, and World War II begins. Some of your fellow medical students leave the University to enlist in the military, and you realize that there will soon be much more suffering in the world. You add extra classes to your schedule – you are determined to be the best doctor you can be.

Completing your studies in 1941, you must decide whether to remain in Scotland, possibly filling in for a doctor who has joined the military, or returning home to get your license to practice in the U.S. Germany has bombed Scotland several times already, and Edinburgh has been hit. On the other hand, German submarines are lurking in the North Atlantic, making sea travel risky.

If you decide to return home to the United States, turn to page 14.

If you choose to remain in Scotland, turn to page 15.

Columbia University's College of Physicians and Surgeons would be a wonderful medical school for you, you feel, as you could live with your parents to save money – Columbia is not far from the Bronx, and it has an excellent reputation for training brilliant doctors.

But the president of the college, unhappy with the large number of Jewish applicants, decided in 1918 to limit the number of Jewish students in the school; like many other elite colleges, it will accept only a very small fraction of Jewish applicants. You are not among these lucky few.

Your parents grieve over your disappointment, and come up with several suggestions. You could apply to Long Island University's Medical School; or, you could go to your mother's brother, your uncle Solomon, in Chicago, where there's a fine medical school at the University of Illinois, which does not restrict the applications of Jewish students.

If you decide to try Long Island University, turn to page 12.

If you decide to pursue medicine at the University of Illinois, turn to page 8.

If you decide to spend a year working and saving money, go to page 13.

Long Island University is in Brooklyn, too far to commute every day from your parents' home. Many nights you stay with a fellow student, enjoying the hospitality of his parents.

His mother, Deborah, is a member of the Hadassah Medical Organization, a large society of Jewish women founded twenty-five years ago, in 1912, to promote public health and train medical professionals in Palestine. There are hundreds of thousands of Jews living there, as well as a large Arab population, and many suffer from typhoid, dystentery, malaria, and a dreadful eye disease called trachoma.

One night a guest joins the family for dinner: Deborah's friend Rae Landy, a nurse in the U.S. Army Nursing Corps. She spent several years before the Great War in Jerusalem, helping Hadassah build clinics in poor areas, and training young people in first aid and nursing skills.

You learn that, recently, Nurse Landy spoke with America's First Lady, Eleanor Roosevelt, about the success that Hadassah has had improving public health in Palestine.

Deborah turns to you. "You should consider going to Palestine yourself when you're finished medical school. Jewish refugee children from Germany are arriving every day, and they need doctors. What a wonderful opportunity to care for the people who are building the Jewish nation!"

You remember this evening several years later, in 1941, when you finish medical school. When you read the news about what's happening to the Jews in Hitler's Europe, it's clear to you that your people must have their own homeland and be able to defend themselves.

If you decide to travel to Palestine to treat young Holocaust refugees in a Hadassah clinic, turn to page 19.

If you choose to work for Palestine's first medical center on Jerusalem's Mount Scopus, turn to page 20.

You take the civil-service exam and find a job processing chemical samples in a police lab in downtown Manhattan. One Saturday afternoon, you decide to go to the Metropolitan Museum of Art on Fifth Avenue in Central Park.

On the museum's grand marble steps, you see a familiar face. It's your high school biology teacher, Mr. Schaffmaster! You call his name and he recognizes you instantly. You were one of his favorite students at DeWitt Clinton.

You tell him that you've had no luck getting into medical school. He urges you to cheer up. You have other choices.

"Do you remember how excited you felt in biology class?" Mr. Schaffmaster asks. "But I was even more so. Every day, students peppered me with so many questions – and each question was my opportunity to open a door for them, into a new world of knowledge. It has been the greatest honor of my life to be a teacher. Perhaps this is something that would be very satisfying for you as well."

It's true, you remember – being in the science classroom was a thrill. You have never considered becoming a teacher, but now it takes hold of your imagination.

Your sister Rebecca recently graduated from the Hunter College High School for Intellectually Gifted Young Ladies – just a few blocks away on 94th Street. The following Monday, you take your college diploma to the office of the school's principal, and are scheduled for an interview.

In September, you walk into the high school and begin a long and honorable career as a biology and chemistry teacher. In the years ahead, your students will include Ruby Dee, a future award-winning actress, and Elena Kagan, destined for the Supreme Court.

You will inspire hundreds of your other students to enter fields of scientific research, engineering, forensics, and medicine. And they will remember you for the rest of their lives. ✿

You return to New York by ship in June of 1941, and it is a tense four days; all the passengers are worried sick about the German torpedoes. Your family greets you at the sea terminal.

Arranging to take the New York state licensing exam, you have a few weeks of free time to relax, visit old friends, and read the war news from Europe. Hitler conquered France last year, and Britain is alone in the fight against fascism.

One day in a Third Avenue deli, you notice a familiar-looking man eating lunch and reading an academic journal.

"Mr. Saperstein?" you say. He looks at you, puzzled. "Hello. You visited my sick sister in 1926, with Dr. Hinton."

"Ah, yes!" he exclaims. "You're the kid who recommended saline spray. Good to see you! What have you been doing?" You tell him of your medical studies in Scotland, and that it was he who inspired you to think about becoming a doctor.

He is delighted to hear this. "By the way, when I received my U.S. citizenship, I changed my name. Now I'm Albert Sabin. I'm studying viruses, especially the polio virus. Tell me about your epidemiology classes in Scotland."

A lifetime of friendship begins. When the U.S. enters the war in December, he joins the Army as a medical consultant, and you go with him as his assistant. You help Dr. Sabin develop vaccines for dengue fever and Japanese encephalitis, which strike many troops serving in the Pacific.

After the war, you go with him to the University of Cincinnati to work on creating a live-virus vaccine for poliomyelitis, the crippling disease that had struck President Roosevelt and tens of thousands of others around the world.

In 1960, the Sabin vaccine, injected into sugar cubes, is administered to 180,000 school-children, and it protects them completely. Polio is cured! Your career in medical research is celebrated. ✿

You remember a guest lecturer in one of your surgery classes called Miss Herzfeld. In Britain, it is customary to call surgeons "Mr." or "Miss," but there is no mistaking that she is a very talented doctor. In fact, she is the first practicing woman surgeon in Scotland.

This interesting fact, and her Jewish name, prompts you to send a note asking to meet her, and she is delighted to have tea with you one afternoon. At the age of 51, Gertrude Herzfeld has accomplished more than most doctors would in ten lifetimes. She is the chief surgeon at the Edinburgh Hospital for Women and Children, a fellow of the Royal College of Surgeons, and she has founded a school and a clinic for handicapped children. She teaches medical students, too.

"Did you grow up here in Scotland?" you ask.

"No, I was born in London. My parents emigrated from Austria. They lived in Vienna, which is a wonderful city, but the mayor hated Jews and would not allow them to work in municipal government. So they emigrated to England, and to study medicine I came here to Edinburgh."

"What part of your work do you love the most?"

She thinks a moment. "I get the most satisfaction when I help a baby begin a normal, healthy life. I see so many who are born with hernias, with orthopedic abnormalities, even severe cosmetic issues. I can fix these problems surgically. It makes me as happy as if they were my own children."

You understand this woman's passion for her work; it is much like your own. You ask whether you might study pediatric surgery with her, and she says it would be her honor.

In the years that follow, you learn not only medicine from Miss Herzfeld, but also patience and determination. In time, you become a renowned pediatric surgeon, and a lifetime of healing children is your gift to your adopted country. ✡

You have heard from a medical school colleague that the Jewish General Hospital in Montreal has recently established its first research laboratory, and is looking for project leaders. Investigating further, you learn that this Canadian hospital, founded almost a hundred years ago during a cholera outbreak, has a reputation for disciplined, ambitious research not only in infectious disease, but in many other forms of pathology.

But the Latin you learned in high school, which is so important in all the sciences, is not going to help you get around Montreal! You will need to speak French for that. Buying a "French for Travelers" book and a 78 rpm recording, you practice French for weeks before boarding a train to begin your new career investigating the role of various minerals in human metabolism.

The work is interesting and satisfying, and you are soon contributing knowledge about nutrition and diseases to the medical community.

And your terrible French accent is a particular source of amusement for a young lab chemist at the hospital, who invites you home for a family Shabbat dinner. Within two years, you are married, and begin a brilliant vocation in scientific research. ✡

On December 7, 1941, the Japanese air force strikes the United States naval installation in Pearl Harbor, Hawaii. In a terrible moment, your country is at war.

In peacetime, the Army had 1,200 doctors. But 50,000 more will be needed during the war, and you are one of the first to enlist. Before shipping out to the Pacific theater of war, you spend eight weeks training enlisted men with the first-aid skills they need to be medics.

You arrive at an aid station in the Solomon Islands, near the front line, early in 1942. Here, you treat soldiers who have suffered combat injuries, first giving them morphine shots, and then sulfa or penicillin to prevent infection. You administer injections of the drug atabrine to protect the men from malaria.

You cannot save every wounded warrior. But your presence so close to the field of battle means that you can provide immediate treatment, and you save five to ten lives every day. Many of those men are able to return to their military units.

Several times, you are flown to jungle bases in Burma on a Piper Cub aircraft to help evacuate casualties. These tiny planes can hold only one injured soldier and his doctor.

Part of your job is to prevent disease in the military bases. You learn fast about insect control, since mosquitoes carry malaria. Also, millions of pints of blood donated by civilians back home have to be preserved safely once they arrive.

By the time the war ends in August 1945, you've been promoted to the rank of Lieutenant Colonel. Like 550,000 other Jewish Americans, you've served bravely in the fight against fascism. You decide to stay in the Army, and are assigned to the Walter Reed Army Medical Center in Washington, where you spend the rest of your career developing treatments for battle-related injuries and post-traumatic stress. ✡

Answering an advertisement for a medical technician in the Office of the Chief Medical Examiner's Office of the City of New York, you are invited to come in for an interview. The assistant medical examiner who meets with you is generous with his time, and pleased to answer your many questions.

You learn that this office investigates thousands of deaths in the city each year, to learn what causes them, and whether they are natural or inflicted; this information is used in civil and criminal court. The work of this office also helps city officials form public health policies. Their new toxicology lab analyzes chemicals to learn whether they affect living organisms. In other words, they study poisons. The medical examiner's staff identifies human remains, which supports the work of the city's police department.

The Medical Examiner's office is a place where you can not only work to improve public health, but also help bring criminals to justice. It seems like a great place for a scientist.

A few days later, you are offered a job as an assistant technician. Your very first assignment is to investigate samples of drinking water in an area of Queens where a lot of people are suffering a bacterial illness. After just an hour at your microscope, you identify a coliphage microbe, and you guess that fecal matter has found its way into the water supply. A phone call to the health department sends an inspector to the sewage facility, and sure enough, a leak is found that's been contaminating the system.

A big success on day one! Your work has saved hundreds of people, maybe more, from a painful and dangerous illness. It's clear that this is the job for you. ✿

The United States has not yet entered the war when you graduate from medical school in May 1941, but it has been raging in Europe, Asia and the Middle East for several years.

In Germany, things have gone from bad to worse. The 1938 Nuremberg Laws keep Jews out of public life, education, and most professions. Jewish children were not allowed to attend elementary school. An organization called Youth Aliyah has been formed to rescue these children from the Nazis, and they are arriving in Palestine by the thousands.

The Hadassah organization sends you to their clinic in the youth village of Bet Shemen in central Palestine. Here, several hundred children, many of them refugees from the Nazis, live under the care of volunteers who teach them about farming and cooperative living.

As the doctor in charge of these children's health, you encounter a variety of issues. Many of the children are, understandably, depressed and anxious. Some have immune disorders, infections, and lung diseases. You treat them with the supplies that arrive every month from Hadassah ladies in the United States: sulfa drugs, vaccines, X-ray film, and bandages. It's wartime, so the children are on limited food rations. Hadassah is feeding 25,000 children every day, as well as providing free clothing and medicine to British military forces stationed in Palestine.

It's a struggle every day, yet somehow you survive the war and the 1948 struggle for Israel's independence. Your life is unlike anything you could have imagined back in the Bronx.

You realize that Israel is your true home, you meet a Jerusalem-born medical technician who captures your heart ... and within a year, you are a happily married citizen of the new nation of Israel, committed forever to the security of the Jewish people and their homeland. ✡

It is 1941, and you've just received your medical degree. You are committed to practicing medicine, but also interested in training other young doctors. When you learn that the Hadassah Medical Organization has recently opened Palestine's first medical center and teaching hospital, you decide to have a look for yourself.

After the Ottoman Empire found itself on the losing side of the first World War, its Middle East lands were divided among the victorious nations. The British were given the mandate over Palestine, and now that another world war has broken out, there are British military installations throughout the territory.

Since you studied surgery, you're invited to visit Hadassah's new neurosurgery department on Mount Scopus in Jerusalem. You're assisting in surgical procedures when, in December, the Japanese bomb Pearl Harbor, and the U.S. enters the war. You are asked to coordinate the distribution of the drugs and other medical supplies that American Hadassah chapters are sending to Palestine.

When you're not busy with that, you are helping to train the nursing students at the new Hadassah School of Nursing. The students there are learning chemistry, venipuncture, wound care and pharmacy skills, and you know their skills will be saving lives every day both in peacetime and war.

Both Jewish and Arab patients are treated at Hadassah's facilities, and one day you're astonished to see an entourage of Arab men wearing regal robes accompanying King Faisal of Iraq into the hospital; he is seeking medical treatment. Most of Hadassah's patients are Jews, but no Arab, poor or royal, is refused treatment.

The Hadassah Medical Organization is staffed by some of the world's most talented and devoted medical professionals, and you decide to stay there and help train the next generation. There are triumphs and tragedies as the new nation of Israel is born, and you feel you are part of something great. Eventually you move to an apartment in the neighborhood of Ein Kerem, where you marry and raise a family of proud sabras.

Chapter Two

I Want to Be an Actor

People in every ethnic group are driven to become performers. To re-create yourself as a character, and interpret a writer's words in a totally originally way – this is like a calling, something inside that doesn't let you be contented with anything else.

Fortunately, it's a calling that doesn't call too many, because an actor's life is insecure and generally impoverished. Not many Jewish parents, I think, encouraged their children to be actors. The world is already uncertain enough.

However, there was a strong Yiddish theatrical tradition brought over from Eastern Europe, and comedy has been a Jewish art ever since Mordecai and Esther. In America, many Jews became directors, theater owners, filmmakers, producers and actors.

The Jewish actors you may encounter in this chapter – which takes place in the really old days, the 1940s and 1950s -- include the Marx Brothers, Sid Caesar, Jack Benny, Mel Blanc, Danny Kaye, Gertrude Berg, Leslie Howard, Luise Rainer, Morris Carnovsky, Sanford Meisner, Luther Adler and his sister Stella Adler, John Garfield, Edward G. Robinson, Lionel Stander, Sylvia Sidney, Lillian Ross, Judy Holliday, and Kirk Douglas. The writers who gave them their lines are George S. Kaufman, Moss Hart, Lillian Hellman, Clifford Odets, Norman Ginsbury, Albert Maltz, Mel Brooks, Neil Simon, Woody Allen and Carl Reiner. And the directors who put it all together include William Wyler, Billy Wilder, and Lewis Milestone – though hundreds more will follow in later years.

My sincere thanks go to my theater friend, Jane Lamphier Atkin, and my Hollywood cousin, Elenie Mansalis, for their advice.

It is 1933, and you are ten years old. You live with your family in the Dorchester section of Boston, Massachusetts. Your street is squalid and noisy with the pungent smells of East European cooking and the sounds of Yiddish conversations among the Jewish immigrants of this area.

On days when you're not in school or playing stickball with your friends, you cross Blue Hill Avenue and roam around Franklin Park. Sometimes you and your friends visit the zoo there, and sometimes you just walk around looking at people and imagining stories about them.

But your favorite thing to do is go to the movies and the theater. When you have a quarter, you can go see a Marx Brothers or Laurel and Hardy comedy, or a thriller like King Kong or The Invisible Man. Occasionally, you see crime movies or musicals. If you were allowed, you'd see a Mae West film. But she's far too scandalous for your parents to approve.

On a really special occasion, your parents take you to see a performance at the theater. You board the streetcar and get off at Seaver Street, then walk to the Franklin Park Theater. Performances there are in Yiddish, your parents' language. Some of the plays are comedies, but some are terrifying, like *The Golem* by Leivick Halpern which features a rabbi who loses control of his giant clay monster, and *The Dybbuk* by S. Ansky, in which a young woman is possessed by a vengeful spirit.

You decide you want to be an actor. What magic, to take a script and create an entirely new person, a character, and tell a story!

You wonder which you'd prefer: to act on a stage, and see and hear your audience's responses to you -- or in movies, where you can't see your audience but have more ways to create the story.

If you love movies more, turn to page 23.

If you love the stage more, turn to page 24.

Movies are magic. As the actor Jimmy Stewart said, "You're giving people little tiny pieces of time that they'll never forget." You're constantly fantasizing about acting in movies, and wonder if there's any path that could make your dream real.

At the magazine stand in the corner store, you look at the latest issues of *Photoplay* and *Modern Screen*. Some of the movie stars in those magazines started out just as poor and unknown as you -- yet now are larger than life on the silver screen. Someday, you're sure, you will break into that enchanted world, and be a star too.

In high school, you spend free time in the library, reading about actors and directors. You join the drama club, and try out for every school production. You ask the teacher who directs the school plays to recommend movies with great actors. She tells you that, for comic acting, you should see *My Man Godfrey* with Carole Lombard and *Pygmalion* with Leslie Howard. For dramatic acting, she tells you to see Laurence Olivier in *Wuthering Heights* and Luise Rainer in *The Good Earth*.

If you prefer serious or dramatic acting, turn to page 24.

If you prefer comic acting, turn to page 26.

You spend every available moment reading classic plays of Shakespeare, Ibsen, Shaw and Chekhov, and also modern works by Eugene O'Neill, Lillian Hellman, George Kaufman and Moss Hart.

During the Depression, movies and theater are escapes from poverty and hopelessness. Theaters lower ticket prices to keep their audiences and continue employing directors, actors and production crew.

In 1935, to keep theater people working, President Roosevelt sets up the Federal Theatre Project. Fifteen thousand playwrights, actors, and stage technicians are hired by the government to re-open theaters, and to put on productions in schools, factories, even hospitals. Admission is usually free, and many Americans now can see plays for the first time.

That summer, your mother falls ill, and you're sent to stay with cousins in New York. You're on a train to Broadway, home of the Barrymore acting family, the Ziegfeld Follies, and vaudeville!

One night you attend Clifford Odets' play *Awake and Sing!* at the Belasco Theater. It's about a poor Jewish family in the Bronx. Interestingly, the names on the playbill indicate that the director and all the actors are Jewish. Morris Carnovsky, Sanford Meisner, and Luther and Stella Adler apparently aren't worried that anti-Semitism may limit their careers. Only one has changed his name to sound less Jewish – John Garfield. That actor used to be Jacob Garfinkle.

Stella Adler, playing the role of Bessie Berger, rivets your attention. She seems actually to *be* that character. There is no trace of an actress there. She doesn't portray Bessie and her feelings – she actually *is* that tortured, desperate mother, and after the final curtain comes down, you wonder how she will become herself again when she leaves the theater.

If you write Miss Adler a letter asking her advice, go to page 27.

If, when you return to Boston, you rely on the advice of your English teacher, turn to page 28.

One evening after the war ends, you're having dinner with your cousin Michael, who has just returned from service in the Air Force. He perks up when you mention that you dream of acting in films.

"When I was tail gunner on a heavy bomber, some fellows were making a movie about it," says Michael. "Major Wyler was the director. You've probably heard of him. He directed *Mrs. Miniver* a couple of years back."

Mrs. Miniver was the 1941 film that showed millions of Americans what it was like to live in London while Germany was bombing it. It had won six Academy Awards – including one for best director. "You actually met William Wyler?" you ask Michael, astonished.

"Yeah, Major Wyler. He enlisted as soon as we got into the war. Him and his film crew came on bombing missions with us. He's a brave guy. Did you ever see that film? *The Memphis Belle?* It was about our B-17."

You don't recall seeing that film, but you're impressed. "Mike," you say, "Would he remember you? Do you think there's any chance I could meet him?"

"Oh, sure. We used to talk for hours. Want me to write to him?"

You definitely do. Your cousin keeps his word, and a few weeks later, he calls you.

"Major Wyler says he's working on a new film for Goldwyn and they're going to start shooting in about two months. He says for you to show up on day one and you can be an extra."

What a break! You'll not only meet the great director, you'll have a part – a tiny one – in his next film.

If you decide to go to California immediately, and wait there with no re-sources for the film to start shooting, go to page 29.

If you decide to work and save money first, then go, turn to page 30.

In 1945, you are 21 years old. You now live with your New York cousin, and have a job taking tickets at a movie theater just a few blocks west of the famous Broadway theaters.

Any time a new movie opens in New York, you're in the crowd of autograph seekers waiting for the stars to emerge. One chilly evening it's the premiere of Billy Wilder's new film *Double Indemnity*, at the Roxy on West 50th Street. The film's stars, Barbara Stanwyck, Fred MacMurray and Edward G. Robinson, will soon come out to greet their fans.

When the doors open, the crowd surges past the red velvet cordon, toward the actors. Mr. MacMurray has accepted an autograph album to sign. Edward G. Robinson pulls his gloves from his pocket. He doesn't notice his wallet fall out. You duck down to retrieve it for him. The fans are noisy and the flashing cameras are blinding; it's hard to get his attention. On impulse, you call out in Yiddish, "Reb Goldenberg! *Do iz dayn baytl!*"

Hearing his real name, Robinson turns and sees the wallet in your hand; his eyes widen. *"Oy! Mayn baytl! A groyse dank!"* And he smiles at you and takes his wallet. He puts his arm around your shoulder, and pulls you next to him, delighted to be speaking his mother tongue. *"Vilst du essen mit ondz?"* he says. You're astonished and thrilled: he's asking you to join these stars for dinner!

In a moment you are sitting next to him in a long black limousine, taking you to New York's best-known restaurant, Sardi's. The famous movie gangster asks you your name, where you're from, and what you do. He seems amused and interested that you want to act in films.

"Well, you can sit next to Wilder, he'll tell you what to do," he says. The director, a friendly and honest fellow, offers you ideas for your career.

If you decide to accompany Edward G. Robinson to a war bond rally and afterwards accompany him to his next film set, go to page 30.

If you decide to go with Billy Wilder to Hollywood and be an extra in his next film, go to page 32.

You write a fan letter to Stella Adler, telling her how moved and inspired you were by her performance in *Awake And Sing.* You also tell her your hopes of becoming an actor. You mail it to her in care of the Belasco Theater, wondering if she will ever read it; she must get thousands of letters like yours.

Amazingly, you receive a handwritten answer a week later. She writes:

> *If you know that you can truly believe the reality of a character, not just pretend to believe, then I encourage you to follow your dreams. You should always play yourself – but remember that each of us is many different people. Find the character in yourself.*
>
> *By the way, I think you should look for community-theater productions that have roles for young people, and audition for them. Don't bother with school drama clubs. They are directed by amateurs who will only instill bad habits.*

You treasure this advice. You decide that as soon as you get back to Boston, you'll scan the casting calls and audition for kid roles. In the meantime, you will read everything you can find about acting technique.

The more you read, the more convinced you are that an actor shouldn't be *telling* the audience about the action in the play; the actor should be *experiencing* it, and this will create real feelings and responses. It is a totally new approach to theater, and when you've finished reading Konstantin Stanislavsky's new book *An Actor's Work*, you are fully committed to "Method" acting.

If you audition for the Footlight Club's production of "Viceroy Sarah," turn to page 33.

If you'd rather audition for a summer-stock production, turn to page 34.

Your English teacher, not surprisingly, loves the theater too. She also happens to run your school's drama club, and she urges you to try out for its next production, *Cyrano de Bergerac*.

For your audition piece, you give the speech from Shakespeare's *The Merchant of Venice:* "Hath not a Jew eyes?" As you speak, you want to convince the teacher of the injustice of your condition. Not only your words, but your voice, your face, and your gestures tell her that you are a human being like everyone else, and she must not imagine that you will suffer silently if mistreated.

It takes a few moments for you to calm your anger and pain: for a few moments, you have actually *been* Shylock. As you finish, your teacher, and several students who've been watching, applaud wildly. You have nailed that speech – and you have won a leading role in the play.

A month later, the play opens and the auditorium is filled with students, family and friends. Nervous and exhilarated, you give your scenes everything you have. When the final curtain falls, the house thunders its appreciation. Your fellow actors buzz with happiness backstage, as members of the audience come in with flowers and hugs. Your parents are so proud they're almost bursting.

You hear several people calling your name. Craning your neck to see through the crowd, you spot two people waving at you: the school's music teacher, and a school friend who's with his family.

If you push through the crowd to the music teacher, turn to page 35.

If you push through the crowd to your friend and his family, turn to page 36.

Buying a plane ticket with money borrowed from your brother, you arrive in Los Angeles in the fall of 1945. With no idea what to do, you decide to seek out the famous director who offered you a role as an extra.

Managing to get past the gate by claiming you were there to interview Mickey Rooney, you wander through the facilities of Metro-Goldwyn-Mayer. You carry a large envelope marked "WYLER." It's empty, but you're the only one who knows that. You tell a secretary that you have an important delivery for William Wyler, and she waves you to an office upstairs.

The door swings open as you knock, and you see several men in shirtsleeves, lounging in chairs with scripts in their hand. The air is thick with cigarette smoke. "Mr. Wyler?" you ask. "Yeah?" answers a middle-aged, broad-faced man without looking up.

"Um, my cousin is First Lieutenant Michael Kaplan ..." you begin.

Wyler interrupts. "Right, Kaplan's cousin. You're looking to be an extra, right?"

"Well, yes, but I'm not sure what to do till then."

"I'll get you something. Doris!" he shouts, "we got room on swing?" Hearing a muffled answer, Wyler says, "Go see Doris. You'll work on sets for a while. We start shooting October 15. Be there at seven AM."

"What film?" you ask him.

"Best Years of Our Lives. Now get lost."

After Doris tells you to report tomorrow morning to the 'swing gang' on a nearby sound-stage, you feel as if your career finally is getting started.

If you decide to celebrate by getting dinner at a nearby restaurant, turn to page 37.

If you offer to carry a package for Doris to Paramount Studios, turn to page 38.

After two months of working in an Upper East Side bar, you set out for Hollywood. At the Metro-Goldwyn-Mayer studios, you find out at which soundstage *The Best Years of Our Lives* will be filmed. You arrive on the first day of shooting and soon have a close-up view of the making of a feature film. And your parents will be thrilled to see you in a drugstore scene; you have no lines, but you can be seen clearly among the customers.

After that, it's easy to get jobs as an extra, once you know how to ask, and you make just about enough money for a tiny apartment a bus-ride away from the studio. Occasionally you take a messenger job, and one Saturday you are assigned to carry a message to the CBS radio studios on Sunset Boulevard. Several actors are waiting there to rehearse tonight's *Danny Kaye Show,* and the envelope you're carrying is marked "Lionel Stander."

You recognize the heavy-faced Stander because you've seen him in a minor role in *A Star Is Born* and as Archie Goodwin in several Nero Wolfe movies. He signs for the documents and asks you in his gravelly voice, "Say, you got a few minutes? The coffee here is terrible. Could you get me some coffee across the street at Sadie's? Black with sugar. Thanks!"

If you have deliveries to make, and don't have time for a coffee run, turn to page 38.

If you have a few minutes to fetch coffee, turn to page 39.

Mr. Robinson, unlike the brutal killers he usually plays in the movies, is soft-spoken and kind. He is also quite intelligent and speaks five languages besides English and Yiddish.

You sit near him at the war-bonds rally where he speaks passionately about the evils of Nazism and implores the audience to buy U. S. bonds in support of America's fighting armed forces.

When he returns to Hollywood, you go with him as an assistant. "My next film is *The Stranger*. I'm a good guy this time – a Nazi hunter!" He's played good guys in many films, but people always think of him as a growly-voiced gangster. He good-humoredly indulges you when you request his famous last line from *Little Caesar:* "Is this the end of Rico?"

Watching the shooting of the film is a revelation. The director is Orson Welles, whose first films, *Citizen Kane* and *The Magnificent Ambersons,* received over a dozen Academy Award nominations. Welles' camera follows the actors as they move between interior and exterior scenes, and you learn that these long takes are very unusual in Hollywood.

At the end of shooting, Robinson is reading a radio script that makes him laugh out loud. You see the title: *The Man Who Thought He Was Edward G. Robinson.* He says, "Want to go to New York? I'm going to do this for CBS. It's a riot. I play a nebbish who wants to be a tough guy."

It sounds like fun. A month later you're at the CBS radio studios on East 52nd Street. The program is *Suspense,* and in this episode the actor plays the opposite of his film persona, and he also plays himself!

One afternoon Robinson invites you to meet a friend of his. In the elevator going down to the lobby, he tells you that he's one of the most prolific writers in Hollywood, but is going through some difficult times now. "Or," says Robinson, "you can take these contracts to NBC and watch Jack Benny do his show this afternoon."

If you go to 30 Rockefeller Plaza to see Jack Benny, turn to page 42.

If you'd rather meet Robinson's writer friend for lunch, turn to page 40.

Billy Wilder is Hollywood's most versatile filmmaker: a producer, screenwriter, and director of comedy, drama, and documentaries.

He describes his current film, which is in the last category. "This is a War Department film for German audiences. We're showing them what the Nazis did to their unwanted population. The Germans recorded these scenes themselves." Wilder has a heavy accent, and you hear a certain tone in his voice. He sees your concern, and explains.

"I began my career in Germany," he says. "I left when the Nazis came to power." He gestures at the horrible images of civilians murdered during the war. "For all I know, those dead bodies could be my relatives."

You assist him as he edits *Death Mills,* learning how movies can affect people's perceptions of history. This film, and others about the Holocaust, will be proof that these atrocities really happened.

"Ach," says Wilder one afternoon, after a day of viewing particularly grueling footage, "too much sadness. Let's go over to the Columbia lot. They're making a funny picture there. We need some laughs."

On the back-lot, a crew is setting up a scene in a military-themed music and comedy revue. Some production staffers are standing in a group shrieking with laughter. As you approach, you see that the amusement is centered on a young man speaking, apparently in Russian, at high velocity. "Look!" says Wilder, "it's Sid Caesar! The pride of Yonkers!"

Wilder introduces you to Sid Caesar as his *"bon ami"* and the comedian switches immediately to high-speed French. It turns out he doesn't really speak any foreign languages at all, other than Yiddish; he's just double-talking in thick accents, throwing in a real word now and then. You patter the same way back at him, and he's delighted.

If you choose to learn comedy from Sid Caesar, turn to page 43.

If you want to return to New York and try to get into radio, turn to page 44.

Not too far from home, on the other side of Franklin Park, is the area of Boston called Jamaica Plain. There, the Footlight Club presents high quality amateur productions of well-known plays.

One cold January day in 1938, you arrive at Eliot Hall to audition for "Viceroy Sarah." It's a historical drama by a British playwright, Norman Ginsbury, who has also translated works of Ibsen and Strindberg into English.

Your audition piece is from *Hamlet*: "O that this too, too solid flesh would melt." The play's director and the artistic director of the theater watch you from the darkness of the third row. They are quiet throughout your speech, and when you finish, they lean toward each other and whisper.

Finally the director speaks to you. "That was very impressive. Very impressive indeed. Have you had any theatrical training?" You respond that you have not. "Interesting," he answers. "Would you be available through March?" Yes, you reply, and you get out of school at 3:30. He smiles, and tells you to leave your phone number with the production assistant.

The next day you receive your very first callback. The director wants you to read for him – and on the spot, you're offered a part.

Over the next six weeks you have nightly rehearsals. You learn about blocking – the directions for where to move and stand while onstage – and about memorizing cues for your entrances and lines. You ask a veteran actor to help you learn an English accent. But you learn the most watching how the other cast members use the director's suggestions.

Opening night is a marvelous success, with a standing ovation from the audience, and many congratulations backstage. The director tells you that you *must* be in his next play.

You are in several more plays before graduating high school in 1940. Then you must decide what to do next.

If you accept a contract for a series of radio commercials, turn to page 44.

If you return to New York and study with Stella Adler, turn to page 45.

There are many summer-stock companies in vacation spots all over New England. Most have resident companies with well-known stage and movie actors who enjoy the freedom and informality of summer stock, and the escape from sweltering New York and Los Angeles.

In June 1938, you ride a bus to Dennis on Cape Cod. The Cape Playhouse is producing George Bernard Shaw's *Pygmalion* this year, and although you've missed the New York auditions, you think you might work on the set and learn something from the actors and directors.

After getting a morning job in a beach café and a cheap rented room, you arrive at the Playhouse. Rehearsals are already underway. Your offer to work backstage for free is accepted, and this leaves plenty of time to watch the actors and their director craft the production.

Leading the cast are Sylvia Sidney and Philip Huston, and you are fascinated watching them try lines different ways until they convey their characters' motivations. You also notice a young man watching the rehearsals. Frequently the director goes over to him to discuss something. You wonder, who *is* this person?

Suddenly it hits you. You have a letter from his sister in your pocket. This is Luther Adler, of the Group Theater, whom you saw three years ago in *Awake And Sing*. Sylvia Sidney, playing Liza, is his fiancée.

During down time, you introduce yourself and tell Mr. Adler how much you enjoyed his play. He's happy to answer your questions about his early years working with his parents in New York's Yiddish theater; many of his other siblings are actors, too.

Mr. Adler tells you that Stella is now working in Hollywood, but is planning to return to New York as an acting teacher. Might you be interested in studying with her?

If you want to take classes with Stella Adler, turn to page 45.

If you want to pursue acting jobs immediately, turn to page 46.

The music teacher throws her arms around you and exclaims how wonderful was your performance. You're surprised and pleased; you don't know her well, but she seems genuinely enthusiastic.

"I would very much like to spend some time with you, working on your vocal technique," she says, and you remember hearing that she had been an opera singer.

"But I'm not a singer," you murmur, trying not to get roped into something you don't want.

"That doesn't matter. You are an actor, and your voice is everything. With some training it will be a much more powerful instrument. Please, give it a chance. It won't be time wasted." That seems to make sense, and you agree to meet her next week after the play has finished.

Vocal training isn't what you'd imagined. She doesn't want you to sing scales. First, she makes you conscious of your standing posture; the way you've been standing, she says, puts a strain on your larynx. Then she has you hum in your normal speaking range, and move your lips around in a number of silly expressions until the humming makes your lips buzz. After a week or so, you're practicing changing the pitch of your voice as you say words. You feel your voice getting stronger and freer.

By your senior year of high school, you've been in every school play and even a few local amateur productions around Boston. Your music teacher tells you there are a number of options open to you after graduation, and she suggests several.

If you want to meet with your teacher's friend who is a talent agent, and start working immediately, turn to page 44.

If you want to spend some time studying Method acting in New York, turn to page 45.

Your friend tells you how much he enjoyed your performance, and introduces his parents. Standing with them is a lovely woman with dark hair. Your friend says, "And this is my mother's cousin, Mrs. Shalleck."

Mrs. Shalleck shakes your hand and smiles. She has a resonant voice and charming dimples. "You have a wonderful stage presence," she says. "You really stand out. It's a terrific production."

You know you've seen that face. Your friend says, "You probably know Cousin Lillian by her stage name, Lillian Roth."

Lillian Roth! Of course you know her! She's a singer and actress, and she's been in lots of movies, including your favorite: the Marx Brothers' *Animal Crackers*. You stare in astonishment and the first thing that comes out of your mouth is "Do you actually know Captain Spaulding?"

They all laugh at the name of Groucho's character, and Lillian Roth says, "Yes, I do. We're going out for some supper now; would you care to join us?"

You make your excuses to your family and join your friend's group at a restaurant nearby. Miss Roth tells lots of stories about the Marx Brothers and repeats the funny things they did and said – sometimes in Yiddish – between takes of *Animal Crackers.* They used to be the bad boys of vaudeville, and now they're the bad boys of film comedy.

Miss Roth has not worked recently, due to personal problems, but she knows a lot of people in New York theater. She suggests that, if you are serious about the art of acting, you should study with the Group Theater there after you graduate high school.

If you finish high school and head to the Group Theater, turn to page 45.

If you want to leave school to be a professional actor, turn to page 46.

With a few dollars in your pocket, you find a restaurant near Hollywood Boulevard and sit near the window. You see a young woman get out of a car and walk toward the restaurant's door; you watch her as she is led to a table. You know you've seen here before, but where?

Suddenly you remember: you heard her perform at the Village Vanguard, a jazz nightclub in Greenwich Village in New York. She had been an extraordinary singer, with a comic wit.

The maitre d' is speaking with her, and, as he leaves, you approach. "Excuse me, please, miss, but aren't you Judy Holliday?" you ask her.

Her blue eyes open wide. "Yes, I am!" she exclaims in her shrill soprano. "Do we know each other?"

"No, but I saw you in New York, at a nightclub, with Betty Comden and Adolph Green," you tell her. "You were just wonderful."

"Well, aren't you *so* nice!" she exclaims, her voice even higher. "Listen, my dinner date just cancelled. Would you care to join me?"

Of course you would. Judy is so pleased that you recognized her, and she tells you about her work. She's just done a play at the Belasco Theatre, and will soon return to Broadway in *Born Yesterday*.

You ask her about her unusual last name. "Oh, I translated it from my real name -- Judy Tuvim. That's Hebrew," she explains. "They say audiences prefer American-sounding names."

Judy Holliday is warm and friendly, and giving you her phone number, asks you to call and tell her how your career is going.

You guard that phone number carefully and start working next day on the Goldwyn soundstage. It's hard work, early in the morning and late at night. In October you report to Mr. Wyler's set and are cast as an extra. With no lines, all you have to do is sit at a drugstore counter drinking soda.

Go to page 41.

While you're leaving Paramount Studios after delivering a package, an intense-looking, pale young man holding a script calls out to you. ""Hey! Can you give me some lines?" This is as close to acting as you're going to get today, so you consent. He hands you the script and shows you where to start.

"What's she like, Walter?" you read your line to him. "Beautiful. I'm married," he answers, looking you keenly in the eye.

You feel unsettled by the blond man's intensity. "I know. I know, you've done all right," you read back.

"I guess so. And you, what have you done?" You sense an undercurrent of pain and desperation in his tone. This is no ordinary actor. The two of you continue to the end of the scene, and at several points he holds up his hand to stop you, thinks about his character, and revises his delivery.

"Thanks! That was real nice of you," he says. He tells you this is his first film: *The Strange Love of Martha Ivers.*

Before he joined the Navy at the start of World War II, he was Izzy Demsky; but he's now taken the professional name Kirk Douglas. While he was saying his lines, you were struck by the naturalness of his acting and the strength of his personality. He's friendly and unpretentious, and interested to hear about your own ambitions.

Watching Douglas on the set seems more interesting than running messages, so you find a spot on the soundstage where you won't be in the way. He introduces you to the director, Lewis Milestone, who's from Kishinev, Russia, your parents' birthplace.

"My friend here was reading the script with me, and doing very well," Douglas tells Milestone. "Really?" the director responds. "Stick around, I have a few smaller roles that aren't cast yet."

You end up with a speaking part, a small one, in the film, and are asked to come back for Milestone's next casting call. It is the first of many. Eventually you build a reputation as a stock actor, and end up working almost constantly in Hollywood. It's happened. You're 'in the movies.' ✿

Mr. Stander takes off his reading glasses when you return with his coffee, puts down his papers and invites you to sit with him. "You an actor?" he asks. You say you're looking for film work.

"You're in the Guild?" No, you say, you haven't joined the union. "Join the Guild. You'll get work, if you're any good," he says.

"Take the pledge!" advises a passing technician. Stander growls.

You ask what that was about. "The Screen Actors Guild is going to require members take a non-Communist pledge," he answers. "It'll be a disaster. People are losing work because of their politics. It's un-American. This is supposed to be a free country."

This seems outrageous. "Isn't there any way around it?" you ask.

"Not for actors. Writers can use a fake name; but we can't use a fake face. I'll probably go back to stage work. Actor's Equity isn't going along with this nonsense. Hey, read something for me."

You read a script with him, and he likes how you build your character. He's contracted to produce a play off-Broadway and he has a part for you. You think about it. This is a dangerous atmosphere, where artists who believe society should be founded on economic equality are being starved. You'll need a protector, even one who himself is being targeted.

You work with Stander on his new play, and later in summer stock. Many are afraid to employ him, but his recommendations are powerful, and you find work in experimental theater and road shows. In 1953 you are riveted by Stander's fearless lecturing of the House Un-American Activities Committee. Asked if he knows anyone who wants to subvert American values, he answers,

"I know of a group of fanatics who are trying to undermine the Constitution by depriving artists and others of life, liberty, and the pursuit of happiness without due process of law ... And these people are engaged in the conspiracy to undermine our very fundamental American concepts."

Stander's bravery is inspiring. You both go to Europe where actors work freely, and have notable careers in avant-garde films. ✿

A gentle-looking, heavy-lipped man reading a newspaper is sitting alone at a table in Eisenberg's Sandwich Shop on Fifth Avenue. At your approach, Albert Maltz stands to shake hands.

"Albert worked on the screenplay for *The Red House*,'" Robinson tells you as you sit down and pick up menus. "He invents wonderful characters. Noble, strong characters."

Maltz shrugs in a melancholy way. Despite his talent, he is not a popular man these days. Robinson prompts him to explain.

"Look, I hate war. War is horrible," Maltz says. "War is always about territory, about property. But I never wanted America to make peace with the Nazis. The Nazis were evil, and had to be defeated. I believe that property should be equally distributed; I lean towards the Communists who are working for that goal. When Germany invaded the Soviet Union in 1941, I supported us getting into the war. I love my country and we were fighting the good fight. But now, this terror of Russia is nonsense. They're more afraid of us than we are of them."

"This is why Albert isn't allowed to work in Hollywood. They think he's a no-good Commie," says Robinson. "Hell, some of them think *I* am, too! They want us to testify to Congress and tell them who our co-conspirators are. But there isn't any conspiracy! And if we don't name names, we're blacklisted. Nobody hires us. It's a rotten situation and it's destroying a lot of good people."

Robinson himself is losing work because of the blacklist, and Maltz can't submit his scripts under his own name. This doesn't seem like the America for which so many fought and died.

After lunch, Robinson asks if you'd like to go over to the Copacabana nightclub and watch a new young comedian who's just come home from the Coast Guard. "Sid's the pride of Yonkers, New York!" he says.

If you decide to meet Sid Caesar at the Copacabana , turn to page 43.

If you go to Hollywood and work as a messenger while trying to break into film, turn to page 38.

During the shooting of *The Best Years of Our Lives,* William Wyler allows you to watch the dailies, the film of each day's shooting. The film is about American soldiers' and sailors' difficult adjustment to civilian life at the end of World War II. Those who didn't fight in the war cannot understand the experience; only the veterans themselves, including Mr. Wyler, can empathize with each other. You think of your cousin Michael's long silences, knowing you'll never comprehend his pain.

Standing behind the director, you quote Shakespeare's *Henry V:* "For he today that sheds his blood with me shall be my brother."

Wyler hears the sincerity in your voice. He turns to look at you. "You like Shakespeare?" he asks in his mild Alsatian accent.

"Of course," you answer, and he asks you to say the entire speech.

At the end of your recital, the director is silent for a moment. "Very convincing," he finally says, "very convincing. What's your name again?"

Wyler likes your voice and particularly your ability to listen. He says that understanding the other characters is a very important step in creating a character. He brings you along when he starts shooting his next film, and you are thrilled to meet brilliant actors like Ralph Richardson and Audrey Hepburn.

Although you never become a big star, you play many minor roles, working with talented directors. You feel lucky that you live in the world of your dreams – Hollywood. ✡

Jack Benny's show is broadcast at NBC's Radio City studios at 30 Rockefeller Plaza. As you open the door, you hear shouting.

"Well, call the writers back to take out his lines!" a producer is yelling. "Can't," says another, "Sam's home with his sick kid and Arnie's not answering his phone."

A hassled-looking man in shirtsleeves turns to look at you speculatively. "Hey!" he says, "can you do an impression of Peter Lorre?" Of course you can. In a wheedling German accent, you whine, "It wasn't me, I swear! It's my knife but I didn't do it!"

He grabs your arm, and he snatches someone's script and thrusts it at you. "Tonight's show is a sendup of *Casablanca*. Peter's stuck in some airport. You can handle these lines, right?"

Eddie Anderson, who has overheard, puts a friendly hand on your shoulder. "Sure you can. Nothing to it," he promises. Then Jack Benny himself strolls over. "Is this our new Peter Lorre?" he asks. You nod speechlessly, and Jack smiles at you. "You haven't got a *thing* to worry about. We're gonna have some fun with this script! Have you had dinner yet? Eddie, let's run through the lines together and then go out for dinner."

Unbelievable! You're about to appear with two of radio's biggest names – Jack Benny and Rochester. At dinner, Jack is warm and attentive, and his assurances calm you considerably. Despite his reputation as a cheapskate, he tips the waiter generously.

Your lines during the program go well, and you even get some laughs from the comedy pros. Most significantly, you attract the attention of a round-faced actor named Mel Blanc. You've heard his voice hundreds of times: he is Bugs Bunny, Daffy Duck, Woody Woodpecker. Today, he's Jack's old wheezing Maxwell car. He likes your voice and offers to teach you some tricks. In the next few months, you learn to impersonate a crying baby, a barking dog, an angry crowd, and lots of other useful sounds.

Soon, you are known as a talented voice artist, and get so many job offers that you can't take them all. Thank you, Mel Blanc! ✡

"Are you from Yonkers?" you ask the comedian. "My uncle lives there – he works in a carpet factory. His name's Jack Weintraub."

"Jack Weintraub?" exclaims Caesar. "Jack and Bessie? Sure I know them. They used to come into my parents' luncheonette all the time. Best audience I ever had. Your uncle and aunt, eh?"

Caesar is a sketch comedian, performing from a script but also improvising. As a child, he listened his parents' customers and imitated their foreign accents, entertaining them with hilarious, meaningless speeches. This, and his skills as a saxophonist, launched a career in the Catskills resorts and the revue stage.

After making one more movie and then a Broadway variety show, Caesar returns to New York for a stint at the Copacabana nightclub. He likes you, thinks you're quick and funny, and asks if you want to get into television. You do, and you help him rehearse sketches while he waits for the other performers to arrive for the *Texaco Star Theater* broadcasts.

Several years later, you follow him to his first NBC series, sponsored by the Admiral appliance company. You appear in minor roles in a few sketches – but in six months, the show is cancelled. Admiral can't manufacture all the televisions people want to buy!

Finally in 1950, Sid Caesar's most famous program debuts: *Your Show of Shows*, which combines an opening monologue, sketch comedy, and songs. You sit in on the writers' meetings, which include the geniuses of the age: Mel Brooks, Neil Simon, Woody Allen, Carl Reiner and Steve Allen.

Spending several years working on *Your Show of Shows* is like getting a college degree in comedy. You realize that although the funny lines get the laughs, many comedians work off other performers' straight lines, and those must be delivered perfectly by the "straight" partner. This seems to be your talent.

In your career you work in several comedy teams, both improv and sketch, and are able to support yourself with nightclub gigs and television appearances. Over the years, you meet and work with some of the brightest lights in American entertainment. ✡

Your resonant speaking voice and clear delivery land you a contract with the Procter & Gamble Company, which sponsors radio programs. Many of these entertainment shows are fifteen minutes long, with the sponsor's commercials at the beginning and the end.

At the sound studios of the Columbia Broadcasting Service, you read scripts that urge listeners to buy Ivory soap, laundry detergent and shampoo. Procter and Gamble sponsor so many radio dramas that people sometimes call the shows "soap operas."

Since the programs are usually broadcast live, you get to meet the actors. Your favorite is Gertrude Berg – you have been listening to her radio show *The Goldbergs* since you were a child. She tells you that she got her start writing skits in a Jewish summer resort in the Catskills. In the old days, Jews weren't permitted to stay in most vacation resorts, so a few entrepreneurs built their own.

Gertrude plays Molly Goldberg, the "Yiddische mama" of a family of immigrants from the Bronx. Their day-to-day situations are familiar to millions of first-generation Americans, and Gertrude is one of the most successful radio writer-performers in the country.

She takes a shine to you, also, and after your commercial contract runs out, she asks you to be her assistant and to take on occasional roles on *The Goldbergs*. In a few years, you work with her on her Broadway adaptation *Me and Molly*. You are seen there by so many theater people that you begin receiving offers of stage work.

Radio has brought you back to the theater world you love, and you enjoy a fulfilling career as an actor and even, occasionally, as a director. You have opportunities to mentor other aspiring performers, which, in many ways, is the sweetest pleasure of all. ✡

When you arrive in New York, you wait tables in a restaurant during the day and see as many plays as you can afford. Listening to theater talk in lobbies during intermission, you learn that the New School in lower Manhattan is about to start a Dramatic Workshop, and that Stella Adler will be a member of the faculty.

Socking away every extra dime, you prepare to be a student again. At the New School, you hear many German and East European accents. The university is crowded with Jewish academics who have fled the onslaught of the Nazis, and found a home here in New York, teaching appreciative students.

When Miss Adler arrives and her classes begin, you are fully enveloped in the work of creating yourself as an actor. You find you must leave some old habits behind. For example, she teaches you not to remember your personal experiences to help you in a role. Instead, you must study a scene's circumstances as your character, who may be a very different person. What you do onstage must reflect the character's own choices, not your own.

You are struck by how completely Miss Adler believes in her characters. A favorite story about her is when her character was supposed to take a gun from a drawer and shoot someone on stage. When she opened the drawer, there was no gun. So she whirled around, pointed her finger and shouted "Bang!" Her recollection of this moment was that the audience, and the cast, were so captured by the reality of her character that they never noticed that there was no gun.

After several years, you feel you have developed the skills you need for serious drama. You attend auditions, and your utter conviction in your roles rivets both directors and audiences. Stella Adler considers you one of her most brilliant students, along with Marlon Brando, Judy Garland, and Elizabeth Taylor. She recommends you to several directors. Your career skyrockets and you become one of the most respected actors in America. ✡

Clearly, a stage career should be launched in New York. You arrive in Manhattan and look for an inexpensive place to stay. Eventually you find a very small apartment which you will share with two other people. Fortunately they are musicians who don't mind the late-night arrivals typical of theater people.

Breaking into acting requires a combination of hard work and good luck. Every week you buy a copy of *Variety*, the entertainment trade magazine which is like a Bible to film, television and stage people. In *Variety* you can find news, reviews, schedules for upcoming productions, and, most important, the dates and locations of auditions.

Keeping an open mind about what kind of roles you want, you attend every audition you can. You see other 'starving artists' like yourself, who will accept any role they are offered. You hope that casting directors will see in you exactly what they're looking for.

You get a small part in an off-off-Broadway play that only runs a week; then a better part in a musical that runs for several months. A reviewer mentions your performance in the *New York Times*, and you buy a huge stack of copies. The next time you audition you bring the clipping to show the director, who calls you back to read again for a major role. But someone else is selected and you go back to pounding the pavements.

It's all very dispiriting. One afternoon, you're in a restaurant, eating the cheapest meal they serve, wondering how to come up with next month's rent. In the next booth, a couple is discussing show business. You overhear one of them mention that an actor in a new show has fallen ill, and, as it happens, you know the play quite well.

You run to the theater, find the producer, and without any introduction, deliver one of that character's big lines. The producer practically drags you by the arm to a telephone to call the director.

Hard work has paid off, and good luck has kicked in. You step into the role that evening and give it everything you have. The audience loves you, and in the next issue, *Variety* mentions your rescue of the play.

You order a telephone for your apartment, because now directors are calling *you*. Congratulations on the start of a great career!

Chapter Three

I Want to Be a Cowboy

The enduring perception of the Jewish immigrant to America is a Yiddish-speaking, urban East European refugee. But before the great 1883-1920 influx of that group from the Pale of Settlement, another population of Jews emigrated from Germany, looking for economic opportunity.

The German Jews were generally of a higher economic class than the later arrivals, and brought the Reform philosophy of Judaism with them. Some stayed in Eastern cities. But others, with a pioneer spirit, struck out for the West, ready to build an entirely new kind of life. These included peddlers, doctors, teachers, and, yes, the occasional cowboy.

Some of the western-bound Jews you might meet in this chapter include businessmen Levi Strauss, Wolf Bluestein, Morris Loeb, Sol Spiegelberg, Bernard Lutz, Isidore Bush and Nathan Appel; abolitionists August Bondi, Jacob Benjamin and Theodor Weiner; politician Isadore Dyer; and artist Solomon Carvalho.

My thanks to the gracious Señora Diane Snyder Brown.

You are ten years old when your family decides to leave Germany and come to America in 1850. There have recently been protests and rebellion all over the German Confederation, and your parents are worried about the outcome. They are tired, too, of the confined life that Europe imposes on Jews. They want freedom.

You are among the earliest Jewish settlers in St. Louis, Missouri, where your father sets up shop as a tailor. A Hebrew day school has just been organized, and you attend for a few years before you get a job in a stable. You muck stalls, groom the horses, and keep the equipment in good repair.

The struggle for freedom is not confined to the past. At your Passover seders, while you listen to the old story of the ancient Hebrews' exodus from slavery in Egypt, you remember what you saw one night on the bank of the Mississippi River. Three silent human figures climbed down from a small cave in the riverbank, and boarded a flatboat that waited there. In the moonlight you saw a ferryman push off with an oar, and the boat glide upstream. Across the Mississippi is Illinois, a free state, and you know that these are slaves making the same kind of journey that your ancestors did.

You learn one day from your boss at the stable that a large convoy of Texas longhorn cattle are about to arrive at the St. Louis stockyard. He allows you to leave work early to watch the excitement. As you're about to leave, you receive a message from a neighbor, Mrs. Stern. She's asking you to watch her little boy while she attends a meeting of the Hebrew Benevolent Society.

If you pretend you never received the message, and go to the stockyard, turn to page 51.

If you decide that going to the Sterns' house is the right thing to do, turn to page 52.

In 1854, Texas Longhorn cattle were driven along the Shawnee Trail, which ended in several railheads in Missouri: Independence, Sedalia, Kansas City and St. Louis. There, they were loaded into railcars bound for markets in the Great Lakes and the East.

Arriving at the railyard, you locate the corrals by listening for the shouts of men and lowing of hoofstock. Leaning on a fence, at a safe distance, you watch mounted cowboys drive hundreds of exhausted cattle into the pens. The dust and smells are powerful.

The last of the herd is corralled, and the iron gate clangs shut. A young cowboy nearby, looping his whip on his saddle horn, takes off his hat and wipes sweat from his face. You bring him a drink of water from the pump, and he gratefully drains it.

"Hooo-eee!" he whistles. "I sure do thank you. I've been riding since sunup and finished my water a while back."

"Did you bring the cattle all the way from Texas?" you ask.

"Nine hundred mile, yes I did, me and the boys," he answers. "And Trapper here," he continued, patting his horse's perspiring neck. "Say, I never been in St. Louis before. Know where I can stable Trapper, and maybe get me a bed?"

You walk your new friend Tim to your boss' stable and offer to groom his horse; but, as tired as he is, Tim will allow no one but himself to care for Trapper. A cowboy's best friend is his horse.

You tell Tim that you, too, dream of being a cowboy, and he says the work is hot and difficult, and lonely too. But the pay is good, and if you love the open sky and the company of the stars, it's a good life. "You should get yourself down to San Antone," Tim advises. "That's where I'm from. Lots of ranches there."

Leaving Tim at the stable, you walk home thoughtfully.

If you skip dinner to lie on your bed and read about Texas, go to page 53.

If you join your family and their guests for dinner, go to page 54.

"Thank you so much for helping me out," says Fanny Stern as she pins on her huge, elegant hat. "Jacob won't be any trouble. Just let him play with his toys, and watch him if he wants to go outside. Oh, also, I'm expecting my brother Levi today or tomorrow; he's coming in from Kentucky. If he arrives while I'm out, please show him the guest room and tell him I'll be back very soon."

While you're watching the toddler gallop around on his stick-horse, there's a knock on the door. You open it to see a dark-haired young man with muttonchop sideburns. He politely removes his hat and introduces himself as Levi Strauss.

After you help him unload his luggage from the hired carriage, and take it up to his sister's guest room, you offer Levi some refreshment and ask him about his travels. Like his sister, Levi has a Bavarian accent, as they arrived in America as adults in 1847.

Levi plans to expand his family's dry-goods business to California, where a recent gold strike has attracted thousands of miners hoping to strike it rich. "Those miners will be disappointed," says Levi. "Merchandising is the only sure way to success." He'll sell tents and other necessities in San Francisco.

"California is an immense region," Levi tells you. "I'll need partners to expand my operations. You say you love the West; I think I will, too. Maybe, when you're a few years older, you could come out to join me. The wide-open spaces will be much more enjoyable if you don't have to worry about money."

This Levi Strauss seems like a very smart man. You think about the lives of the cowboys you've read about. They have lots of big sky and roaming buffalo, but really, very little freedom: they have to obey the trail boss, and there's no quitting if the sun is baking or your back is breaking. Maybe the life of a merchant would be more pleasant; and you'd still have the big sky and the mountains.

If you decide to find yourself some other western territory and maybe make a lot more money striking out on your own, turn to page 55.

If you decide to join Levi out west when you're eighteen, turn to page 56.

Texas is what your dreams look like. Formerly a Mexican province, it became the 28th U.S. state eight years ago, and its citizens retain a proud and independent spirit as their heritage. A land of cotton farmers and cattle ranches, Texas is the picture of American freedom and unlimited possibilities.

As a teenager you work long hours at the stable, using free time to develop your riding abilities. Sometimes your boss buys a wild or 'unbroken' horse, and he teaches you how to tame and train it, which is a valuable skill both on the open range and for cattle drives. You even find an old cowhand to show you how to rope, though you practice on a fence-post rather than a running calf.

When you turn eighteen, you bid farewell to your family and set out for Texas. Your boss is sorry to see you go, but he wishes you well, and offers you one of the older horses in the stable if you decide to ride the whole way.

If you decide to take up your boss' offer and ride toward San Antonio, turn to page 57.

If you decide to take a riverboat down the Mississippi and buy a horse near the Gulf of Mexico, turn to page 58.

Your parents' dinner guests are the Bondi family – Naftali and Marta, and their twenty-year-old son August, a sailor who has just returned from a river journey on a freighter.

August does not join in the pleasant table conversation, and you see a sad, haunted look in his dark eyes. You ask what troubles him, and he looks at you a long time before deciding to speak.

"My family arrived in the port of New Orleans at the end of 1848," he says in his gentle Viennese accent. "There, I saw what I wish I could forget. The slaves, dressed in nothing but ragged sacks, screaming under the whips of their taskmasters. The weeping mothers in the slave-market, parted forever from their children. I see these horrors elsewhere, too, in places my ship docks along the Gulf of Mexico. If I learned nothing else from the Torah, I learned that oppression and slavery are evil, and all righteous people must dedicate their lives to free their fellow men."

His intensity is riveting. You have never met anyone so passionate about justice. During the next few years, whenever he is home from his voyages, you spend time discussing slavery and abolition with August. One day in 1855, he tells you about John Brown of Springfield, Massachusetts, who with his five sons has moved to Kansas to support the Free State settlers who who oppose slavery.

"Look here!" August says, showing you an editorial in the *New York Tribune.* "The Free Staters are requesting freedom-loving Americans to come to Kansas. They are being attacked by border ruffians who want to drive out anyone who would vote for Kansas to become a free state. I'm going to establish a trading post there, with my friends Jacob and Theodor, and we will join John Brown's militia to protect the Free Staters. Will you join us?"

If you want to resist slavery without the use of violence, turn to page 59.

If you decide to join August Bondi when he goes to Kansas with John Brown, turn to page 60.

You continue working several days a week at the stable, but for other days you find a job at a general store owned by recently-arrived Isidore Bush and his father, Jacob.

As a store clerk, you learn about the goods your customers prefer. Ladies buy needles, thread, lace, ribbons, cloth and clothing patterns; nearly everyone wears homemade clothes. Tea, coffee, tools and combs are popular, as well as eyeglasses, bedding, mirrors, and ready-made curtains from the East Coast. Occasionally, you sell a stove or a sewing machine. Penny candies in round jars on the counter are inspected daily by interested children.

Having saved your wages, you arrive at adulthood with a small bankroll and dreams of the West. You've exchanged letters with an old neighbor, Nathan Appel, who now freights merchandise in Tucson, Arizona, a twenty-one-day journey from home. You have enough money to ride the Butterfield Overland stagecoach to Tucson, and some left for supplies to sell to householders in the area.

You buy your $160 ticket, bid farewell to your family and settle into the Concord stagecoach, wedged between sacks of U.S. mail and crates of tools and nails. As impatient as you are to reach Arizona, you appreciate the stops at the relay stations or 'stages'; your muscles ache from the hard seat and the bumpy ride.

Leaving Missouri, the coach passes through Arkansas and into Oklahoma. The wild Texas prairie stirs your imagination; sometimes you see herds of cattle grazing, and the occasional cowboy. Your old dreams re-surface, and as the coach rolls over the Rio Grand at El Paso you wonder if you'll ever ride the plains. You listen to people at the relay stops, and realize that your German and English fluency won't be enough; you'll need to ask Nathan to teach you Spanish if you're going to sell dry goods in Arizona.

If, on arriving in Tucson, you look for refreshment in a saloon, turn to page 61.

If, when you arrive in Tucson, you immediately set out to find Nathan Appel, turn to page 62.

Levi Strauss tells you that the thousands of Gold Rush miners will need tents, and he'll make a fortune supplying them. After becoming an American citizen, he departs for San Francisco by boat in 1853. He says he hopes to see you in California someday.

One day, an engineer named Egloffstein comes to the stable to buy horses for an expedition. It will begin in western Missouri, end at the Pacific Ocean – and be led by Colonel John Fremont.

You are amazed! Colonel Fremont was the explorer who, with the legendary Kit Carson, had mapped much of the West and Northwest. Now he'll try to chart a course for a rail line to the Pacific.

"Do you need someone to tend the horses?" you ask, hopefully. Mr. Egloffstein hesitates; you are very young. You say you'll take no pay, and he says that with your parents' approval, you may.

A month later you are assembled with two dozen others, including Fremont, a distinguished Mexican War soldier and former senator, in Independence, Missouri. As you ride northwest on the Spanish Trail toward the Rocky Mountains, you strike up with an interesting man named Solomon Carvalho. He's an artist and photographer hired to record the journey. Born in Charleston, South Carolina, Carvalho is an Orthodox Jew of Portuguese descent. By trade a portrait painter, he has now taken an interest in the recently-invented daguerreotype process of recording images.

As you cross the Continental Divide toward central Utah, the snow and bitter cold are oppressive. Food becomes scarce and one by one, the horses are shot and eaten. The party is forced to leave behind some of their equipment; Carvalho buries his precious cameras. Finally, lame, exhausted, and starving, the expedition straggles into the Mormon settlement at Parowan.

If you have had enough of this difficult expedition, and want to wait here till spring, and then ride to California, turn to page 63.

If you want to continue riding with Fremont, turn to page 64.

Your boss' parting gift is an eleven-year-old buckskin mare named Belissa; you and she are old friends, and she does not object to being loaded with your possessions and ridden out of town one crisp September morning.

You travel through Springfield, Missouri, the Indian settlement at Tulsa, and the bustling cattle town of Fort Worth. When night falls on the prairie, you set up camp, and heat beans and dried beef over your fire, and sleep in your bedroll. When you find yourself in a town, you look for a Jewish community and are always invited to share home hospitality.

You arrive in San Antonio to find a town rebuilding itself after the destructive Mexican War. On every street, men are building houses, and carts are hauling goods and supplies. You find a house with a sign in the window offering a room to rent, knock on the door and are greeted by Señora San Miguel. Five silver dollars buys you two weeks' room and board.

Dinner is served in the modest dining room. A crucifix hangs on the wall, and portraits of Catholic saints are everywhere. Before bringing out a huge dish of beef stew, the lady pauses to light two candles on a table in the rear of the house. This seems strange; the candles don't seem to serve any purpose. You search through your Spanish phrase book and finally ask her, "Por que las velas?"

She smiles at you. "Hoy es viernes. Es la tradición de mi familia. No sé la razón."

Lighting candles because it's Friday? This would make sense in a Jewish home. But the San Miguel family is clearly Catholic. You ask no more questions, but converse sociably with the children, who try to teach you more Spanish. After the meal, they invite you to their small garden, where a flimsy wooden hut stands, decorated with grape clusters. "Por que?" you ask, pointing. "Es la primera luna llena del otoño," they tell you, and after paging through your phrasebook, you understand the hut is there because it's the first full moon of autumn.

Turn to page 65.

Saying goodbye to your family, with your entire savings rolled up in your pocket, you stand at the port of St. Louis watching bales of cotton being loaded onto the steamboat *Natchez V.* In a crowd of hundreds of fine gentlemen and ladies, laborers, immigrants, and tourists, you board Captain Leathers' vessel for the voyage down the mighty Mississippi, all the way to the Gulf of Mexico.

At the great port of New Orleans, you disembark and begin your search for a good horse to take you west to Texas. But first you glimpse a dreadful sight; in the domed rotunda of the St. Louis Hotel, dozens of humans are being sold as slaves. The luxurious hotel contrasts starkly with the suffering of the Africans, as they are separated from their families and doomed to lives of misery and pain. The sobering memory does not leave your mind, as you ride the long journey toward Galveston.

You rent a room with a merchant's family and learn what you can about Galveston. The city has many German residents, including Jews, as well as Mexicans, and they have recently elected Michael Seeligson as their mayor. Though Texas is a slave state, you find strong anti-slavery feelings among these people, and after making some new acquaintances, you come to a decision. You will postpone looking for ranch work until you have done everything you can to help fugitive slaves escape to Mexico.

A city alderman named Isadore Dyer is among your new friends. Like many Galveston immigrants, he is anti-slavery, and he tells you in strictest confidence the address of a local woman who helps slaves reach freedom. Until 1861, when you join the Union Army, you ferry runaways to boats bound for Matamoros, Mexico. You know it's the most important thing you'll ever do.

After the Civil War ends, you and several other former soldiers buy a farm near Beaumont and begin growing rice. When oil is discovered on your property in 1901, you are able to transition to a comfortable retirement, supporting the arts in Beaumont, and working with Wolf Bluestein and Morris Loeb to build the town's first synagogue at Broadway and Willow Streets. ✿

When you tell August you don't wish to fight, he says there's another way to fulfill the Divine mandate to liberate the oppressed.

He tells you of a network of white abolitionists, freeborn and freed slaves, and Native Americans, who help runaway slaves move between safe houses on the way to free states and British North America, north of the 49th parallel. It is dangerous work, and must be done in absolute secrecy, usually at night. Capture will mean hanging for you, and savage beatings for the slaves.

You think about being a cowboy. More than anything, cowboys love adventure and freedom. But right here in Missouri, there are people with miserable lives and little hope of freedom. Justice for them is more important than a life of driving cattle to stockyards.

You are sent to a farmhouse a few miles north, where the Missouri River splits from the Mississippi, to meet an abolitionist woman named Sarah. Her barn is a 'safe house' where she takes care of fugitives and tells them the next stage of their journey; she needs a messenger to let the next station know who was about to arrive.

On this particular route, fugitives cross both rivers by night into Illinois, and continue through Springfield up to Lake Michigan where boats take them across. You are receiving instructions from Sarah at nightfall, when two men, a woman and a small child approach. Frightened and tired, they need water and a place to hide.

You squat to talk to the terrified child and reassure him that, if he's quiet and brave, his family will soon be free in the "Promised Land." He gazes at you with huge brown eyes, and finally smiles. You set off toward a church up-river, which has a hiding place under the floorboards, leave your message, and return to Sarah's farm, noting landmarks which will help the slaves find their way.

When the Civil War begins, you take the "underground railroad" route to Butler, Illinois, to join the Fifth Regiment Cavalry. You fight for the Union cause, to end slavery in America; and when it's over, you mount your horse and ride off into the west. ✿

With August Bondi, Theo Weiner and Jacob Benjamin, you head for Ossa-watamie in the free area of Kansas, where as settlers they are entitled to receive a land parcel. They bring items to stock a trading post, including Springfield muskets: the Border Ruffians who aim to make Kansas a slave state aren't known for gentleness.

You and the others join the Kansas Regulars, and soon the Ruffians pay a visit. They burn down your cabin and steal the livestock, and warn you to leave the territory if you value your lives. "Look there!" shouts August indignantly, pointing. "See those Federal troops? They're doing nothing, nothing, to protect us!"

But someone else is. John Brown has led a raid on a Border Ruffian stronghold, killing a dozen pro-slavery leaders. The battle is on. The next day, you, August, and Theo join John Brown's attack at Black Jack Creek, where Henry Pate's forces hold two of Brown's sons hostage. The gunsmoke and the screaming are hideous. During a respite, you ask Theo if he's scared. He shrugs.

"Sof odom moves," he quotes in Hebrew – the end of man is death – and he aims his musket to continue firing. The struggle continues for five long hours, but your side finally is victorious. Henry Pate is captured and exchanged for Brown's sons.

John Brown has an ambitious dream. He wants to establish a safe homeland for fugitive slaves, and several years later, he and his followers attack the federal arsenal at Harper's Ferry, Virginia, to obtain weapons. But Brown's attempt fails, and he is hanged in 1859 for treason.

You didn't follow Brown to Harper's Ferry; though you share his ideals, you can't support violence against the Federal government. The war begins in 1861, and you board a steam packet upriver to Keokuk, Iowa, to join the 2nd Regiment Infantry in the Union cause. You serve throughout the war, surviving dysentery after the bloody Battle of Shilo, and are mustered out in July of 1865.

Then you join an army comrade whose family is going west to buy a cattle ranch. Your dream of being a cowboy comes true. ✡

Strolling up Stone Avenue, you find a hospitality establishment and walk in. You find a place at the bar and order a beefsteak and a beer. While waiting for the meal, you look around at the tradesmen, ranch hands, and miners in the saloon. A prosperous-looking gentleman nearby catches your eye and nods at you.

"Just arrived in town?" he asks. You tell him yes.

"It's a nice place. I won't be here long, though. I'm scouting a few mining opportunities. Name's Sol Spiegelberg, of Santa Fe."

"Pleased, I'm sure," you say, surprised to encounter a fellow Jew.

Spiegelberg asks you about your plans. He's a good listener, and soon you have told him your intention to peddle dry goods, and your love of the wide-open spaces that brought you so far west.

"Well, sure seems like you have a solid background in merchandising," Spiegelberg muses. "If you're not committed to Tucson, maybe you'd like to try your fortune in Santa Fe. My brothers and I have a mercantile operation there, and we've branched into banking and trade with the Indians, too. If being cooped up indoors isn't for you, we're about to invest in copper mining, and we'll need someone to keep an eye on the mine operations."

This man strikes you both as a straight shooter and a shrewd businessman. He certainly seems connected to all sorts of opportunities. Feeling you cannot let this chance pass, you sign on with Sol, and within the month you're riding your big chestnut mare across the painted desert of northern New Mexico, inspecting copper mines and visiting Indian trading posts. You are as free as any cowboy – but you're not slowed down by herds of cattle.

During the War Between the States, you serve both your employers and the Union cause by conveying provisions to the First New Mexico Volunteer Cavalry. Ultimately you buy a house in Santa Fe and become deputy to Sol's brother Willi, who has been elected mayor. The West is now in your blood, and there you stay. ✿

Tucson is a blisteringly hot Spanish town occupying a flat mesa overlooking the Santa Cruz River. At Tucson's registry office, you inquire where you might find Mr. Nathan Appel, merchant. The elderly clerk says, "At this time of day, when he's in town, he can often be found taking refreshment at that hotel across the plaza."

Making your way to the adobe hotel, you spy two bearded gentlemen in the shade of the front porch. You see that one is your old St. Louis neighbor, and he rises to hail you enthusiastically. "I always believed I'd see you again," he cries, and introduces you to his companion, Mr. Bernard Lutz, who has set up a post to trade with local Apache Indians.

After an hour of genial conversation, you explain that you want to learn Spanish in order to do business here in southern New Mexico, and you recalled that Nathan is fluent in many languages. The two men smile broadly at each other. "We aren't mocking you, friend," says Nathan, "we're smiling because, just before you arrived, Bernard was wondering aloud how to find a bright and hardworking youngster who wants to ride the peddler's circuit down to Sonora and Chihuahua, and trade with the Indians."

Mr. Lutz adds, "If you're as bright as you seem, maybe you'd consider learning Spanish *and* Apache. I'd supply you with the stock and a buckboard wagon, and we'd split the profit. When you get tired of traveling, I'd be proud to make you a partner."

This is how your career as a merchant begins. Bernard Lutz is an amiable business partner, and becomes a lifelong friend as well.

And you still have frequent opportunities to ride the prairie and sling a gun. Nathan employs you from time to time to guard his freight as it moves between Tucson and Sonora. Slouched in the saddle, hat tipped low over your eyes, you think, "If my yiddische mama could see me now." ✡

The Mormon governor, Brigham Young, brings Fremont's party to the new settlement of Salt Lake City, where you will convalesce. After recuperating, Colonel Fremont retrieves the buried equipment and continues along the 38th parallel toward San Francisco.

You, Egloffstein, and Carvalho stay among the Mormons until you're completely recovered, and gratefully receive gifts of horses and supplies from your hosts. You ride together as far as Stockton, a supply center for the nearby gold country. Parting from your comrades, you find a place to stay with a member of Stockton's new Jewish congregation, Ryhim Ahoovim.

Obtaining a supply of cloth, notions, and household goods, you load up your horse and ride toward the southeast to visit isolated homesteaders. Some mining communities already have their own trading posts; you make the acquaintance of Henry Angel, whose general store gives Angel's Camp its name.

You visit the same customers every week. Most of them live so far from established communities that a shopping trip is near impossible, so they always welcome your visits. And they can see how curtains and tablecloths look in their homes before they buy. Your prices are lower than the shops', and you sell goods on credit, picking up payments during subsequent calls. For some farm families, you are the only outsider they ever see, and they eagerly listen to the news you bring of the wider world.

Soon you buy a buckboard to carry more goods and take the load off your mare. The investment pays off and customers start depending on you for a wider variety of supplies. Eventually you must decide: should you use your profits to set up shop somewhere, as most successful peddlers do? Or keep riding?

Compromising, you buy a home in Stockton and marry into a family lately arrived in San Francisco from Boston. But your shop will keep its four wheels. There's just something about those lonely pioneers that appeals to you. You will remain their lifeline, their confidant, and their friend. ✡

Leaving Carvalho and Egloffstein in the care of the Mormons, the expedition moves on toward the Pacific Ocean. You arrive in San Francisco in April of 1854, and Colonel Fremont files his optimistic report that a railroad will be able to pass through the Rockies.

It's not hard to find Levi Strauss & Company on a main street in the rough and boisterous town. His is not the only dry-goods store, though; there are others, mostly with Jewish names. Levi is delighted to see you and asks whether you've found accommodation and employment, as he wishes to help you with both.

You are appointed a purchasing agent, and have an opportunity to explore your new surroundings. The largest racial minority here are the Chinese, who suffer the same discrimination and violence that your own people experienced in Europe. Your position in this new nation is on the upper side of the power divide, among white people. You incorporate your Jewish identity into your American-ness, and your family's memory of oppression inspires you to help lift the burdens of oppressed people right in front of you today. Like your boss, you support local charities, and you set an example of acting respectfully to the company's employees of all races.

After you've been working for Strauss for many years, he shows you a letter he's received from a tailor in Reno named Jacob Davis. This tailor has devised a way to place rivets at the stress points of the pants he makes, so that they last longer. The two men patent the new duck-cloth pants, creating "waist overalls" that won't tear as easily as regular pants. What an advantage for miners, builders and woodworkers, and what a great use for Levi's tent cloth!

Business booms, and you're busy morning till night manufacturing and shipping the new "XX" jeans all over the country. You are part of a great American mercantile success story. And after you've banked your salary, raised a family and retired, you find time for your original dream: riding through the mountains of the Sierra Nevada, as close to heaven as you can be. ✡

As you stroll through the town, looking at the houses and their kitchen gardens, you see no other wooden huts either at Spanish or Anglo homes. The San Miguel tradition is apparently not widespread. The hut is clearly a sukkah without the name, and the candle lighting on Fridays sure seem like a Shabbat tradition. Why are these Catholics different from all other Catholics?

Trying to remember your grade-school American history lessons, you recall that the Spanish conquistadors started arriving in the New World in the late 1400s. Doubtless, their ships carried many sailors, cooks, navigators; could some of them have been Jews fleeing the brutal Spanish Inquisition?

You've always liked to think about history as if you yourself were experiencing it. If you had lived in Spain when being Jewish was a capital crime, what would you have done? Pretend to be Catholic, flee the country, or submit to the flames? Probably you would have escaped, as the ancestors of Señora San Miguel did. Over the centuries, without Jewish education or community, the religion was forgotten – but not all of its traditions.

But you came here to ride the range, and so you set about learning what cowboys do, and how to get a job. Texas cattle live semi-wild, and their brands identify their owners. Cowboys separate their bosses' cattle to bring them to different pastures, or, sometimes, to market. A customer in the nearby dry-goods store tells you about a ranch that needs hands for a roundup.

The work is challenging, and you make plenty of mistakes, enduring the jeering of more experienced cowboys. But you stick with it, and develop formidable roping and riding skills. Soon you're being hired for cattle drives several times a year, and the rest of the time you're training horses for this difficult work.

At night, gazing into the campfire, you think about the unknown Jews of Texas – unknown even to themselves.

Chapter Four

I Want To Be A Reporter

*The allure of America for most immigrants was its promise of equality –
an enormous change from the Jewish experience in Eastern Europe. The
U.S. Constitution enshrined freedom of expression as the law of the land,
a guarantee that no one, no matter how powerful, could prevent the publication of truth. This was more than liberation: it was an assurance of
justice.*

*Inspired by this sacred commitment, and with gratitude and loyalty, a
large number of these new Americans decided to become journalists.
They devote their careers to writing the first drafts of history.*

*The Jewish broadcast journalists you might encounter here include Mar-
tin Agronsky, Marlene Sanders, Daniel Schorr, David Schoenbrun, and
Howard Cosell; also newspaper people Miriam Ottenberg, Art
Buchwald, and Carl Bernstein; magazine editors Morris Schappes and
Kermit Lansner; photographer Alfred Eisenstaedt, and New York Times
publisher Arthur Ochs Sulzberger.*

*My profound appreciation to Jeff Lunden, Robert M. Campbell, and Kim
Pearson for their assistance.*

It is 1945. You are fourteen, and live in the Strawberry Mansion neighborhood of West Philadelphia. World War II has just ended. Dozens of your neighbors, cousins, and friends begin to return from the Pacific and Europe, telling war stories that astonish you.

When you begin high school in the fall, you join the staff of the school newspaper, because it seems like fun. You interview a new teacher and write a profile of him; you attend school board meetings and report on issues interesting to students; and you cover the race for junior class president. Seeing your byline, in the newspaper that all the kids read, is exhilarating.

By senior year, you decide that reporting news is a vital mission. People depend on news media to learn what's happening in their neighborhood, nation and world. If they cannot trust the information they receive, they can't participate meaningfully in democracy. Providing truthful reports is almost a sacred commitment.

In 1949 you enroll in the journalism program at Temple University. Attending at night, you also take classes in English, political science, business, law, and history. By day, you work as a copy runner at the Philadelphia Inquirer, the city's major daily morning newspaper. After a story's been written and approved by a copy editor, a bell rings and you grab it and rush it to the typesetters, who put it into columns, to be laid out on the newspaper's pages.

Your parents' neighbors are related to a television newsman named Martin Agronsky, now based in Washington, D.C. They offer to ask him if he needs a research assistant. He responds that he'll allow you to follow him on assignments and introduce you to important people. But when you graduate Temple, you're also offered a job as a culture writer at the Philadelphia Evening Bulletin.

If you decide to 'shadow' Martin Agronsky at ABC, turn to page 69.

If you'd rather take the job at the Bulletin, turn to page 70.

You can't pass up a chance to learn journalistic skills from Martin Agronsky. Last year, the National Association of Broadcasters honored him with the Peabody Award for distinguished broadcast reporting. He earned this at ABC radio by covering Senator Joseph McCarthy's persecution of Americans he believed were Communist sympathizers. You remember being impressed by his coverage of the 1948 national political conventions.

You take the train to Washington, and catch up with the genial Agronsky as he's about to leave for Capitol Hill. He invites you along. "Journalism is the search for, and exposure of, truth," he says in the taxi. "McCarthyism is the opposite. It's accusing people of subversion or treason without any regard for evidence. So we have to stay on this senator like a bulldog. He can't be allowed to create his own twisted reality and sell it as truth."

Senator McCarthy has dedicated the Permanent Subcommittee on Investigations to the task of exposing Communists wherever he imagines them to be. Agronsky says that McCarthy has a gift for manipulating journalists. "He'll make sensational accusations just before the wire services send out their news releases. There's no time to check his facts. So he's basically writing the reports for us. Reporters don't even try to find out who the 'card-carrying Communists' are! Thomas Jefferson said that the people should get full information from the newspapers. Any journalist who simply funnels politicians' statements is no journalist. And no patriot.

"Check everything you hear before you repeat it. Especially when your source stands to profit by hiding the truth."

You watch Agronsky phoning congressional aides and others who have access to facts, questioning them about McCarthy's accusations. You're invited to make some calls yourself. Soon you are learning how to find sources and check their statements.

If you accept an offer to fill in for a Washington correspondent of the Philadelphia Inquirer, turn to page 71.

If you want to shadow Agronsky a while longer and then work in television news at ABC, turn to page 72.

You were hired for culture desk, but the Bulletin's police reporter is retiring. You are asked to shadow him, take over the crime reports, and decide whether that's what you want to do.

Police headquarters, called the Roundhouse for its unusual architecture, is at Eighth and Race streets. You sift through police bulletins about burglaries, assaults, and street fights to find stories important enough to send out a general assignment reporter.

One summer morning you are returning from an overnight visit with a friend near Bryn Mawr College. A vicious heat wave is plaguing the area, and your car windows are open to catch the breeze. Passing through Penn Valley, you smell smoke, and follow the sound of sirens to a mansion engulfed in flames.

Edging as close as you can to the firefighters, you see a woman in a robe watching the blaze, hands over her mouth. You ask her what she knows. The woman, a cook, says between sobs that it's the home of George and Mary Bartol; Mr. Bartol is president of the Philadelphia Bourse, a commodities exchange, and his wife is a descendant of Dr. Benjamin Rush, who signed the Declaration of Independence. You scribble everything in your notebook.

You are questioning the fire chief when the body of Mrs. Bartol is carried out of the mansion. Mr. Bartol is rushed to a hospital.

Racing back to your car, you drive to the newsroom, park illegally and type an account of the disaster in less than ten minutes. The metro editor reads it, sends out a photographer, rings the copy bell and the story is rushed onto the front page. You have scooped all the other papers with the tragic story of the Bartol fire.

After a few years on assignments, you're promoted to assistant metro editor. Eventually you're offered a high-paying job at the Washington Star; but more and more people are getting their news from television, and you think that might be interesting.

If you'd like to be a consumer reporter in Washington, turn to page 73.

If you want to break into television news in New York, turn to page 74.

You find an apartment a few blocks north of Dupont Circle, and the Bulletin pays your moving expenses. You cover news from Capitol Hill, while another Bulletin reporter serves as White House correspondent and bureau chief. You get acquainted with congressional staffers who let you know about upcoming debates and votes, and can get you interviews with members of Congress.

In 1963 you go back to Philadelphia a week before Thanksgiving to spend time with your family. On Friday, you drop in to the office of the national editor, and are chatting when the wire service teletype bells start to ring. Three bells mean an urgent story, but the bells keep ringing. Five bells mean a bulletin – but there are six, seven, eight, nine. Ten bells is a flash. The teletypes keep ringing. You and everyone else run to the machines.

The United Press International clacks out the flash: *"Dallas Texas - Kennedy seriously wounded perhaps fatally by assassin's bullet."*

There is a microsecond of stillness, then everyone starts running to the phones, to the televisions, to the typewriters. You are reading the incoming reports on the teletype when the national editor yells to you, "Get on a train!" So you fly down three flights of stairs, cross 30th Street to the Pennsylvania Railroad station and catch the next express to Washington. The news has already been broadcast on radio; you see people crying on the train.

The body of the slain President is flown to Washington, and his Vice-President, Lyndon Johnson, is sworn into office on Air Force One. The next days are a blur of shock and grief around the country and the globe. But you have to control your emotions, because your bureau chief asks you to focus on Congress and President Kennedy's legislative legacy, and also to interview ambassadors and civil rights leaders about their views of Johnson.

If the excitement of the White House beat is what you really want, turn to page 75.

If you really don't like the rushing and the pressure of daily news reporting, and would prefer to analyze current events, turn to page 76.

After several years with Martin Agronsky, you have impressed him with your aggressive investigation style and concise writing. He introduces you to television producers at ABC, and you do several stints as as assistant producer, writing copy for anchors and maintaining communication with reporters. When Agronsky travels to Israel in 1961 to report on the trial of Nazi war criminal Adolph Eichmann, you accompany him. The testimony shakes you badly; it's difficult to separate your emotional reactions from the story you're witnessing. Having brought your Nikon, you spend spare hours photographing everyday life in Jerusalem.

At ABC you get to work with Marlene Sanders, a correspondent who previously had written and produced radio and TV documentaries. She asks you to fact-check scripts and pre-interview guests. Sometimes you obtain visas for crews working overseas.

Her courage is extraordinary: though the war correspondent has the most dangerous of all journalism posts, she insists on going to Vietnam to report on the conflict. She is one of the first women to do so. You hesitantly volunteer to go with her, but it's too nerve-wracking, and soon you return to the safety of New York, coordinating battle reports by phone. Sometimes you meet freelance and assignment photographers who have covered stories with her, and they tell you about their work.

The first time you see Ms Sanders in the anchor's seat, it's a shock. A woman has never presented the national evening news. But you realize there's nothing unreasonable about it. She's poised and articulate, commands every detail of every broadcast, and connects with the audience at least as well as any male anchor.

But the problem with a half-hour broadcast, you feel, is that even important news must be presented in just a few minutes. You want to delve deeper into the implications of events.

If you want to be a news analyst rather than a reporter, go to page 77.

If you become interested in bringing stories to the public with photographs rather than words, turn to page 78.

A rising star at your new employer, the Washington Star, is Miriam Ottenberg, who started as a police-beat reporter in 1937. Ever since then, she's investigated crimes committed by everyone from fake charities to the local car dealer. She's incensed by criminals who use the anonymity of businesses to sell faulty merchandise or overcharge for their services. She also reports on the federal agencies that prosecute them.

Laws protect the public from dishonest vendors and service providers. But law enforcement can't be everywhere, and consumer agencies don't have the staff to watch over every food distributor, appliance dealer and contractor. Sometimes, it's a news reporter who uncovers unfair or dangerous business practices.

Miriam asks you to help her investigate some phony home-improvement contractors. The two of you sit in her house, waiting for the shady businessmen to visit and give estimates for repairs; your job is to seem very simpleminded, and to operate the tape recorder hidden under the kitchen table. After they leave the house clutching deposit money, she transcribes the tape while you follow their trucks to learn where they live. Exposing their racket makes a great story, and it's a big help to law enforcement.

"A reporter should expose the bad and campaign for the good," she tells you over appetizers at the Washington Newspaper Guild's awards dinner. "That work can take many forms. You, for example, I know you're committed to telling the truth, but you also have a great sense of humor. Maybe you'd be good at political satire, as a way to inform people when elected officials try to obscure what they're really doing. Want to spend some time with Art Buchwald at the Post?"

But another goal pulls at you: providing commentary and reflection on the issues of the day. You feel news cannot consist of short summaries, but deep background and many points of view.

If you want to write in depth about national events, turn to page 79.

If you decide to learn from Art Buchwald how political humor can educate a more skeptical public, turn to page 80.

For several years you've been an avid follower of Edward R. Murrow, who's assembled at team of brilliant, fearless reporters at CBS. You send your résumé and some of your clippings to a producer, and you enclose your editor's recommendation.

The only offer is as a starting associate producer, basically a gofer, but you grab it. On your first day, you're told to pick up the Moscow bureau chief arriving at Idlewild Airport; he is coming home for good, since the Soviets won't let him stay there.

"It's hard to win sometimes!" says Daniel Schorr as he settles into the passenger seat. "The Russians don't like me because I don't cooperate with their censors. And President Eisenhower seems to think I'm distributing communist propaganda. So – here I am."

You ask him what he's going to do. He says, "Not change a thing. Journalists have the right to report the news without *any* government interfering. So people didn't like my interview with the Soviet premier; who cares? I'm not here to make them like me. My job is to uncover corruption. The military and the CIA don't like me either. I must be doing something right."

A million Germans living under Communist rule have migrated to West Germany, and hundreds more try to cross every day. You accompany Schorr to the border to interview the migrants, and sometimes split up to get as many stories as possible.

One professor tells you that he knows that Russian Communism isn't the paradise it pretends to be; dissidents are imprisoned and their families persecuted as well. A farmer reports that his fields were seized by the Communists as part of their "collective agriculture" program. Fear and desperation are everywhere. You write up the accounts and send them to CBS in New York, and Schorr films his television reports. In mid-1961, East Germany starts building the Berlin Wall to prevent escapes.

If you feel this type of reporting is too intense, and you'd rather try sports journalism, turn to page 81.

If you want to continue to work with Daniel Schorr, turn to page 82.

Your first task as a White House reporter is to relieve the Post's chief correspondent by taking 'pool duty' – when nothing's happening on the grounds, you sit in the West Wing, recording who's entering and leaving. Sometimes you stake out the White House lawn for hours, in all sorts of weather, in case someone important makes a statement. You share a desk with the paper's correspondent in the basement, and occasionally notice evidence of rodents.

You and your colleagues endure these conditions throughout Lyndon Johnson's presidency. Reporting on the President during the Vietnam War is definitely one of the nation's most important journalism jobs. America is sending more troops and equipment to fight the Communists, but at the same time, Johnson wants to spend more tax money on his War On Poverty, Medicare and Medicaid, and public broadcasting and the arts. "With limited resources, how will the President order his priorities?" you ask his press secretary, but you get no clear answer.

The war continues. A new President, Richard Nixon, takes office in January 1969. When the New York Times' publisher, Arthur Ochs Sulzberger, expands the paper's reporting staff, you're temporarily assigned as an investigative assistant in the Washington bureau. Early in 1971, you and some other reporters are asked to evaluate a massive military document that the Times has just received, and edit it for publication. It reveals that the Vietnam war was secretly expanded to include bombing campaigns against Laos and Cambodia; the papers also record the opinion of military strategists that the war could never be won.

"Isn't this dangerous – and illegal?" you ask Sulzberger. "These documents are classified!" He answers, "Oh, it's a risk, all right, for us, and for Daniel Ellsberg, who gave them to us. But it doesn't threaten national security, or the armed forces. All it does is embarrass the government. So they stamped it secret. That was wrong. The American people have a right to see them."

If, after the Pentagon Papers are published, you feel you need to plan a little vacation, turn to page 83.

If you want to accept an invitation from the managing editor of the Washington Post, to work in their Washington bureau, turn to page 85.

Many Jews in Russia had supported the Communist revolution in 1917. They had suffered so much under the Tsars, and believed Communism would overthrow the wealthy class and let everyone share equally in the work and profits of industry and agriculture.

The Soviet premier, Josef Stalin, had been America's ally against Hitler during World War II, but he turned out to be a very brutal dictator. He ordered fake trials, assassinations, executions and deportations of millions of his political enemies. The ideals of Communism were so violently betrayed that many of its supporters, in Russia and worldwide, were completely disillusioned. American Jews, who had thought Communism would bring an era of justice and equality, were shocked by the Stalin's murders of thirteen Yiddish writers in 1952 – part of his campaign to end Jewish culture in the Soviet Union.

You've been reading the political commentary in a quarterly magazine called *Jewish Currents* for many years, appreciating its critical articles about society from a leftist perspective. It used to represent the views of the American Communist Party, but broke away when Stalin's purges became known. You write to Morris Schappes, the magazine's editor, asking to submit an article about the Johnson administration and the escalating Vietnam War.

"I look forward to reading your material," he writes back. "When I learned you worked with Agronsky covering the McCarthy hearings, I thought, now there's a journalist with stories to tell. You know, I spent some time in prison for 'failing to remember' the names of left-leaning faculty members at City College."

You write some analytical pieces criticizing President Johnson's Great Society goals, and evaluating the American anti-war movement. *Jewish Currents* brings your work to thoughtful, educated readers who are re-considering their political identity.

They respond well to your scrutiny of political and social issues. You start receiving invitations to address conferences and advise social-service commissions. You're helping society clarify its values and goals during a chaotic time in American history. ✿

Since you've always wanted to travel in Europe, you rent a room in Paris in 1965 and work as a 'stringer,' writing analyses for American newspapers about France's efforts to unify Europe.

One evening you are having dinner with a French public-radio news producer, and she sees someone she knows come into the restaurant. She invites the middle-aged man to sit at your table, assuring you "This is someone you need to meet."

"May I introduce Monsieur David Schoenbrun," she says. "During Germany's occupation of France, when I was a little girl, it was David's voice I heard broadcast from Algiers. Listening to him, I had hope that my country would someday be liberated."

You coax the journalist to tell you the details. He served in the U.S. Army Military Intelligence, and posted war reports while assigned with the French after D-Day. Afterwards, he worked at CBS with the legendary investigative reporter Ed Murrow. More recently, he was the only American correspondent stationed at the French garrison at Dien Pien Phu in Vietnam. Now he freelances and lectures about Europe and Israel.

Recently you've been wondering whether getting a graduate degree in journalism might advance your career; you ask David's advice. "Absolutely not," he responds firmly. "Decide what you want to report on, and learn it cold. Get the history, get the culture of the institutions, learn the language. Then investigate the stories. The only valuable reporting comes from experts."

He has clarified the issue for you, and it doesn't take long to decide that your real interest is the future of the Western countries' alliances. You read the international relations journals and attend lectures and conferences, study French and German, and talk with every embassy staffer who has time for you.

When you have a firm grasp of the theories of diplomacy, negotiation and treaties, and have gained access to the power brokers of the European communities, you begin writing about international relations. Soon, you have a weekly column that is syndicated in several major news magazines. Famous reporters quote your opinions. Congratulations on a distinguished career! ✡

You've noticed that people reading a news story sometimes don't understand it unless a picture shows them why it's important. Knowing why public figures do what they do, and how they feel about it, compels readers. Most journalists don't focus on this, mainly recording when, where, and how an event happened.

But many times when you have seen, in a photograph, an interesting facial expression or a surprising visual contrast, and realized that this image told the real story. A neighborhood playground's significance can be seen in the face of a child seeing it for the first time. A photograph of survivors picking through rubble eloquently tells about the misery of a bombed-out city. Your favorite picture was taken in 1945 by Alfred Eisenstaedt: a sailor kissing a nurse in Times Square, on the day Japan surrendered. The jubilation of the entire country is seen in that one image.

It's not just luck that makes a great photojournalist. It's knowing about a situation before it unfolds, and deciding what you're looking for. This makes it easier to position yourself to take the most eloquent picture. A lot of the work happens before you even uncap your 35-millimeter Nikon.

While staying in Washington in 1972, you learn that on March 22, the Senate will vote on the Equal Rights Amendment which outlaws discrimination on the basis of gender. A demonstration by its supporters is predictable, and you take the Metro to the Capitol building well in advance of the Senate's call to order.

A crowd of mostly women is growing in front of the building, and police have closed off the block to traffic. The crisp, cool air is warmed by the excitement of the demonstrators. Many are holding signs declaring the equality of women and men.

You notice a woman with a baby daughter in her arms. Her emotion is clearly apparent, and you think her hopeful face reflects the importance of the vote. You frame your shot, focus, and wait. The woman lifts the baby high in the air, and the sunlight catches the tears running down her cheeks. It's your 'money shot,' and it's perfect. You develop and print it in an Associated Press darkroom, bring it to an editor, and by evening it's an iconic image of the women's rights movement. Your reputation is made. ✿

One day you're visiting an art gallery in Long Island, New York, and your companion introduces you to a friend of the artist who is exhibiting his work there: a big, shaggy-headed fellow named Kermit Lansner. "You two are in the same business," she says.

Mr. Lansner has just been promoted to the editor post at News-week, and he asks you what you do.

"Well, I've been assisting Miriam Ottenberg at the Washington Star, but I'm not sure I want to stay in newspaper work," you tell him. "It's all about brevity, it's too much scrambling to move on to the next thing, you know? I like to write more in depth."

"What have you written about? Lansner asks.

"I just sold a 3500-word article to the New Yorker about 'white flight' out of Baltimore into the suburbs. And The Star published a series I wrote about people's consciousness of air and water pollution, and how it affects their habits."

"Send me your clippings," he responds, "and if you're as versatile as you sound, we might have room at the culture desk."

A stack of your best work is on Lansner's desk at Newsweek a few days later. Soon you get a call: can you interview the Manhattan district attorney about drug use in private high schools?

The magic word "Newsweek" gets you an appointment at the New York County DA's office. You get your questions answered, spend the next day fact-checking, make some more phone calls and then pull an all-nighter writing the piece.

Three weeks later, "Prep and Privilege" appears in the magazine. The senior editors really like it. You're invited to join the staff. You find an apartment in Queens, and start working on your first assignments. A museum reinvents itself; a newly-formed orchestra struggles with its artistic philosophy; cuts in federal funding threaten arts programs in schools. You investigate and write about these, describing cultural trends and providing interesting perspectives. It's a fulfilling specialty and you do it well. ✿

Miriam calls him and learns that he's in Manhattan for a taping of the Dick Cavett show. He agrees to talk with you. You hope that he'll be smoking a cigar, because that's classic Art Buchwald.

He's sitting in a small restaurant, reading the New York Times, and greets you in the gravelly voice you've heard on TV.

"So you write political humor," he drawls pleasantly. "No, I don't ... I want to learn about it," you stammer. "Well, maybe you can," he continues. "Now's the time to find out. If you can't write political jokes while Nixon is president, then it's probably hopeless. You know, I love Nixon. I worship the quicksand he walks on," Buchwald says as the waitress delivers his banana split.

"Okay, start here," he advises. "What do you think is an absurd aspect of the Nixon administration? Really ridiculous."

"Uh, maybe ... the money being spent on the war?" you venture.

"Good! Good, that's good," Buchwald responds. "I happen to know that every Viet Cong we kill, costs the Pentagon $300,000. Now, how could we spend that money more effectively?"

You begin to see how this works. "Well," you muse, "they really hate us ... they hate our way of life ...."

"Yes! That's right! Because they don't *have* our way of life!" he shouts. "Okay, take that $300 grand, offer each Viet Cong soldier a U.S. passport, a house in the suburbs, a color TV and a country-club membership. Boom! The war's over. Bring the boys home."

Back at your apartment, you spend the afternoon looking out the window, organizing your pencils. What's silly about Nixon? You could never understand his paranoia, how he seems afraid of college students at demonstrations, even though he's so much more powerful. What would he confess during a therapy session?

Once you have the idea, it's easy. You compose a hilarious imaginary transcript. Tribune Media buys it, and wants another. You write about a domestic surveillance agent spying on the wrong family. Tribune loves it -- and you've made Miriam laugh! ✡

When your beloved Philadelphia Athletics moved to Kansas City, you were left without a baseball team. Though you're now a New Yorker, you can't root for the Yankees, your A's hated rivals – and the Dodgers and Giants have left New York for California.

But in April 1962, an expansion team is added to the National League, and you tune in with interest to the first WABC Radio pre-game show introducing the New York Metropolitans. Former Dodgers pitcher Ralph Branca is analyzing the team's prospects with the outspoken host of "Speaking of Sports," Howard Cosell.

You remember Cosell from a radio show years ago, where Little Leaguers interviewed pro athletes. With his guidance, the boys managed to get answers when most reporters couldn't, like when they asked Yankees right fielder Hank Bauer how he felt about being benched by Casey Stengel. Now Cosell himself is grilling sports figures. Clearly, this is an entirely new reporting style. You take the subway to the Polo Grounds to try to meet him.

Cosell is heading toward the clubhouse entrance as you arrive, shouldering a Phono-Trix tape recorder. He says he'll be pleased with your company; would you carry these microphones for him?

This man is the enemy of vague or evasive answers. He doesn't spare his subjects' feelings or ask softball questions. In the locker room, he asks Gil Hodges whether, because of his recurring knee injuries, he was considering retirement. It's a tough but justified question. Hodges is a great slugger but clearly is slowing down.

"These athletes have responsibilities. The fans depend on them," he says to you afterwards. "They have to be held to a standard. And that goes for the managers and owners, too. There's no place for exploitation or discrimination. Never let them off the hook."

Like every fan, you follow Cosell's career. Sometimes you're shocked by his abrasiveness, but you're always impressed by his principles and commitment to fairness. Trying to be just as tough, you start covering high school football games, eventually doing live reports on local television and eventually writing a sports column for a tabloid. You even get to cover the World Series. What a great way to make a living! ✡

Assisting Daniel Schorr is a roller coaster. In 1962, a "checkbook journalism" incident goes wrong when he offers money to a West German group digging a secret escape tunnel under the Berlin Wall, in exchange for television rights for CBS. But it's a trap; the Communists know about it and the U.S. State Department persuades Schorr to back off, and the escape is cancelled.

In 1971, President Nixon writes a list of twenty people he considers his political enemies, and it's sent to White House lawyer John Dean. Schorr obtains a copy, and reads it on live TV before looking it over. He's shocked when he sees his own name. Apparently his investigations of the Presidency have touched a nerve, and when Schorr recovers, he is very pleased.

After publishing details of illegal CIA activities, including the attempted assassination of Cuban president Fidel Castro, Schorr is forced to resign from CBS, and you both end up working for smaller independent television stations for awhile.

In 1979, the Atlanta Braves baseball team owner, Ted Turner, decides that a 24-hours-a-day cable television network could be profitable. He launches CNN, and sets up news bureaus around the world, broadcasting live events, everywhere. Other TV networks struggle to keep up. Turner hires Daniel Schorr as its first news anchor. You become an associate producer, overseeing scripts, running the teleprompter, and setting up reporters' feeds.

However, Schorr criticizes Turner's editorial ethics, and so his contract is not renewed in 1985. National Public Radio seizes the opportunity to sign up the award-winning journalist as its senior news analyst. He provides commentaries for *All Things Considered* and *Weekend Edition*, which are carried on all the network's 900 radio stations nationwide. His voice is regularly heard in millions of American homes.

He is a tough guy, but also kind and loyal, and he makes sure your career is also secure. He gets you a job as a news producer at NPR, where you set up interviews with newsmakers, write scripts, edit taped conversations and create promotional audio clips. You become an important part of the independent voice of public radio. ✿

Your college friend calls; he's been hired to teach at Indiana University. He's driving out there in August. How about a road trip?

It's a nice break from your routine, and after a two-day drive, you help Sam move into his apartment. There's no air conditioning, and you're broiling, so Sam suggests that you could take advantage of his University privileges to use the pool.

You arrive with Sam at the athletic facility with trunks and towel, but stop short at a sign on the locker room door: "Pool closed till noon for training session." A staffer, seeing your disappointment, remarks, "If you're a fan, you might want to watch the guy training. He's an Olympian medalist. You can go up to the bleachers."

You take a poolside position to watch the Hoosiers' swimming coach, Don Counsilman, conferring with a dark-haired athlete in the pool. You hear the coach say, "I'm going to look at the film."

The athlete pulls himself out of the pool, and since you're an Olympic fan, there's no mistaking that big black mustache. It's Mark Spitz, who won gold at the Pan American Games in 1967, the Mexico City Olympics in 1968, not to mention ten gold medals at two Maccabiah Games in Israel. You've read that he wants to break an Olympic record for medals next year in Munich.

Waiting for his coach to return, Spitz strolls over to sit near you, and you nod. "Hi," he says. "What's up?"

"Just waiting for the pool!" you answer, grinning.

"Go ahead, I don't care. I'm Spitz," he says and puts out his hand.

You introduce yourself as a New York Times political reporter, and he's interested in discussing the CIA and the war in Vietnam. At 21, he's an intelligent and informed college student, not just a superstar athlete. Just a week ago in Chicago, he set world records while qualifying for next year's Olympics, but sometimes he likes to talk about something else for a change.

Spitz works for several more hours on the freestyle stroke, and then he and Counsilman call it a day. He's headed for the cafeteria, having just burned thousands of calories, and invites you to come along.

"So, will the Times send you to the Olympics?" he asks you.

"Don't I wish! But the Times has a huge sports staff. It would be great, though," you say wistfully. "Never been to the Olympics."

"If I think of any way to get you there, I'll call you. Let me have your business card," he says.

"Whether or not I get there, I'll watch every race," you promise.

But by June 1972, President Nixon's problems are accelerating. The Washington Post reports that the Democratic National Committee offices at Washington's Watergate Hotel have been burglarized, and the burglars seem to be connected to White House staff. The Times needs you to interview for background and fact-check articles. Attending the Olympics must remain a dream.

In the moments when you're not writing about the shady financial dealings of the Committee to Re-Elect the President, you watch proudly as Mark Spitz sets four individual world records in freestyle and butterfly, and three relay event records.

He has just won his seventh gold medal – an Olympic record – when a world-shattering tragedy eclipses his victory. Palestinian terrorists kidnap eleven Israeli athletes in the Olympic Village. Agonized, you watch television footage of Spitz, with six armed guards, being evacuated from Munich for his own safety. A German rescue effort goes wrong, and the hostages are murdered.

Hopes for a safer world have been shattered. You understand Mark Spitz when he says, "Here we were 27 years after World War II, and madmen are still killing Jews because they're Jews."

You ask your editor for time to study and report on the evolution of global terrorism and security, and he agrees. You shuttle from Israel to The Hague back to Washington, interviewing experts and policy-makers. You write a series of articles to raise awareness of the patterns of civilian-targeted political violence. Within three years you are an acknowledged expert and trusted analyst. ✡

Most of the Washington Bureau staffers cover the White House, Congress, the Supreme Court and the executive departments, and you are soon busy attending various Senate hearings, sitting behind the photographers and taking copious notes in shorthand.

But two young Post reporters aren't doing any of this. A break-in is reported in June at the Democratic National Committee's offices at the Watergate Hotel, and one of the burglars is an ex-CIA agent connected with the former Attorney General, John Mitchell. This seems to point to a horrifying possibility: that President Nixon himself was covering up, maybe even directing, criminal activities intended to insure his re-election.

Carl Bernstein has been covering less-important news about local Virginia politics, and his colleague Bob Woodward was new to the Washington Post. Their editor feels nervous about accusing the White House of obstructing justice, but Woodward and Bernstein convince him to let them follow the trail and get more evidence.

You sense that this is going to be a huge story, and stay close to the young reporters as they telephone their sources. Occasionally, they ask you to keep calling Republican insiders when they rush to meet secretive informants who are afraid to speak by phone.

Their investigations uncover evidence that the Committee to Re-Elect the President has been illegally wiretapping Democrats. The Senate establishes a committee to find the truth, and Nixon fires several aides, his lawyer, and the Attorney General. The lawyer, John Dean, tells the Senate committee that Nixon's conversations have been recorded on audiotapes. This is the "smoking gun," proof that extensive crimes have been committed and hidden. It's over. Richard Nixon, in August, 1974, becomes the first President to resign from office. The Vice-President is sworn in.

America is stunned at these unbelievable events, and politics will never, ever be the same. Journalists have reached into the nation's most powerful office and held the Chief Executive accountable. The free press has proven that, in a democracy, no one is above the law. You are proud to be part of this profession.

Chapter Five

I Want To Run a Business

In the 'old country,' Jews practiced a wide array of trades. They were artisans, tailors, carpenters, merchants, doctors, teachers, furriers, glaziers, and scribes, to list a few. But life was restricted and dangerous. The Russian Tsar conscripted their sons into the army for 25-year terms, forced them to live within limited borders, and allowed, even encouraged, murderous pogroms.

In contrast, America, the Golden Land, promised freedom, protection under the law, and unlimited possibilities for hard workers. Prosperity was possible for all. So street vendors became shop owners, and shop owners built growing companies.

You probably know hundreds of brand names that began as small Jewish businesses. This chapter will offer two commercial paths: the food business and the clothing or "shmatta" business. The Jewish food entrepreneurs you might encounter here include William Rosenberg, founder of Dunkin' Donuts, and Murray Lender, the bagel man. Harry Attman and Abe Pariser helped feed Baltimore, and Nathan Handwerker popularized kosher hot dogs on Coney Island.

Among the early clothing designers are Ida Rosenthal, Calvin Klein, Sally Milgrim, Nettie Rosenstein, Mollie Parnis, Anne Klein, Carl Rosen and Hattie Carnegie. You'll also notice the great Jewish retailers: Adam Gimbel, Edward Filene, Benjamin Altman, Bergdorf Goodman, Henry Sonneborn, Hecht's, Hochschild-Kohn, Hutzler Brothers, Stewart's, Stanley Marcus, and Joseph A. Bank.

I am deeply grateful to my sister-in-law Susan G. Weill, Michael Wex, and the eminent deli man, Paul Sia.

It's a warm summer day in East Baltimore, Maryland, in the year 1915. School won't start for many weeks, and you're free as a bird to wander down noisy, smelly, exciting Lombard Street.

Pushcarts throng the sidewalks, full of pots, pans, shoes, clothing, bread, pickles, fruit, and crates of clucking chickens. Peddlers shout in English, Yiddish or Italian, trying to be heard above the other hawkers. *"Frish fleysh!"* calls a meat vendor, *"Bellisimi abiti!"* cries a clothing vendor, and above all, the wail of the bagel man: *"Koyf zhe beygelekh!* The customers' shrill haggling is deafening.

The buildings behind the pushcarts are tenement apartments, storefront religious schools called Talmud Torahs, sweatshops, and some dry goods stores and butcher shops whose owners are successful enough to have moved on from carts to rented space. Laundry hangs from upper-story windows. Many immigrants from Eastern Europe settled here to scratch out a living, a short distance from Baltimore's harbor, where they got off the ships.

Unlike many of your immigrant neighbors, you're getting an education. Now you're pondering what to do when you finish school. Running your own business seems so much better than working for wages. You'd have to take on the risks, and work hard, but the rewards in dignity and income could be considerable.

Your Lithuanian father is a tailor, and he's taught you sewing skills, and an appreciation for fine fabric and clothing style. So the "shmatta" business could be a natural choice for you.

On the other hand, the lovely, pungent odors of Jewish cooking intoxicate you. Harry Attman has just opened a deli nearby on Washington Street. On days when you have an extra dime, Harry makes you a pastrami sandwich that melts in your mouth. Or, you could choose savory corned beef, whitefish, beef tongue, brisket, salami, or chopped liver – with a pickle. The men behind the counter seem so happy. How great would it be to run a deli!

If you'd like to set up a tailor shop, go to page 89.

If you'd rather try the restaurant business, go to page 90.

Your parents have been making and mending clothes for four years, and through careful saving, they've accumulated almost enough money to rent a storefront on Lombard Street. The B'nai Abraham and Yehuda Laib Family Society, founded by earlier Jewish immigrants who 'made good,' provides a loan to help your family furnish the shop, and buy tools, fabric, thread and an additional Singer Red-Eye sewing machine.

Your customers are mostly men. Some work in business and need to look good to impress bosses and customers; some want a suit for Shabbat, and to outfit their sons. Others are courting young ladies, and don't want to look like *schlubs*.

The new style in suits is slim and youthful-looking. Jackets are shorter. Sleeves are straighter and less puffy, and feature an elegant four-button cuff. Fitted vests are popular, but as men put away their pocket-watches and start wearing wrist-watches, many stop wearing vests altogether.

As soldiers begin to return from Europe after World War One, you start hearing requests for high-waisted jackets that evoke a military look. You also notice fewer high-button shoes. Men want comfort and convenience, and they're wearing oxfords and soft, unstarched collars. They want to look young and stylish.

Young women, too, are experimenting with new clothing designs. You see them wearing sailor blouses and cravats, and observe that the long tubular dresses are giving way to shorter, pleated skirts that allow freer movement. The broad brims of women's hats are getting smaller – to show off the new bobbed hairstyles.

This seems to be a time of change and exploration in dresses and suits. More people are willing to break old traditions with new fashions. The more you think about it, the more you feel that new styles will catch on. However, American prosperity is expanding -- there's also a growing demand for men's conservative business wear.

If you want to begin selling new women's fashions, turn to page 91.

If you want to reach new markets for your menswear, turn to page 92.

Attman's Deli is fully staffed by the Attman family, but there are plenty of other Jewish food shops on "Corned Beef Row." One day after school, you wash up at home and then walk into the first deli you see. You pass shelves full of pickled tomatoes and Wissotzky tea, and sausages and smoked salmon in the glass cases. The air is pungent with the scent of pepper and cured meats.

A man in a white apron is slicing rye bread in the back, near the tables. "Excuse me, mister," you call. He looks up, still slicing.

"I'm looking for a job. Do you need someone?" you ask. He grunts, looks down again, and shakes his head.

An idea comes to you from somewhere. You lean forward. "I can slice lox so thin you can read a newspaper through it," you say.

The deli man stops slicing. "An interesting skill."

"So, can I work here?" you pursue. He finally smiles. "My friend, I respect your spirit. As a matter of fact, my wife is having some tsuriss with her kishkes. She should stay in bed, the doctor says. I could use some help. But only a short time maybe," he warns.

That's fine with you! "I can come here straight from school!" you promise. His face darkens. You offer, "Okay, I can quit school."

It's a deal. Next morning at six, you report to Mr. Goldfarb who sets you up in the back room stuffing cabbage leaves with ground beef, onion, rice and eggs. When those are boiling in tomato soup, you learn how to mix pickling spices to rub on hunks of belly beef. It takes up to four weeks to cure the meat, spice and smoke it. After it's boiled and steamed, it's finally pastrami.

Mr. Goldfarb sends his meats to a smokehouse over a mile away, which costs money and time. You wonder whether having a smoker on site would be more efficient. But he says he can't make the investment now. Maybe you could visit the B'nai Abraham and Yehuda Laib Family Society, asking for a loan against your wages to buy a meat smoker and set it up nearby.

If you choose to start a meat-smoking operation, turn to page 93.

If you want to learn the fine art of deli carving, go to page 94.

Not every woman, you reflect, can afford to go to a dressmaker; and many have joined the workforce, leaving little time to make their own clothes. Spending more time outside their homes, women want to stay up to date with fashion trends. This is why manufacturers are starting to produce cheap ready-to-wear clothes, and marketing them to department stores and through the Sears mail-order catalogue.

You see other changes in young women customers, too. World War One and the Spanish flu epidemic killed tens of millions of people. Life seems short, and women want to enjoy it, and the company of young men, freely and without restrictions. Gaining the right to vote in 1920, women leave behind their chaperones and tight, restrictive Edwardian clothing. They smoke cigarettes and dress in slender, sleeveless dresses, preferring to be informal and companionable with their boyfriends rather than demure and mysterious. Embracing the "flapper" style and the freedom it celebrates, they dance wildly at jazz clubs.

Few women are wearing those uncomfortable corsets anymore, so you design a bare-backed chiffon dress with a high hemline and a beaded fringe. Laying out and cutting a prototype, you visit an East Lombard Street sweatshop and engage a contractor to produce two hundred dresses in five sizes. While you wait for them, you carry samples to Baltimore's department stores, like Hecht's, Hochschild-Kohn, Hutzler Brothers, and Stewart's. A few buyers agree to your price and place orders. With the profits, you plan to add some new dresses and expand your marketing.

Your dresses are popular, and you enlarge the shop to hire your own seamstresses, cutting out the middle-man. In a few years a dressmaker named Ida Rosenthal in New York has invented and popularized the Maidenform brassiere and women's fashions become less boylike and more feminine. You start to produce curve-hugging clothes.

If you try to reach the "working women" market, turn to page 95.

If you are more intrigued by the Paris "haute couture," turn to page 96.

There are already major Jewish men's clothing companies in Baltimore, like Henry Sonneborn and Joseph Bank, and you want to be one of them. Business is booming. Millions of Americans have joined the work force. Ready-made clothing is in high demand.

However, manufacturing and selling are two huge jobs, so you ask your sister to join you as a traveling salesperson, carrying samples to buyers in out-of-town retail stores and collecting orders. She's adventurous, and knows a lot about clothes, so she agrees. In 1924 she buys a large valise, fills it with your best suits and shirts, and boards a train to go clinch some deals.

Wealthy Americans have been ordering lounge suits from Saville Row tailors in London, and less well-off men try to copy them. But you notice some innovations that your customers like: striped shirts instead of white, wider pants, and leather belts instead of suspenders. Accessories, too, are the rage among the 'smart' set – bow ties, scarf ties, brightly-colored gloves, pocket squares, and bowler, derby and homberg hats.

There are some troubles in the factory, however. A representative of the Amalgamated Clothing Workers of America visits you at the shop, saying that your employees cannot live on $26 a week, and that working eleven hours a day is ruining their health. If you don't treat them better, they will probably unionize and go on strike. You throw him out, but he's made you think. You know your workers personally, and depend on them. It cuts into your bottom line, but you raise the hourly wage to 45¢.

Your sister brings back orders for flannel and wool tweed suits, and your workers can hardly keep up. You hire more people. Your label becomes better known; maybe it's time to expand into shirts and ties. The Baltimore Commercial Bank is willing to loan you some of the money you could use to buy your own building.

If you consider cutting wages so you'll be able to afford to buy an additional factory, turn to page 97.

If you don't like taking risks, and keep your operation in its present rented space, turn to page 98.

Meats, fish, and even some cheeses are smoked over burning wood as a preservative, and to add the sharp flavor that consumers love. For the capacity to smoke sufficient amounts of food to turn a profit, you'll need a very large industrial smoker; and if you want to sell to kosher retailers and restaurants, you might want to consider buying two: one for meat, one for milk products.

You dream big, and ask the Jewish mutual aid society to lend you money for two huge smokers, and for enough money to rent your own space. They agree to back you, and even before the machines arrive, you're passing out handbills in every restaurant in Baltimore, offering your services for a low introductory rate.

Once the smokers are installed and a wood supplier is found, you test them on some of Goldfarb's stock, and perfect your method. You soon receive enormous cuts of beef from customers who want that perfect, savory pungency. Cutting and arranging the meat on steel racks, with enough room between them so oak and hickory fumes can reach every surface, you set the thermometer at 200 degrees, and wait three days.

Your customers are pleased with the results, and within a week you're taking delivery of sausages, liverwurst, and turkey. You're not smoking pork products, because you would lose your *kashrut* certification, and most of your customers; but you have lots more room in the smoker that should be used. Not too many restauranteurs are sending you cheeses like ricotta, gouda, or provolone to smoke. You have to decide whether to abandon your kosher customers and take in hams and bacon, or possibly buy some salmon, cod, mackerel, herring, and sardines, and wholesale your own brand of products.

If you decide to leave the kosher specialty and begin smoking 'treif'meat, go to page 100.

To start your own smoked fish product line, go to page 101.

Mr. Goldfarb must like you a lot, or else he wouldn't be willing to teach you the secrets of carving. Slicing the beef and creating the perfect sandwich is a fine art, known only to a few. Jewish delis are judged by their sandwiches. One morning before any customers arrive, he calls you to the back table. Brandishing a very sharp, narrow knife, he tells you to pay attention.

"Pastrami," he says, "has a thin skin on the outside that you can't eat. See?" He points to a silver membrane, and you lean close to look. "Now. Hold the blade against the grain of the meat, and very carefully take off the skin." You slide the knife under the membrane and it seems to come off easily.

"Slice the beef very thin, you big show-off 'You-can-read-a-newspaper-through-it,'" and you cut through the black peppery surface. The soft pastrami slides into perfect slices. You cover two pieces of rye with spicy brown mustard, and Mr. Goldfarb lifts the warm, pink meat onto the bread, adds the top slice and cuts it in two. He hands you half the sandwich and takes the other. The first rich, fatty bite seems to melt in savory glory.

"Did I ever tell you," says Mr. Goldfarb, his mouth full, "about the time a fellow asked me for a corned beef with mayonnaise?" You nearly choke as he shakes his head sadly.

Years pass. You learn how much garlic to add to the half-sour pickle barrels; you decide to boil matza balls in chicken stock to boost their flavor. Renting rooms next to the deli, you expand, adding more seating and installing brighter lights. Mr. Goldfarb makes you a partner and adds your name to the front window.

The stock market crashes in 1929, and its effects filter quickly through the population. A quarter of American employers are unemployed. Business suffers, and you have to lower prices and cut frills. But the deli survives, a comfort for many Baltimoreans who can forget their troubles awhile with a plate of brisket and a glass of Dr. Brown's celery tonic.

To explore a bigger market for your products, go to page 102.

If you and Goldfarb decide to open a second deli out of town, go to page 103.

The U.S. begins supplying materials to Britain before entering the war in 1941. You feel the effects immediately. Some female employees leave to work in munitions plants, and most men join the armed forces. Many of your machines sit idle for want of workers.

One day in 1942 you're at a cousin's wedding in Boston, and you find yourself at the same table as a flashy young man named Carl Rosen, and his wife Shirley. He started as a cutting-room sweeper at his father's firm, Puritan Fashions, and he hopes to be the chief executive officer. "Women are changing their attitudes about clothes," Shirley says. "They're wearing trousers in the factories, but they want them outside of work. Look at their everyday life."

You've heard your female relatives complain that shampoo is getting scarce and expensive, and joke that maybe they should wear hats. But then you start thinking: women in factories had to keep their hair away from the machinery; why not market a sort of turban, for safety and to cover unstyled hair?

Turbans are familiar -- glamorous actresses like Merle Oberon and Hedy Lamarr wear them in the movies. They're simple enough to make quickly. If you can get into the Sears catalogue, or a major retailer, you could sell millions of them.

Bergdorf Goodman on New York's Fifth Avenue orders two thousand, and you coax retired tailors to your shop to help fill the contract. The turbans are a huge success. Other retailers place orders.

You invest capital into velveteen and corduroy for cold-weather outerwear; no wool, because it's needed for military uniforms. For summer, you are among the first to make two-piece swimsuits and cotton separates, which remain popular after the war ends. Your label is seen in all the best department stores.

And, many years later, at a Press Week reception in New York, you run into Carl Rosen again. He is now CEO of Puritan Fashions Corporation, and he looks very happy. "You remember we talked, long ago, about women's pants?" he asks. "Well, I've just signed a license with Calvin Klein. Puritan's about to introduce a totally new concept. *Designer jeans!* I think it's going to be big." ✡

The U.S. enters World War II in December 1941, and the effect on the clothing industry is immediate. Silk, which mostly comes from Japan, is unavailable. Women have just started getting used to nylon stockings, but now the government needs nylon for parachutes, ropes, and tents; so stockings are almost impossible to find. Wool, rubber and metals are also needed for the war effort, but Washington doesn't want to ration materials as the British do. The War Office wants civilians voluntarily to buy less fabric.

President Roosevelt asks Stanley Marcus of the Nieman-Marcus department stores to find a solution. Marcus wants clothiers to recycle old designs so consumers won't feel tempted to buy new clothes. It's not good for business, but it will help beat Hitler, and your industry is just as patriotic as anyone. Marcus also formulates "Limit 85" for women's clothing: skirts can't be lined, belts and coat lengths are restricted, and quilting is banned.

Paris is losing its place as the capital of high fashion. While France is occupied, designers there have been dressing the wives of German officers, and Coco Chanel is discovered living with a Nazi. American Jewish innovators are bringing their ideas to high fashion, and you take an opportunity to sit in on consultations with Nettie Rosenstein, who is introducing high-end printed dresses with matching gloves. Sally Milgrim on Fifth Avenue is turning out brilliant ready-to-wear, quality outfits. Older women are thrilled with the flattering gowns of Mollie Parnis.

The 1950s brings an explosion of prosperity and consumer spending. It's clearly a great time to explore new markets, and you learn that a young designer named Anne Klein has guessed that young women are tired of cute buttons-and-bows little-girl fashions. Her Junior Sophisticates company offers stylish, cultivated looks for young buyers. You rush to introduce your own line of grown-up wear for teens, marketing debutante gowns, cocktail dresses and sleek casual wear.

The loud and shocking sixties decade inspires you to model mini-dresses in loud, splashy colors, and, barely able to keep up with orders, you expand your factory. You have the knack for jumping on trends, and it pays off. By the time you retire, your fashion line is a household word. ✿

In 1926 one of your best customers persuades you to buy tickets to a charity dinner given by a Jewish organization he supports. Reading the program, you see that the evening's honoree is the philanthropist Edward Filene, who with his brother runs Filene's Sons clothing store founded in Boston by their father, William.

Another guest tells you that it was the Filene family that developed the "department store" concept first introduced by Adam Gimbel in Indiana. He adds that Edward was disturbed by the extreme poverty of many American workers, and had launched the nation's credit union movement. Because of this, employees who can't get bank loans or afford high-interest shark loans, can use their credit unions to buy a home or deal with emergencies.

It's a pleasure to meet the elderly Mr. Filene. When you ask about his business, he describes his workers instead of his merchandise. At Filene's, employees help resolve disputes between management and labor. They receive health benefits, work five-day, 40-hour weeks, and use the company's medical clinics and insurance programs. They even get paid vacations.

This moment is a life-changer for you. You've met a successful businessman who lives the Jewish ideals of justice and human dignity, and practices a humane, respectful capitalism. Instantly you decide to be like Edward Filene. A week later, you visit him in Boston to resume the conversation. He convinces you that it's the workers' purchasing power that drives business expansion. For everyone's sake, they must have shorter hours and higher wages.

Regretfully you think of your employees' pathetic pay, and the wealth their labor brings you. Wasting no time, you implement Mr. Filene's profit-sharing incentive plan in your factories, sharing your success with the workers. Appreciative and loyal, they help your business survive the Great Depression of the 1930s and re-tool to manufacture uniforms and tents when the U.S. enters World War II. In the fullness of time, you retire happy and fulfilled, knowing that you've married your ethical traditions to the opportunities given to you by your beloved country, America. ✡

Baltimore's clothing businesses are thriving, but the real center of both men's and women's clothing is New York City. After the catastrophic Triangle Shirtwaist Factory fire in 1911, which killed 146 immigrant workers in Greenwich Village, most manufacturers moved north to fireproof factories and showrooms between Fifth and Ninth Avenues, an area now called the Garment District.

You attend clothing-industry events in the District to learn what's trending from other designers and manufacturers. Getting off the train at Penn Station, you pass the great retailers like B. Altman's and Macy's during your short walk to the designers' showrooms. Delivery trucks block traffic to bring materials to the factories, and you have to watch out for aggressive "push boys" steering racks of dresses and suits on the sidewalks.

The fashion business is buzzing, demand for new styles is growing, and clothing companies are expanding – until disaster strikes in October of 1929. The U.S. stock market crashes, and businesses lost most of their value overnight. Millions lose their jobs, and soon a quarter of the country's work force is unemployed.

Naturally, consumer spending drops rapidly; people standing in bread lines do not have money for food, much less new clothes. You are aghast when you see newsreels of families losing their homes and begging for basic needs. This national emergency calls for sacrifice and ingenuity. You read in the *Baltimore Sun* that flour and animal-feed companies have started printing their cloth sacks in pretty designs, so that impoverished farm families can make them into clothes for their children.

For the sake of your business, and your customers, you get the idea of selling clothing patterns alongside your other merchandise, and set your staff to work drawing technical illustrations and writing instructions that the consumer can follow. You contract with a printer to publish each of your designs in eight different sizes, and package them in large, full-color photo envelopes with your company's name emblazoned across the front.

The customers who loved your styles now can make your clothes themselves for a small fraction of the cost, and feel well-dressed. Times are tough for a while, but your firm survives and your customers stay loyal. A decade later, the nation has recovered from the Depression, but many of your employees are off fighting World War II or making weapons in factories. Sewing at home becomes a patriotic duty and a necessity during fabric rationing. Your pattern sales soar; consumers enjoy adding their personal touch.

You are co-chairing a War Bonds event at the Metropolitan Museum of Art, and pull up a chair near your friend, designer Hattie Carnegie. You knew her way back when she was Henrietta Kanengeiser, running messages for Macy's.

"You really inspired me with your pattern sideline," Hattie says. "I'm going to give these snooty couturiers a little *knip*. Check out next week's *Life* Magazine. I'm offering their readers the pattern of my favorite high-end dress for 15¢. This is a $175 frock I'm talking about."

"Nice!" you respond approvingly.

"It's wartime, you know? So everyone's making sacrifices. I do it for the boys," she adds, tucking in some hors d'ouvres. ✡

One night you lie awake, thinking about how to expand your business. You have already half-decided to begin smoking non-kosher meats, targeting customers outside the Jewish community. Suddenly a memory comes to you: your grandma Rivka, back in Kovno, where you were born. You called her Bubbie.

Bubbie refused to leave Lithuania when you and your parents and sisters emigrated, and you haven't seen her for many years. You remember watching her cutting *lokshen*, noodles, to make kugel. In your mind, you tell her that you're about to start selling *treif* meat for a living. You can see her soft brown eyes become sad. "You'll trade in *treif*, and soon you'll eat *treif*," she says in Yiddish. "And when you eat *treif*, no longer you'll be a Jew."

This thought is not going to help you sleep. Bubbie continues, "Better you should make *goyische* food that's kosher."

'Goyische food that's kosher.' That odd phrase is still with you the next morning as you stumble wearily toward your smoke-house. A friend sees you in the street and calls your name. "Say, I just came back from a week in Coney Island," he exclaims. "It's beautiful. And, you should know, there's a Galicianer there named Handwerker. He's selling hot dogs for five cents from a stand on Surf Avenue, and oy, is he making a killing!"

You stop, dumbstruck, in your tracks. It's a sign. It's *got* to be a sign! Of course, hot dogs are a popular American street food, but you don't know of anyone making *kosher* hot dogs in Baltimore.

As if in a dream, you wander into a butcher shop to see if you can find out how to make hot dogs. The proprietor sends you to a wholesaler, where you learn that all you'll really need is a meat grinder and a manual filling machine. You already have a smoker, and know a source of the kosher sheep intestines they call 'natural casing,' and you can probably come up with a spice combination as good as Nathan Handwerker's.

Within a few months, you've mastered the recipe and process, and a year later you're supplying restaurants all over town with kosher hot dogs that explode with a juicy snap at every bite. You name your line "Bubbie Dogs," and a hundred years later, Americans still love them. Thank you, Grandma Rivka. ✿

As a child in the old country, the only fish you ever ate was *schmaltz* herring, a fatty fish prepared with onions, oil, salt and pepper. You heartily hated it. Once, however, you had the opportunity to taste smoked salmon, which a relative had brought back from a business trip on the Baltic coast. It remains one of your favorite foods, a close second to brisket.

The poor immigrants eat herring and chub, and sometimes on Shabbat have the rare treat of the chopped carp called "gefilte" fish. But you think that there's a market for more luxurious food items, like whitefish and mackerel. You could sell to the "appetizing shops" where East European Jews buy fish and dairy products, as well as pickled onions, bagels, rugelach, and halva.

With a rabbi supervising your smokehouse's *kashrut,* you install stainless-steel racks with tray shelves for brining fish. You devise a cold smoker with hanging racks for the sides of salmon. It separates the heat box from the food compartment with a metal pipe, so the smoke will reach the fish without much heat, at temperatures no higher than 86°. You smoke your first batch of brined salmon belly, and slice yourself a sample. The lox's pungent, woody campfire flavor is sheer happiness.

The rabbi is satisfied that the fish is *parve,* always separate from milk and meat. You then experiment with sable, mackerel and whitefish. Finally you're satisfied: each tastes exactly as it should.

Deciding to name your smoked delicacy line after your mother, you ask a printer to design labels, and invest in a plastic wrapping machine to vacuum-package the products. At first you hawk your merchandise in person, *schlepping* samples to restaurants and shops, taking orders from owners. After a little success, you hire someone else to do this. Finally a deli owner suggests that you contact one of his regular customers, a radio comedian, and find out if you can sponsor his show occasionally.

It costs considerable money, which you must borrow, but it pays off. The very first day your delicious smoked fish is described on the radio, large orders start pouring in, and soon you have to rent the next-door building to ramp up production. Mazel tov! ✡

Delis like yours, which serve only meat and *parve* products, are not the only cherished food institution in the Jewish community. There's also the appetizing store, which stocks fish, dairy, and other non-meat items, and the bakery, where the weary immigrants, without time or energy to bake, buy their familiar challah, knishes, babka, rye bread and onion *bulkes* or rolls.

You are a big fan of bagels, and since they're not found in any deli – it's unthinkable to make a *fleischig* sandwich on a bagel, and of course you have no dairy – when you're not working, you sometimes stroll around East Baltimore, sampling different bakeries.

One day, you stroll up Fremont Avenue and stop in at Pariser's bakery. The aroma of warm rye bread embraces you. Abe Pariser has been trading here for over forty years, and you find him in the back of the shop. He greets you as you arrive. He's just finished a making a dense concoction of flour, salt, water, malt syrup and yeast, and is now rolling the dough into round, thick strips and coiling them into circles. A large kettle of water bubbles next to him. The recipe is closely guarded. If he had still been mixing, he wouldn't have let you into the back room.

"So what do you hear from your cousins in New York?" you ask.

"Oy, they're *meshuggeh* in New York," Abe sighs. "To sell bagels, you gotta be in the Bagel Bakers Union. Try to set up shop with your *bubbie's* secret method, they'll hustle you out of town so fast, your feet won't touch the floor." He shrugs, dropping bagels in to the boiling water. "New York. *Feh!* Better to be in Baltimore."

In few seconds, Abe lifts the boiled bagels out of the water and lays them on baking sheets. Out of the oven, they'll be the chewy delight you love, with shiny hard crusts. You're happy to wait.

When World War II begins, you leave the deli with Goldfarb's children, and join the Navy, serving as commissary steward on a supply ship in the Pacific. There's no lox or pastrami on board, but the sailors, remembering the hunger and the soup kitchens of the Depression, are enthusiastic about your cooking. After the war, they go home to tell their local restaurants that they want your deli products. You start getting phone calls – and within a year, you've become a major specialty food supplier! ✡

You enlist in the U.S. Army after Japan bombs Pearl Harbor in 1941. In the service, you meet people very different from you. When you return, you feel that America seems to be changing. After fighting alongside people of many backgrounds, Americans are more conscious of each other's lives and experiences.

One way this is apparent is a willingness to try different cuisines. Chinese and Spanish restaurants open in mixed neighborhoods, and do business with many ethnic groups. People are cooking Italian and Irish dishes for their families. Traditional foods of the South, brought north by millions of African Americans, find enthusiasts in many communities. Polish, Greek, Indian, Caribbean, French, and other flavors become part of the culinary landscape.

This is true also of Jewish foods. Many Americans are becoming familiar with matza balls and knishes. But outside of the nation's Jewish neighborhoods, bagels are unknown. The recipe is complicated and the method time-consuming. In 1961, you see an item in a trade magazine that tells you a big change is coming.

"Daniel and Ada Thompson of California Register Bagel Machine Manufacturing Corporation," notes the headline. A bagel-making *machine*. It will roll and form the dough. It will make thousands of bagels per hour. Is this good or bad, you wonder.

During a visit to New Haven, Connecticut in 1963 for a nephew's graduation from Yale, you visit the New York Bagel Bakery on Baldwin Street. The Lender brothers have taken bagel-making to a whole new level. Murray Lender shows you their new onion and raisin-and-honey bagels. They're cut and frozen in polyethylene bags; the bakery makes thousands of these packages, selling them to delis, restaurants and Catskills hotels. "The problem is," says Murray, "people don't understand a roll with a hole! My wife goes around to supermarkets, demonstrating how to put spreads on bagels. Our mission is to bagelize America!"

Murray's brother Marvin, an engineering genius, essentially invented the bagel factory. "Bagel dough is heavy and thick; if you try to make bagels with doughnut machinery, you wear it out," Murray explains. "Marvin monkeyed with the mixers and the belts, expanded the building, and we're fully automated now."

But Murray is the family's marketing genius. To create a place for bagels on America's tables, he makes deals with orange juice and cream cheese companies: they'll include Lender's Bagel coupons in their packages, and bagel bags will contain their coupons.

Murray Lender's biggest achievement is convincing the country to accept frozen foods. Supermarkets are growing larger, and fewer customers are going to the grocer or the bakery. Consumers now are convinced that frozen food is healthy, not just convenient.

Freezing food means it can last on market shelves for weeks, even longer. And supermarkets and groceries aren't the only places that could move lots of bagels. A Boston man, Rosenberg, has launched a chain of breakfast shops that's becoming very popular. Hoping to connect him to the Lender factory, you suggest to him that Dunkin' Donuts add mass-produced bagels to its menu.

"Nisht gut," William Rosenberg tells you. "Have you tasted those factory bagels? They're *drek*. There's no crust. And no taste at all. The inside is soft like a pillow. A real bagel has to be fresh – it gives your face a workout to eat it, you know? Dunkin' Donuts will never sell Lender's *drek* bagels. We do fine with doughnuts. If we ever want to sell bagels, we'll make them fresh in-house."

Well, this is a philosophical problem. Is it better to join the trend of mass-produced food, which could be a huge money-maker, or maintain the old, smaller-scale traditions of hand-carved meats and food cooked and prepared by people, not machines?

Then a romance blooms for you in Boston, and you ask your partner Goldfarb whether he wants to open a second deli up north. Business is good, and he agrees. Your new establishment in Framingham attracts a growing, appreciative crowd of regulars, all sorts of people who love your soup, your stuffed derma, and most of all, your succulent sandwiches. Soon you're a pillar of the community, a business leader and a philanthropist supporting local hospitals, charities and service organizations. Well done!

Chapter 6

I Want To Work For Justice

The book of the prophet Isaiah exhorts us: "Learn to do good; seek justice, defend the oppressed. Take up the cause of the fatherless, and plead the case of the widow." And in the thousands of years since those words were written, the Jews, who so often have been victims of injustice, have cherished them as a central creed of our people.

In recent times, Bella Abzug, a fearless American who battled her entire life for the rights of the powerless, said, "Judaism has had a very profound effect on me. Jews believe you can't have justice for yourself unless other people have justice as well. That has motivated much of what I've done."

Both in history and in our own time, our people have been at the forefront in the cause of equality for minorities, women, the disabled, immigrants, and the LGBTQ community.

Too many rabbis to count have been in the struggle; some you may meet here are Jacob Rothschild, Joseph Glaser, and Joachim Prinz. And others supporting Dr. Martin Luther King, Cesar Chavez and John Lewis -- in the streets and in the courts -- include William Taylor, Marshall Ganz, Bella Abzug, Albert Vorspan, Kivie Kaplan, Jack Greenberg, Jerry Cohen, and Betty Friedan. Some Jewish organizations organized for the same purposes are the Hebrew Immigrant Aid Society, the International Rescue Committee, and the Religious Action Center of Reform Judaism. Possibly you might even run across an interesting anti-war group called the Yippies.

It's a warm Sunday morning in October 1958, and you're eating breakfast with your sisters at home in Atlanta. Sunday school at the Hebrew Benevolent Congregation starts in two hours, and your confirmation class will be working in the temple's sukkah, getting ready for the Simhat Torah festivities. As you reach for the orange juice pitcher, the phone rings, and your mom answers.

"Hello, Celia," she says. Then she screams. You drop the pitcher.

When she can speak, your mother repeats the dreadful news. Overnight, the Temple was bombed. There is extensive damage.

At first, your mind is too numb to think. Who could do a thing like this? To attack a place of worship ... but then you remember that four African-American churches in Alabama have been bombed in the last two years. All of their pastors were civil rights leaders -- like your rabbi, Jacob Rothschild. He's given sermons and written newspaper editorials advocating the integration of the nation's public schools. His family has been threatened and harassed because of it. Now you understand what just happened. You are shocked, terrified, and soon, you are very angry.

In time, the temple is repaired. You go back to the business of being a high school student, and begin applying to colleges. Sometimes on Sunday mornings, you walk into African-American churches and sit quietly in the back during services, wondering how the congregants endure the hatred they face every day.

In the spring, you are accepted by a number of colleges, and decide on Vanderbilt University in Nashville, Tennessee, to study history and sociology. You arrive on campus in August of 1959.

There are no black undergraduates at the university; as a Southerner, you aren't surprised. But one day you see a notice on a bulletin board, inviting all those interested to a series of workshops sponsored by the Southern Christian Leadership Conference. Participants will learn the tactics of non-violent direct action, preparing to resist the separation of blacks and whites in bus systems across the South. You are intrigued; the president of the SPLC is a young Baptist minister from Atlanta, Martin Luther King, Jr., who had helped organize the Montgomery bus boycott in 1955.

So you show up at the first meeting, in the basement of the Clark Memorial United Methodist Church, and find it crowded with young black and white people. Many are Vanderbilt and Fisk University students. You find one of the few empty seats, next to a Fisk sophomore, sit down and introduce yourself. "Pleased to meet you, I'm John Lewis," he says genially, shaking your hand. "Have you met Mr. Lawson yet?" No, you have not.

"He studied *satyagraha* in India," John explains. "It was Gandhi's method. He believed that violence obscures truth, and opponents must be overcome through patience and compassion. I'm not sure this method will work on the White Citizens Councils and Alabama police departments, but I'm willing to try," he says.

White Citizens Councils are groups of local segregationists who want to keep black and white Americans separated in schools, neighborhoods, and public facilities. Many whites hated the 1954 Supreme Court decision *Brown versus Board of Education,* outlawing segregated schools, so Councils' membership has grown.

James Lawson, a graduate student at Vanderbilt's Divinity School, comes to the front of the room and greets the crowd. He explains nonviolent resistance, and you love that it begins with the acceptance of suffering without retaliation for a just cause, and negotiation with dignity for all.

In January, the students put those new skills into action. You join peaceful sit-ins in Nashville's lunch counters, asking that black customers be served alongside whites. Onlookers scream abuse; some physically attack. Hundreds of students are arrested for refusing to leave. But the peaceful protests are rewarded on May 10, when the city's lunch counters are finally integrated by law.

When you graduate Vanderbilt in 1963, you are fully committed to the struggle for justice in the United States.

If you decide to go to California to work with Rabbi Joseph Glaser, who is campaigning to protect the rights of farm workers, turn to page 108.

If you want to become a lawyer and work to pass federal civil rights laws, turn to page 109.

Rabbi Joseph Glaser is the executive vice president of the CCAR, which represents the nation's Reform rabbis. They work for the economic rights of all people, pressuring the U.S. government to fight the War on Poverty and to send food to Communist China when it suffered massive crop failures. Rabbi Glaser is focused on the poverty and working conditions of California's farm workers.

Knowing your interest in civil rights, Rabbi Glaser soon introduces you to a lean, intense community activist named Fred Ross.

Fred tells you his background. "During the Depression, I worked with migrant workers to form self-government structures so they could negotiate with employers. Our folks fought against school segregation in the Citrus Belt, did voter registration and citizenship classes with the Community Service Organization, that sort of thing. What I do best is train other organizers. That's the key to changing society from the grassroots on up. Listen, you want to help the working class? I have someone for you to meet. He'll organize the farm laborers or die trying."

The day in San Jose when you meet Cesar Chavez, is the day that will change your life. The man's dark eyes smile warmly as he shakes your hand; anyone committed to improving the lives of the agricultural workers is his friend. He and his colleague Dolores Huerta have taken Fred's community organizing tactics further: they want to form a labor union of farm workers, and take the fight against Big Agriculture out of the fields and into the cities.

California's fertile valleys are Chavez' home. From the passenger seat of his battered old truck, you pass endless acres of vegetable and fruit fields; you stand beside him in the scorching heat as he speaks with workers about his vision for a better life. When you say you want to commit yourself to justice for the laborers, Chavez says, "Welcome to *la causa.*" He asks if you want to visit churches, synagogues, and community organizations to teach about the workers' lives, or if you'd rather join the negotiation teams that deal with farm corporations and the Teamsters union.

If you want to garner popular support for the workers, turn to page 110.

If you feel you'd be useful negotiating with owners, turn to page 111.

You enroll at Emory University's School of Law, but two weeks later, you're not in class. Crammed into an old Ford Squire, you and five other students have driven 600 miles to Washington to attend America's largest-ever civil-rights demonstration. President Kennedy has recently announced that he will support laws to protect minority rights, and there's a strong sense that the time is now. Organized by black, Jewish, and Catholic community leaders, the March for Jobs and Freedom is intended to focus attention on civil and economic rights for African-Americans.

The day is blisteringly hot, and the crowds are overwhelming. Many had feared violence, but the people are peacefully singing and holding hands. With binoculars you see celebrities on the Lincoln Memorial steps: Jackie Robinson, Ruby Dee, Sammy Davis Jr., Paul Newman. After the Queen of Gospel, Mahalia Jackson, sings of her vision of a better world, Rabbi Joachim Prinz, who had fled from Hitler's Germany, comes to the podium. He tells the crowd that the greatest shame is silence in the face of discrimination. Finally, Martin Luther King, Jr. addresses the crowd, describing his dream that one day his children will not be judged by the color of their skin, but by the content of their character.

Like the other 300,000 marchers, you are inspired to carry on the struggle for justice. When you get back to Emory, you add an advanced course in constitutional law to your schedule. You have several mornings without classes, and spend them at the office of the Southern Christian Leadership Conference, which has been organizing sit-ins and boycotts of segregated businesses. Police are arresting demonstrators, so you assist the volunteer attorneys with researching precedents and preparing motions for court.

The campaign continues heating up during your law school years. There are voter registration drives in the deep South, and in 1964, Congress passes the Civil Rights Act outlawing discrimination based on color, religion, sex, race, or national origin.

If, during a summer break, you decide to work for the Religious Action Center of Reform Judaism, turn to page 112.

If you'd rather work as a Senate aide, turn to page 113.

You ask some kids to teach you Spanish, and spend many months traveling between migrant labor camps, listening to the workers tell you about their lives and struggles.

These Latin American and Filipino laborers pick strawberries, grapes, lettuce, and broccoli, hurrying to keep up with the collection truck. Many of them are children. Their pay is lower than the national minimum wage, and they live in poverty. Farm laborers often work way more than forty hours a week. Conditions and housing are terrible, but they're afraid to complain, because they could lose their jobs or be beaten by their supervisors.

Half of the nation's fruits and vegetables are grown on California farms, which depend on these workers. The New Deal labor protection laws signed by President Roosevelt just thirty years ago don't apply to agriculture workers – farm managers don't have to give them rest or meal breaks, overtime pay, or even basic comfort and safety. Most Americans know nothing about this.

In the Union's small headquarters in Delano, sitting at a table with a telephone directory, you call every synagogue and church in the area, introducing yourself as a colleague of Rabbi Glaser. You ask to come speak with the congregants about farm laborers, and many say yes. With a full schedule, you borrow a car and ask your parents to send money for gas.

You always begin your talks with a quote from Proverbs: "Whoever oppresses the poor to increase his own wealth, will only come to poverty." Congregants listen attentively, and are astonished to learn the story behind the food they eat. "What can we do?" they ask you. You tell them they can participate in voter registration drives, and ask lawmakers to improve labor protections.

Late in 1965, a young civil rights organizer, Marshall Ganz, arrives from Mississippi to help organize the workers. He is a rabbi's son, and asks you whether you could formulate a solid Jewish argument that food grown by oppressed workers can't be kosher.

If you think you're up to that challenge, turn to page 114.

If you're more comfortable helping to make a case within the American legal system, turn to page 115.

The next few years are a whirlwind of activity. You coordinate strike actions, supporting picketers at the fields of the most oppressive employers. In 1967, you volunteer for the presidential campaign of Senator Robert F. Kennedy, who as Attorney General was a champion of civil rights enforcement. He is murdered in 1968, a few months after Dr. King's assassination. You return to the UFW to try to open lines of negotiation with ranch owners.

Cesar Chavez has joined with the Agricultural Workers Organizing Committee in demanding that grape workers receive the federal minimum wage. The growers balk, a strike is called and American consumers are asked not to buy table grapes until a contract is offered and signed. Millions support the workers by refusing to buy grapes. The California Grape and Tree Fruit League, an association of vineyard owners, strikes back, announcing that the boycott is ineffective, and their sales have really risen.

But eventually the opposition begins to crack. Lionel Steinberg, a major grape grower in the Coachella Valley, has led a dozen farm owners to the negotiation table. Steinberg is not particularly happy about paying workers a higher wage, but he accepts reality and also admires Cesar. Lewis Rosenstiel, another grape grower, raises pickers' pay to twice the minimum wage. Finally all the farm workers have their contract, and the boycott ends.

But the struggle continues for years. Lettuce growers in the Salinas Valley refuse to recognize the UFW as a bargaining partner. Fields are sprayed with pesticides with unknown medical dangers, and the giant Teamsters union is negotiating with ranch owners without any consultation with the workers in their fields.

Discontent seems to be growing everywhere in the country. Young people are protesting the Vietnam war, which many see as a pointless, destructive power struggle. Minorities are demanding not only civil rights, but the freedom to express their cultural identity. Women want opportunities outside their homes.

If you read Betty Friedan's The Feminine Mystique, *turn to page 116.*

If, at a family funeral, you hear a story about your great-uncle's survival after WWII, turn to page 117.

In June of 1964, while an intern at the Religious Action Center of Reform Judaism, you hear that the Reform rabbis' conference in Atlantic City is short-staffed, and you volunteer to help. A few days at the beach might be nice.

While handing out keys and packets to the conventioneers, you hear that Dr. King has asked the rabbis, via telegram, to join him and other leaders in St. Augustine, Florida, a city still oppressed by racial segregation and violence. Peaceful demonstrations are in progress, more arrests are expected, and the Ku Klux Klan is on patrol. You leave your post at the welcome table to find Albert Vorspan, the CCAR administrator. "I'm a law student, a RAC intern," you say to him. "I'd like to handle the travel arrangements to St. Augustine and serve as support staff." He agrees.

The next day you, Mr. Vorspan, and sixteen Reform rabbis fly to Florida. You had wanted a few days at the beach ... but this is quite different from your original vision. The beach of St. Augustine's beautiful seaside, designated "whites only," is literally soaked with the blood of peaceful activists who were attacked by white counter-demonstrators. The rabbis join a march to a church where Dr. King introduces them, to tremendous applause.

Anti-segregation actions have been going on here for weeks before your arrival; demonstrators have been shot, and the jails are filled with activists both black and white. You are at the jail, monitoring the treatment of the protesters, when the rabbis are hauled in. They had been holding a 'pray-in' in front of a whites-only motel, serving to distract the police while black and white demonstrators joined hands and jumped into the motel pool. All were arrested.

You were raised in the very dignified Reform tradition, and seeing the rabbis behind bars is a severe shock. But they seem to be in pretty good humor. "Don't make a speech, Dresner, it's too hot," you hear one of them warn. You sneak a camera into the jail and take pictures, and pass the film to reporters outside. Just as you intended, the public is appalled by the images.

If you remain at RAC after getting your law degree, turn to page 118.

If you'd rather be active in electoral politics, turn to page 119.

You follow developments in Congress closely in the spring of 1965. Last year's passage of the Civil Rights Act was in no way the end of the struggle; widespread injustice continues, and police and 'white citizens' groups continue to attack non-violent demonstrators marching for equality and de-segregation. In March, protesters are brutally beaten and tear-gassed on the Pettus Bridge in Selma, Alabama, as they attempt to walk to the state capital, Montgomery. The young man you met a few years back at non-violence training, John Lewis, has been seriously injured.

You get a summer position with a Senator, and move to Washington in May. A voting rights bill is in the Senate and the House, and is being argued in a conference committee. One morning you look up from your work, hearing a familiar voice in the hall. Dr. King and Kivie Kaplan of the NAACP are heading toward the office of Senator Everett Dirksen, one of the bill's sponsors, to try to smooth out an agreement. You get up and follow.

While they wait for the rest of the committee to arrive, you introduce yourself to Mr. Kaplan, telling him that you're studying law. He asks about your plans for after law school, and you say you want to work against economic and employment discrimination. You also note your disappointment that although the Civil Rights Act outlaws discriminations on the basis of gender, American women still don't have equality at work, home, or in family court.

"Well," Mr. Kaplan answers, "If you want to fight racial discrimination in the courts, you need to meet Jack Greenberg. He's the director of our Legal Defense and Education Fund. But if you want to work for women's equality, I'd suggest that you contact Bella Abzug. She's an attorney who does mainly labor law, but she's also been campaigning for the Equal Rights Amendment, and she's been talking about possibly running for Congress."

A few days later, President Johnson signs the Voting Rights Act into law. Dr. King, Rosa Parks and John Lewis attend the ceremony. And you have to decide what to do about your career.

To connect with the NAACP Legal Defense Fund, turn to page 120.

To join forces with Bella Abzug, turn to page 121.

You didn't bring your Bible to California, but perhaps you should have. In a library, you find a Torah translation and turn to Deuteronomy. Soon you find, in chapter 24, *"Do not oppress the hired laborer who is poor and needy, whether he is one of your people or one of the sojourners in your land within your gates. Give him his wages in the daytime, and do not let the sun set on them, for he is poor, and his life depends on them, lest he cry out to God about you, for this will be counted as a sin for you."*

You know that Torah laws provide just a basic concept, leaving rabbinical interpretation to apply them. What's the consequence of violating this particular "do not"? You place a long-distance phone call to your rabbi in Atlanta, Jacob Rothschild.

"The Talmud translates these concepts into concrete reality," he explains. "In this case, the fruit of exploited labor, or *oshek,* is forbidden since it results from a violation of Torah. In a sense, you could say that if workers are oppressed by a farmer while they're picking his crops, those crops aren't kosher."

You thank him and rush back to your typewriter, to compose a passionate article about the lives of the farm workers and your understanding about the meaning of the Deuteronomy laws. You mail copies to every Jewish newspaper and synagogue you know.

Did your message land? In the spring, rabbis are joining UFW protest marches. Chavez declares a national boycott of non-union grapes, and Americans respond – among them, the Boston Board of Rabbis, who declare these grapes forbidden, and Rabbi Haskel Lookstein whose thundering sermon "No man is free who has no economic opportunity" is published in the New York Times. Support for the workers comes from across the Jewish population, from Reform to Orthodox. The boycott finally ends in 1970, when the growers finally sign fair contracts with the laborers.

Eventually you decide to move on to Florida, where the sugar cane industry is making fortunes since the Cuban embargo halted imports. Unfortunately, these fortunes are created on the backs of desperate, underpaid refugee workers. You bring your organizing skills to the Farmworkers Rights Organization, and the rest of your career is an honorable, and holy, fight for labor justice. ✡

Volunteer lawyers generally focus on defending individual workers arrested while protesting. Cesar wishes someone could be the legal representation of the entire organization. In 1967, a tall, very casual-looking lawyer arrives from Los Angeles to do exactly that. This is Jerry Cohen.

Farm workers' civil rights are being violated in lots of places, not just California. Law enforcement officers called the Texas Rangers violently beat striking melon workers, and Cohen wants to file a federal civil rights suit. But the violence must be documented – pictures taken, and witnesses found. With notebook and camera in hand, you see demonstraters beaten, maced, and sometimes killed. You collect evidence to be presented in courts, and in the press, also, which is the court of public opinion.

The powerful Teamsters union wants contracts with the growers without bothering to consult the workers. A Teamster decks Cohen, sending him to the hospital for days. But soon he's back, arguing with judges who have declared picketing illegal, negotiating with ranch owners, and helping to write California's Agricultural Labor Relations Act, which becomes law in 1975.

The UFW organizes and supports hundreds of strikes, boycotts, and farm actions. But eventually, the union's idealism starts to fade, with fighting among the leaders, and discontentment because no actual farm laborers are allowed to be leaders. The UFW is weakened by declining membership. Although farm workers now have better conditions in California, sometimes laws to protect them are not enforced, depending on the political climate.

You know the challenges immigrant workers face, and when you learn that the Hebrew Immigrant Aid Society is helping refugees fleeing Southeast Asia, you want to go back East and work for them. Advocating for refugee Ethiopian, Iranian and Russian Jews, you use the skills you learned in California to lobby lawmakers and community agencies to help them become citizens and get jobs and homes. Soon you are working full-time with HIAS to resettle people from Afghanistan, Bosnia, and Africa. You know that your work fulfills the Torah mitsva, *"You shall not oppress the stranger, for you were strangers in the land of Egypt."* ✡

When World War II ended in 1945, millions of soldiers and sailors returned to the United States, expecting to resume their familiar home and work lives. Most women, whether they liked it or not, left their jobs and returned to their roles as housewives. Postwar prosperity allowed businesses to advertise hundreds of new household products, promising female consumers they'll make housekeeping glamorous, pleasant and satisfying. And television and magazines were full of ads for cosmetics and clothing that women must buy to remain beautiful for their husbands.

But you observe that the 'glamor' of running a household is over-shadowed by restrictions on women's lives. Many leave college so their husbands can prepare for their professions. If mothers work outside the home, usually as domestics or secretaries, they are criticized for leaving their children with babysitters. They earn far less than men, even for doing the same work. If male bosses harass them, they must endure it or quit. If their husbands beat them, few judges will punish them. A woman can't even have a credit card unless her husband co-signs for it.

But most American women cannot explain why they're unhappy until Betty Friedan publishes her book *The Feminine Mystique*. She writes: *"The problem lay buried, unspoken ... Each suburban housewife struggled with it alone ... she made the beds, shopped for groceries ... afraid to ask even of herself the silent question – 'Is this all?'"*

You have noticed that newspaper help-wanted ads are divided into men's and women's jobs. After you've read this book, you understand: society expects these two worlds to be separate. It's not right. Women should be doctors, lawyers, engineers and salespeople as well as men. You know you should join this fight.

You march in New York with 20,000 women in 1970, to mark the Women's Strike For Equality. The speeches make you realize that access to child-care and the ability to choose if and when to have children, are essential for women's liberation.

Women must have power over their own bodies. Joining Planned Parenthood's staff, you publicize their clinics' health and family planning services. You're helping millions of women to access low-cost medical care – and gain control over their own lives. ✡

In 1972, back home in Georgia for your great-uncle's funeral, you hear a story you had forgotten. During World War II, he had been a slave laborer in the Lodz ghetto in Poland, and was among the few remaining prisoners when the Nazis abandoned the area, fleeing the Soviet army. His family was murdered at the Chelmno extermination camp.

Agents of the International Rescue Committee, which had been organized by Albert Einstein before the war, arrived with food and medicine, and transported him and other survivors to Paris. There, in a resettlement facility, he met his future wife. The next year the IRC arranged for them to join his relatives in America.

"This is amazing," you say to your cousin. "I've never heard of this International Rescue Committee. Does it still exist?"

"Of course," she answers. "They supported the Berlin Airlift and relocated Hungarian refugees after the revolution. They assist refugees from Haiti, Chile, the Soviet Union, you name it."

Many Americans are suffering from poverty, racism, and violence, but in other parts of the world, millions are fleeing for their lives from wars and brutal dictators. You wish you could help everyone, everywhere, but for now, you want to look into this IRC. You write to its chairman, Leo Cherne, telling him about your experience with the farm workers and your interest in his work.

He soon responds, inviting you to New York to talk to their operations chief about how you can help. Walking to his office, you see Elie Wiesel's portrait on a wall; he is on the IRC board of directors.

You're impressed by the wide scope of the agency's activities, and learn that they immediately need staff in the West Bengal state of India, to oversee construction of water and sanitation facilities.

There's no reason to wait. A week later, you are in India organizing desperately-needed help for villagers displaced by war. You coordinate volunteer building teams and delivery of materials. Your work supports the health of victims of conflict, and also restores their dignity. Providing this relief is a career as important and rewarding as anything you have ever done. ✡

Back at Emory, you stay in touch with some of the people you got to know in St. Augustine. You have always been proud of Reform Jews' commitment to social justice, and these folks lead political and religious resistance to discrimination. When you get your law degree, you join the Religious Action Center's team.

It is 1966, and the Civil Rights Act has been passed, but prejudice still exists everywhere. Minorities are refused mortgages and apartments by landlords who want their neighborhoods to remain white. No law prevents this bigotry.

Representative Emmanuel Celler of New York introduces a bill that bans discrimination in the sale and rental of housing. He is your hero since he successfully pushed the Hart-Celler Act, making it illegal for the government to consider national origin when deciding whether to admit an immigrant to the United States.

When the National Association of Real Estate Brokers starts pressuring members of Congress to vote against the Fair Housing bill, you ask Reform Jews across the nation to tell their representatives that forcing people to live in segregated neighborhoods is not equality, and that these practices are degrading and shameful. After much negotiating and filibustering, the bill passes in 1968.

William Taylor, the staff director of the U.S. Commission on Civil Rights, who worked tirelessly to pass the bill, drops by the RAC office to celebrate. You ask him what led him to civil rights work. "I grew up in Brooklyn," he answers. "Other than getting cursed for being Jewish, I wasn't aware of prejudice around me. But in 1947 I saw, or rather I heard, what Jackie Robinson had to endure at Ebbets Field. When I started looking for it, I saw it everywhere. Thurgood Marshall – now he's the Solicitor General – hired me at the NAACP. After the *Brown* Supreme Court decision in 1954, I've mostly worked on school desegregation cases."

As the years pass, you lead Jewish delegations to visit their lawmakers in Washington, to advocate for Soviet Jewish prisoners of conscience. You educate the Jewish community about bills in Congress concerning poverty, homelessness, and employment, and train young citizens to exercise their rights to petition Congress. Justifiably, you are proud of your mission. ✡

Like many Americans, you are inspired by young Senator Bobby Kennedy of New York, the slain President's brother. He's spoken boldly against the nuclear arms race and the racist apartheid system in South Africa. Working to fund for anti-poverty programs, he supports Dr. King and farm worker advocate Cesar Chavez.

Kennedy announces his candidacy in March 1968, and two weeks later President Johnson announces he won't run for re-election. You and thousands of other enthusiastic volunteers sign on to campaign for Bobby. In June, he wins the California primary, and surges ahead of Senator Eugene McCarthy. But that night, two months after Dr. King's murder, Bobby is killed by an assassin.

Bitter about the tragedy, and angry about the endless Vietnam war which the U.S. is not winning, you join the campaign of Senator McCarthy, a peace advocate. The country's mood is restless. Young people are rebelling against "the establishment," loudly advocating for peace, love, and mind-expanding drugs.

A group of mostly Jewish activists, including Jerry Rubin, Abbie Hoffman, and Paul Krassner, form the Youth International Party or 'Yippies.' They attract attention with their anti-war theatrics, like nominating a pig for President, and saying they'll disrupt the Democratic National Convention in Chicago, blocking streets and dumping LSD in the water supply. They don't really intend to do it, but the alarmed mayor refuses to grant permits for protesters.

Thousands of demonstraters gather anyway, listening to Phil Ochs singing protest songs. The police respond brutally with mace, tear gas and billy clubs, and the demonstrators throw food and rocks. You hear about it inside the convention, when Senator Ribicoff, during a speech, says the police are using Gestapo tactics outside. The convention is a disaster. In November, Richard Nixon defeats Hubert Humphrey to win the Presidency.

You feel discouraged and hopeless about politics. But after dropping out of the scene for several years to teach at a college, you run for your local town board, win, and later become a state legislator. You spend the rest of your public career fighting pollution as an environmental protection commissioner. ✡

The names of Jack Greenberg and Thurgood Marshall have always been linked in your mind. Together they had argued the 1954 Supreme Court case of *Brown v. Board of Education*, which challenged the segregation of black and white children into separate schools. They argued that "separate" could never be "equal," and thus segregated schools discriminated against black students – and they won. You had made a speech about the decision when you were first called to the Torah at age thirteen.

So if Kivie Kaplan actually wants to introduce you to Mr. Greenberg, you won't hesitate. A week later, you're waiting in his office while he finishes a phone call, looking at the pictures and documents on his wall. In a frame is the first page of a 1961 decision of the United States Court of Appeals for the Fifth Circuit. You can't see the small print, but you know what it is: James Meredith's victory over the University of Mississippi, which had denied him admission because he was black. Mr. Greenberg had argued the case – and is now hanging up the phone.

"So!" he begins, "Kivie says you want to work in economic discrimination. You're at Emory. What have you done so far? How are you at researching? When will you finish law school?"

"Next year," you answer. "Well, I've been arranging Senate hearings on the Voting Rights bill. During college I was a legislative aide for my state senator back in Atlanta. And I'm a pretty thorough researcher. I know my way around a law library."

"That sounds good," he responds. "Send me some of the stuff you've written. Next spring, maybe I can put you to work."

Mr. Greenberg proves to be as brilliant a teacher as he is a litigator, and you're an avid student. A year later, you're attending meetings with members of the Southern Christian Leadership Conference and preparing motions asking courts to allow them to demonstrate throughout the South. Soon Mr. Greenberg feels confident enough to send you to San Antonio to help launch the Mexican American Legal Defense and Education project. You spend your brilliant career defending the civil rights of your fellow Americans. ✡

You are in line to get a seat in a crowded airport café in 1966 when you strike up a conversation with a flight attendant. Ending up at the same table, you ask her, "Say, I always wanted to know – why are all stewardesses so young? I've never seen one over thirty."

The stewardess is amused. "Didn't you read about the Congressional hearings last year? A lot of airlines fire or relocate us at about that age – or when we get married, whichever comes first."

You are appalled. "But that's illegal under Title VII of the Civil Rights Act, if the rules are different for women than for men."

She shrugs. "That doesn't really matter if the law isn't enforced," she tells you. You inquire if this issue's been taken to court.

"Well, last year the union sued Braniff and won," she says. "The New York State human rights commission is looking into it, but nothing yet. In fact, a guy on the Equal Employment Opportunities Commission said the sex discrimination clause is a joke."

So it's not a surprise to you, not long after this, when you learn that several dozen female activists have started a new organization to defend their rights: the National Organization of Women. You *are* a little shocked, however, to read the platform that NOW adopts: they demand that abortion be legalized, public funding for child care, and passage of an Equal Right Amendment to the Constitution. "These women are going for it all," you think.

The ERA is a compelling proposal, when you think about it. It would end legal distinctions between men and women in divorce, employment, and property; it seems the most effective way to guarantee equal pay and access to jobs. Kivie Kaplan had recommended talking to a lawyer named Bella Abzug about women's rights issues, and you ask a mutual friend for an introduction.

"Are you particularly sensitive?" asks your friend.

"Sure, I'm as sensitive as the next person ... wait, why?"

"'Battling Bella' is very direct. She's honest, and doesn't waste time. Let's say she has a forceful personality. If you think you can handle it, fine. If not, find some other way to help the cause."

You're up for it, and arrange to meet Mrs. Abzug in her Greenwich Village office. She welcomes you pleasantly, wearing her trademark wide-brimmed hat, and gets right down to business.

"You said on the phone you want to work for economic justice. Do you consider yourself a revolutionary?" Hesitantly you begin an answer. She interrupts.

"Sam Adams, Thomas Jefferson, those guys started a revolution. But it's not finished. *We* have to finish it. Jefferson, Washington, they had guts. They didn't stop when they came up against powerful opponents. Today we're up against institutions that don't want to yield an inch. They don't want to give up any control over women's lives, over the profits they make selling armaments, over anything. If you're a revolutionary, there's room for you in this fight. If not, go be nice somewhere else."

Abzug isn't just about women's rights. She fought the un-American Senator Joe McCarthy, and created the Women's Strike for Peace against the military draft and the war in Vietnam. She advocates legal protection for gays and lesbians. And she is determined to get the Equal Rights Amendment passed and ratified.

With so many interrelated goals needing such complex strategies, Abzug needs alert, detail-oriented support staff. You join her team, researching legislative issues and meeting with allies and opponents. When she runs for Congress in 1970, you schedule her appearances and write speeches, and when she takes office, you are her legislative director, monitoring committee meetings and writing statements for her to read on the House floor.

When the Equal Rights Amendment is submitted to state legislatures for ratification, you serve as Abzug's liaison to the National Organization of Women. In 1979, the clock runs out before the required 38 states ratify. The ERA is dead.

Many struggles for equality remain, including sex discrimination in workplaces, birth control and abortion rights, and family and medical leave. You continue to fight the good fight.

Chapter Seven

I Want to Be a Writer

Because we produced the Hebrew Bible, Jews have been called the "people of the book" for centuries. We pray every Rosh Hashana to be included in the Book of Life, and on Passover we conduct our seders by reading from the haggada. Our holiest object is a book – the Torah. And everyone is looking into a siddur during Shabbat and holiday services. I read once that in Germany in the Middle Ages, outsiders observing a synagogue and seeing everyone apparently reading, called the place a schul, or school. Well, we Jews tend to like books.

Among the Jewish superhero comic-book writers you may see in this chapter are Bob Kane, Bill Finger, Jerry Siegel, Joe Shuster, Joe Simon, Jack Kirby, Stan Lee, Lee Falk, and Julius Schwartz. The "usual gang of idiots" at MAD Magazine include Al Feldstein, Will Elder, Dave Berg, Al Jaffee and William Gaines. Some of the great children's authors of our people are H.A. and Margaret Rey, Sydney Taylor, Maurice Sendak, Bennett Cerf, Shel Silverstein, Donald Sobol and Judy Blume. And the heroic Harper & Row editor, Charlotte Zolotow – never forget the role of editors.

Jewish writers for adults mentioned here are Arthur Miller, Viktor Frankl, Primo Levi, Anne Frank, Howard Fast, J. D. Salinger, Leon Uris, Herman Wouk and Lionel Trilling. Dominant in science fiction: William Tenn, Avram Davidson, Jack Dann, Harlan Ellison, and, of course, Isaac Asimov. Humorists S. J. Perelman and Leo Rosten are here, and songwriters Abel Meeropol and Tom Glazer. Jewish cartoonists include William Steig (who created Shrek), Jules Feiffer, and Saul Steinberg.

You may also encounter some of the great television writers: Mel Tolkin, Neil and Danny Simon, Selma Diamond, Mel Brooks, Carl Reiner, Lucille Kallen, Woody Allen and Larry Gelbart.

Life begins for you in the pleasant residential area of Washington, DC, called Crestwood, in the 1930s. Your home is a short distance from Rock Creek Park, and you can also walk to the National Zoo any time you like; it's part of the Smithsonian museum system.

Your father works at the U.S. Government Printing Office and your mother is a third-grade teacher. Mom taught you to read before you started school, and you love books. Sometimes you read after bedtime, with a battery-powered lamp under the covers.

You breeze through children's classics from England like *Winnie The Pooh* and *The Wind In The Willows,* and American books too, like the *Wizard of Oz* and Mark Twain's stories.

You also like the new Timely and Detective Comics magazines, where muscly champions of goodness and democracy have thrilling adventures fighting evil, and you can look at them while reading the stories. The world is a scary place as Hitler's forces are overwhelming Europe, and to escape into another world where superheroes beat bad guys is comforting. Each month you wait impatiently for cartoonists Bob Kane and Bill Finger to publish a new Batman adventure, and for Jerry Siegel and Joe Shuster to share more Superman stories. Your favorite is Captain America, created by Joe Simon and Jack Kirby – you like that his superpowers come from American ingenuity, unlike Superman who's from Krypton. Batman has no superpowers, he's just terribly clever.

You yourself aren't much good at drawing, but you like to make up stories and write them out on typing paper, reading them to your family after dinner. Your parents urge you to show them to your teacher, who is so impressed that she sends several to a children's story contest. Several months later you receive a certificate with a blue ribbon. "I must be pretty good at this!" you think.

During junior high school, you often get in trouble for not paying attention in class, generally because you're reading a book under your desk, or staring into space while thinking about a story line.

If you decide to search the local library for story ideas, turn to page 125.

If you find no new comic books at the newsstand one day and buy a New Yorker *magazine instead, turn to page 126.*

In 1947, at the nearby Mt. Pleasant Public Library, standing in line at the checkout desk, you see a bulletin board with drawings from a recent children's art show. One picture catches your eye. It's a man standing in front of the U.S. Capitol, ripping off his business suit to reveal some sort of superhero costume. You go over to identify the artist; she is Mollie, a student at your school.

Finding her next day in the cafeteria, you tell her you liked your drawing in the library, and ask if she's ever drawn a comic strip. No, she says, she can't think of any stories. You ask her about the character in her picture. She answers, "I thought it would be interesting to draw a superhero who's a Congressman but secretly he's an action hero who fights crime."

It sounds pretty weird, but that's no problem, so you and Mollie start your collaboration. You have a hero, so you devise a German naval officer as the bad guy, his sidekick, and some prominent citizens. You create a story about a German submarine cruising into the Chesapeake Bay. As you fill in the narration, you feel so excited – this is exactly how Stan Lee brings the Destroyer to life! In a few weeks, you have a complete story pencilled in 108 panels across six large boards. You leave Mollie to ink the strip while you try to figure out how to publish *Capitol Commando*.

You beg your parents for a train ticket to go to the World Science Fiction Convention in Philadelphia in August. Mollie and you wrap the precious boards in tissue paper and arrive at the hotel ballroom excited to meet the cartoonists. Sure enough, there's Phantom's creator, Lee Falk, signing autographs. While you're waiting to meet him, Mollie gestures toward a pleasant-looking man with glasses, name-tagged Julius Schwartz. He published *Time Traveller*, the science fiction magazine, and now he's at All-American Comics; he hired the men who draw Flash and the Green Lantern. Schwartz looks at your comic strip and says you have a talent for telling stories for kids, and also for science fiction and fantasy. "Which one pulls at your mind?" he asks.

If you want to write stories for kids,, turn to page 127.

If it's science fiction and fantasy that stir your imagination, turn to page 128.

The *New Yorker* magazine is obviously meant for grownups, which makes it far more interesting to you, and you pay the news vendor and bring it to a park bench, paging through it and eating an apple. You first notice its cartoons – hilarious, biting cartoons which mercilessly mock pretentious urbanites. Then you page back and look for interesting articles. That's the day you first encounter S. J. Perelman, writing about the farm he'd just bought.

When I first settled down on a heap of shale in the Delaware Valley, I too had a romantic picture of myself. For about a month I was a spare, sinewy frontiersman in fringed buckskin, with crinkly little lines about the eyes and a slow laconic drawl. After I almost blew off a toe cleaning an air rifle, though, I decided I was more the honest rural type. I started wearing patched blue jeans and mopped my forehead with a red banana (I found out later it should have been a red bandanna).

Today, thanks to unremitting study, I can change a fuse so deftly that it plunges the entire county into darkness. The power company has offered me as high as fifteen thousand dollars a year to stay out of my own cellar.

This writer is clearly a master of language, and he outrageously skewers anyone who catches his attention, reducing all his targets to ridiculousness. This is real power, you think. You try out his style on people around you. "Mademoiselle Haleine Mauvaise oozes through the classroom, snooping into her students' exercise books, trailing the sour bouquet of last night's *oeufs brouillés* across their labored verb conjugations ..." This stuff is fun to write, though it won't make you any friends among the teachers.

You enter Columbia University in 1950, majoring in Western literature, studying with literary critic Lionel Trilling and writing for a student magazine. You like making readers laugh, but you know very well literature's ability to point out society's injustices. Arthur Miller's plays *All My Sons* and *The Crucible* cry against greed, xenophobia, and moral irresponsibility. An essay couldn't convey these truths so powerfully; it is the art that speaks.

If you focus on humorous social/psychological satire, turn to page 129.

If your imagination leads you to more serious explorations of humanity, turn to page 130.

Even while a kid yourself, you have a higher regard for children's ethics, their sense of right and wrong, than for adults. It was adults who have committed all the brutal war crimes, and, although it was also adults who defeated those fascists, you kind of wish that children were in charge of all the important decisions.

Julius Schwartz, the great comic book editor at Detective Comics – DC for short – is obviously someone who has never lost his inner child. He looks at your storyboards and tells Mollie that he thinks she should be in fine arts, not comics, because her drawings tell their own story about the characters, not really related to the narration. He tells you that you should experiment with stories about kids, with real-life settings. Maybe you'll eventually create some new genre of comic strip. But for now, he says, write stories.

The stories you liked as a kid were *Curious George* by H.A. and Margaret Rey, and Sydney Taylor's *All-of-a-Kind Family*. But you never found any books about your world. So you begin a story about a group of urban children who are bored with school and looking for something to do that's exciting, but not actually illegal.

Get That Horse Off This Train is finished about the time you graduate high school, and, not being shy, you mail it to Bennett Cerf, founder and director of the publishing firm Random House. You like his joke books, and you've seen him on TV as a game show panelist, so you feel as if you know him.

A major surprise comes in the mail a few weeks later: an acquisitions editor at Random House likes the story but won't publish it on its own. She invites you to meet with a staffer to develop eight or ten companion stories that they might publish as a collection.

Writing the stories is exhilarating, hard work. You spend a lot of time staring out your window, trying to squeeze ideas out of your brain. After two years of working at a library, attending college part-time, and window-staring, you have a manuscript titled *Way Past Bedtime*. Your editor loves it but scribbles a thousand suggestions, sending you back to your desk for another six months.

To keep writing traditional children's books, turn to page 131.

If you want to break the mold and try something new, turn to page 132.

Science fiction has always stirred your imagination; it leaves behind what's known and ventures into time travel, parallel universes, and life on other planets. You started reading *Amazing Stories* since you were ten, particularly enjoying fantasies by Isaac Asimov and Howard Fast. Asimov's first story was "Marooned Off Vesta":

Eagerly he searched the skies for the little blue-white speck that was Earth. ... It had often amused him that Earth should always be the first object sought by space travelers when star-gazing, but the humor of the situation did not strike him now. However, his search was in vain. From where he lay, Earth was invisible. It, as well as the Sun, must be hidden behind Vesta.

Asimov, an actual scientist, is an intelligent fantasist who writes near-plausible stories, drawing readers into unreachable places and times. In college, you read his *I, Robot* and *Foundation*, and almost everything else that Astounding Science Fiction and the Gnome Press publishes. The magazine also introduces you to William Tenn, who uses satire and humor in "Child's Play" and "Venus and the Seven Sexes."

There are other science fiction fans at college, and you write some stories for these friends. Your starting point is the story of Shamir the worm, who, according to Jewish folklore, assisted King Solomon in cutting stone to build the Temple in Jerusalem. You posit that Shamir was a visitor from another quadrant of the galaxy who went on to build pyramids in Mexico and Stonehenge in England – but plans to return to his home planet with recommendations on the best way to conquer Earth.

The students like your stories very much, and recommend that you submit them to publishers. "Don't limit yourself," they recommend. "Your stories could appeal to both kids and adults."

If you send your manuscript to Charlotte Zolotow at Harper and Brothers, turn to page 133.

If you send your manuscript to William Gaines at EC Comics, turn to page 134.

Reading the *New Yorker* is even more enjoyable now that you're in school in New York, and you read other regular contributors besides Perelman. A favorite is Leo Rosten, writing under the pseudonym Leonard Q. Ross, who, before the war, taught English in night classes to immigrants. He has invented a character he calls Hyman Kaplan, a night school student, who approves of the rules of English, but doesn't think they apply to *him*. Kaplan dominates the classes, which are taught by a hapless Mr. Parkhill.

"Vell, 'Honest Jake' Popper vas a fine man, mit a hot like gold. Ufcawss, Jake Popper vasn't a beeg soldier; he didn't make Valley Fudges or free slafes. Jake Popper had a dalicatessen store…in his store could even poor pipple mitout money, alvays gat somting to eat – if dey vas honest. Jake did a tramendous beeg business – on cradit. An' averybody loved him.

"Vun day vas 'Honest Jake' fillink bed. He had hot an' cold vaves by de same time' – vat ve call a fivver. So averybody said, 'Jake, lay don in bad, rast!' But did Jake Popper lay don in bad, rast? No! He stayed in store, day an' night. He said, 'I got to tink abot mine costumers!' An' he got voise and voise. De doctors insulted odder doctors. Dey took him in de Mont Sinai Hospital! Blood confusions dey gave him!"

The *New Yorker*'s cartoonists tell stories in a different way, describing characters in drawings, they skewer their insecurities and pretensions with a punch line. William Steig draws a fat husband asking his dowdy wife, "Whither goest thou so gaily attired?" and a woman in a park saying to a statue, "I just love your poetry!" You also are a fan of Jules Feiffer and Saul Steinberg's cartoons.

Cartoons are like vignettes, tiny plays frozen in a single idea. You love stage comedies, and are intrigued by cartoonish characters coming to life, sometimes voicing your own feelings and frustrations. You invent your own character: Hubert Low, a nondescript department-store clerk constantly passed over for promotion. Hubert mutters his judgments about more successful employees, which only the audience hears. He morosely celebrates his rivals' downfalls, but is never promoted.

If you decide to write Hubert into a television pilot script, go to page 135.

If you think you'd like to write for film, turn to page 136.

The years after World War II are prosperous and creative in the United States, but the genocide of the Jews in Europe pervades the public consciousness, partly because so many American Jews are connected to, or witnessed, Hitler's atrocities. And many of those Jews are writers. A concentration camp survivor named Viktor Frankl records his experiences in *Man's Search For Meaning* in 1946, followed the next year by Primo Levi's autobiographical *Survival in Auschwitz*. Then *The Diary of a Young Girl*, by the teen-aged Holocaust victim Anne Frank, is published posthumously in English in 1952. With a foreword by Eleanor Roosevelt, *Diary* immediately becomes a best-seller.

A lot of fiction of this time tells of anxiety and alienation. J. D. Salinger's *Catcher In The Rye* describes the confused hopelessness of a teenager who cannot find meaning in his life. In *The Caine Mutiny*, by Herman Wouk, the moral rightness of fighting fascism is affirmed, but it also depicts the cowardice and bullying that sometimes occurs in the difficult, surreal setting of a Navy ship in wartime. Howard Fast's *Spartacus*, about a Roman slave uprising, is inspired by the noble but doomed resistance of European ghetto fighters against the Nazis. And Leon Uris writes *Mila 18*, a fictionalized account of the Warsaw Ghetto uprising in 1943.

You are in a nightclub one evening to hear the legendary Billie Holiday, feeling mellow and lost in the beauty of her rich, smoky voice. At the end of her second set, she sings Abel Meeropol's song *Strange Fruit*. It's a thin metaphor for the agony of lynching victims in America. "*Southern trees bear a strange fruit – blood on the leaves and blood at the root. Black bodies swinging in the southern breeze; strange fruit hanging from the poplar trees.*"

The lyrics burn the heart of the listener, and the melody makes them unforgettable. No story, or even poem, has ever moved you like this song, and after you have absorbed its impact, you wonder that it's never occurred to you to set your thoughts as songs.

If you want to find a musical partner to write songs, turn to page 137.

If you'd rather write short stories and novels, turn to page 138.

After a number of rewrites, Random House children's literature division accepts your manuscript, sends you a contract and a modest retainer check. You feel energized and optimistic, and begin work on your next project, *Please Don't Call My Parents.*

Way Past Bedtime is published and vigorously promoted to libraries, bookstores, schools and teachers' organizations. It generates a lot of interest and you are interviewed on radio and even on a children's television program. Your contract with Random House requires you to travel to book fairs and librarian conferences, which is actually more fun than you had predicted.

The next decade is spent writing more books for pre-teens, and you enjoy getting occasional fan letters from your readers. You keep attending author events, and one afternoon find yourself at a book festival in Florida, sitting next to a pleasant gentleman, Donald Sobol. Penguin Books just published his *Encyclopedia Brown, Boy Detective.* A copy of it is in front of him on the table, and you start reading it while he's talking to an interviewer.

The Encyclopedia Brown stories are short mysteries set in a small town, and the title character is ten years old. Nobody fools the young detective, who charges 25¢ an hour for his work. To find out how Encyclopedia solves each case, you have to turn to the back of the book, and you are trying to puzzle out the first mystery when Sobol taps your arm -- it's your turn at the microphone.

He is one of many Jewish authors of young people's books whom you feel fortunate to meet during your career. When you become a parent yourself, the writer whose work you and your children love most is Judy Blume. Her books break with tradition, and address the delicate issues that teens find so hard to discuss: divorce, religion, bullying, racism and sexuality. Even Blume's titles, like *Are You There, God? It's Me, Margaret* and *It's Not The End of the World,* are comforting. You sense that she understands that kids want to understand the adult world, but not step into it; and you gain a deeper understanding of that difficult balance that children live, and that adults often forget.

Judy Blume's work helps you write more three-dimensional characters and stories, and you always will be grateful to her. ✡

Way Past Bedtime does well, and you look around for more ideas. Why not observe what kind of stories children in your own family enjoy? You have nieces and nephews, wonderful intelligent kids who are well-behaved and never need to be punished. But they're fascinated by the misbehavior of some of their classmates, and love to tell you about their naughty antics.

Obviously, your young relatives enjoy vicarious thrills. To amuse them, you invent a rotten kid who never listens to her parents, and write stories about her. To avoid trouble with your sister, you make sure your character always ends up suffering consequences. Your editor likes the stories, and they become a very popular series called *Headstrong Hannah*. However, you get a significant number of letters from readers who love Hannah and wish that she could sometimes get away with her shenanigans.

You're not sure that's a good idea. But one day in 1961, you're in a bookstore looking at the new children's titles, and you see something odd from Simon & Schuster, *Uncle Shelby's ABZ Book*. Flipping through it, you soon realize you're reading something very weird. The author, Shel Silverstein, has drawn cartoons with captions for each letter of the alphabet, and they're positively twisted:

See the potty. The potty is deep. The potty has water at the bottom. Maybe somebody will fall in the potty and drown. Don't worry, as long as you keep wetting your pants, you will never drown in the potty.

Should this be in the children's section? You look up the author. He's a cartoonist, poet and songwriter, and his subversiveness has a devoted following. You wonder if this is going to be a trend. Two years later, an illustrator named Maurice Sendak presents his first book, *Where The Wild Things Are*. A boy named Max has been sent to bed without dinner for misbehaving, and his room transforms into a jungle. Max sails away to an island where he is crowned king of a crew of grotesque but adorable monsters.

It certainly seems okay to reward naughtiness in children's literature these days! You decide to set Headstrong Hannah loose. In your next story, she gets elected student body president, and wreaks havoc in her school – and there's nothing the principal can do about it. Your book sales shoot through the roof! ✡

You carry the carefully-wrapped manuscript – your first – to the post office, and watch the clerk carry it to a dispatch bin. In a few days, it will be on the desk of Charlotte Zolotow, children's editor at Harper Brothers. She is a legendary shepherd of talented authors, and you hope with all your might that she will add you to the Harper family.

It takes a month, but the answer arrives, "I felt excitement when I read about Shamir," Zolotow writes. "You tell a good story and kids will want to read it. It's a trifle over-written in places, and I'd like to work with you. Not to shorten it, but to make sure that every word in your book tells something important."

This is it – the doorway to your career has opened. Over the next few months, you travel back and forth between your editor's office and your own desk. You take out unnecessary words and phrases that don't convey meaning, so that your sentences flow more fluently, creating uninterrupted scenes in the reader's mind.

Rock of Ages is the first science-fiction book many children read. You're invited to conventions and panel discussions to talk about the appeal of this category of literature and what can be done to widen its audience. As years pass, you meet many of your favorite writers at these events, and are proud to sign your books for fans a few feet away from where they're doing the same.

Jewish sci-fi authors, especially, love your use of Biblical and rabbinic folklore as sources. Avram Davidson, who draws from medieval legend in his Vergil Magus and Peregrine novels, started out as a Talmudic scholar, and likes to talk to you about the wild imaginations of ancient rabbis; you use several of his ideas in your books. You are thrilled to be introduced to Jack Dann and Harlan Ellison, who, when they hear about your character Shamir, spontaneously begin riffing on Jewish topics with an intergalactic twist.

But the greatest honor of all is meeting Isaac Asimov. He is an expert in many fields and genres; he's even written a *Guide to the Bible*, and graciously discusses with you other Hebrew myths you might use in future stories. With a patron like Asimov, there is no star you cannot reach. ✡

Bill Gaines went into the family business: EC Comics. But his brisk business producing horror comics was ruined by a Senate investigation into juvenile delinquency. After he refused to cooperate with the new 'industry standards,' the publishers who controlled newsstand distribution killed off EC's horror comics.

You hope that Gaines likes your sci-fi and assigns an artist to turn it into comics. And he does like your stories, and invites you to the EC offices in lower Manhattan. Al Feldstein, the editor, welcomes you and offers you a seat. On the walls are outrageous, oversized drawings of fabulous animals, exaggerated landscapes, and rude cartoons, with hilarious titles. The place smells like ink.

"So," Feldstein says, "you write science fiction. I've read your *yiddischer* worm story. It has a certain zany aspect, if you ask me."

In this setting, that sounds like a compliment, so you thank him.

"Here's the situation," he explains. "We've decided to concentrate on building up *MAD* Magazine. Catch!" and he throws you a copy as if you didn't know every issue by heart. "We've got the finest artists around, and great writers, too, but we need more. *MAD* parodies popular culture – a lot of satire. Do you have a good handle on the science fiction kids are reading now?"

Yes, you respond. "Good. Why don't you work on a sendup of, say, Jules Verne, and we'll run it past the gang and see what they can do with it. Let's show you around. Eisenberg!"

A balding artist with a friendly expression looks up from his drafting table. "This is Wolfie," says Feldstein. "Maybe you've seen his work. He signs his stuff Will Elder."

Will Elder, creator of Poopeye and Mickey Rodent, is possibly the finest caricaturist alive today. You follow him speechlessly through introductions to Dave Berg and Al Jaffee, cartoonists you have adored since you were ten.

And that's how it begins. You begin writing for *MAD*, "Humor in a Jugular Vein." The 'usual gang of idiots' develops your funny stories into hilarious cartoon strips. It's such a great job that it never occurs to you to leave. ✡

You pitch your pilot for *Low Life* to NBC. The network has been successful with television comedies like Milton Berle's *Texaco Star Theater* and Sid Caesar's *Your Show of Shows*, and besides, you're related to the secretary of NBC's famous producer, Max Liebman.

Mr. Liebman reads your script, and invites you to come in. "We can't use a situation comedy now," he tells you. "We already have *Mr. Peepers* and *The Mickey Rooney Show*. We'll buy your script and hold it; but I really like your dialogue. Maybe you could sit in on writers' meetings, see if you like sketch comedy."

When you step into the NBC writers' room on the 6th floor of West 56th Street, you know this is comedy's Holy of Holies. Mel Tolkin, the head writer, has the staggering task of organizing the ideas of the funniest writers in television. Sitting unobtrusively by the wall, you listen to the back-and-forth of Neil and Danny Simon, Selma Diamond, Mel Brooks, Carl Reiner, and Lucille Kallen. The comedy-writing process is loud, hilarious, and mildly violent – you see dozens of pencils stuck in the tile ceiling.

You are only marginally useful to the team, and you spend a lot of time writing your own plays which are occasionally produced off-Broadway. Woody Allen and Larry Gelbart soon arrive in the writers' room, working on Sid Caesar's next show, and you love their sharp humor. "All jokes are bitter truths," explains Gelbart, and you begin to see that pain can be re-visioned as great comedy.

Defying the 1960s' bitter truths, Neil Simon leaves television for stage comedy, becoming the most successful playwright since Shakespeare. In 1966 he has four plays, including *The Odd Couple*, on Broadway simultaneously. Mel Brooks and Woody Allen depart to make movies, with even more triumphant careers, and Carl Reiner develops and directs *The Dick Van Dyke Show*.

Larry Gelbart gets an idea for a TV series after seeing a 1970 black comedy film, set in a mobile army surgical unit during the Korean War. When CBS commits to *M*A*S*H*, you are asked to join the creative staff. The hilarious, heartbreaking series, a cry against war and a tribute to the human spirit, becomes an American icon. It's the finest creative effort you could ever have hoped for. ✡

Although of course you're happy that Hitler was defeated, and know that World War II was necessary to do that, you are basically anti-war. You see the military establishment in the 1950s and 1960s as a dangerous confluence of the abuse of authority and mindless conformity. The lives of both soldiers and civilians seem cheapened in the pursuit of questionable goals.

Creative artists are increasingly bold about expressing their objections to militarism and the political and industrial institutions that support it. Movies like Stanley Kubrick's *Paths of Glory* and *Dr. Strangelove*, and Stanley Kramer's *On The Beach* mock popular paranoia about Soviet communism and the nuclear arms race. *Munro*, a short animated film written by cartoonist Jules Feiffer, tells of a four-year-old boy mistakenly drafted into the Army, where mindless adherence to standard procedures cannot admit the mistake.

You write a film script about an enlisted company clerk who persistently seeks logic in incoherent military regulations, and inadvertently surrenders his entire battalion to an enemy as confused as himself. *Scrappy's Command* is produced by an independent film studio and wins several awards. You move to Hollywood to develop scripts for bigger companies and enjoy a good deal of success in commercial films and, eventually, animated cartoons. You tend to focus on cynical characters who generally feel hopeless about their world, but sometimes, against their better judgment, take a chance on optimism.

One day in 1990, searching a bookshop for a gift for Kate Capshaw's and Steven Spielberg's new baby, you come across a new picture book by your favorite cartoonist, William Steig. It's about a grouchy ogre who reluctantly saves a princess, and it sort of fits your sense of humor. You're amused that Steig calls his ogre "Shrek," the Yiddish word for "dreadful," and you think the baby's parents will like it, too.

It seems like they do. Eleven years later, Dreamworks Animation releases the wickedly funny computer-animated *Shrek,* a sendup of fairy tales clearly intended for adults as well as kids. Sequels, TV specials, an entire franchise follow. Well done! ✿

The 1950s, when you graduate college and face the world as an adult, is a troubled period. Americans and Russians are terrified of each other, and oppression crushes many spirits.

You find a job in a public-relations firm, and spend your free time writing song lyrics. Some are about the strength of the human spirit. Others are about freedom and equality, standing up for what's right. Friends with guitars set them to music. They sing them in coffeehouses and house concerts, but none really take off.

At a benefit concert for a union strike fund, Pete Seeger and Tom Glazer sing about the dignity of labor and workers' rights. You used to listen to Glazer's radio show, and his children's songs are very popular. You go up to meet him after the concert.

"I've written all these songs, but I don't know how to compose music," you tell him as he looks over your lyric sheets. He hums as he reads the words. "You don't have to," he finally says. "You can use tunes people already know, as long as they're in the public domain. I used a Bach chorale for *Because All Men Are Brothers*. You know that old song, *On Top of Old Smokey*"?

Sure, it was a big hit for the Weavers. "Yes, everyone knows it," Tom explains. "Here's the words I put to the music:

> *On top of spaghetti, all covered with cheese*
>
> *I lost my poor meatball, when somebody sneezed."*

You laugh at the contrast with the original love song, and thank him for the idea. After hours of listening to the Anthology of American Folk Music, on Moe Asch's Folkways label, you choose good tunes without copyrights. You write a new lyric for "Swing Low, Sweet Chariot":

> *Rise up, beloved people, Rise up and sing for peace*
>
> *Rise up, beloved people, Join your hands in peace.*

With familiar tunes in your ear, writing lyrics is easier. You compose simple songs that tell of your hope for America. Thousands hear them, sing them, and are inspired to stand up for justice. ✡

The best stories are those that begin inside the author. They have settings and characters that the writer already knows well, and deal with issues that he or she has wrestled with. You think about the problems you've faced, and consider which ones your readers have encountered.

One issue that you keep re-visiting is religion. Your family has belonged to a synagogue since you were born, attended services at least on major holidays, and sent you to Hebrew school. Your parents identify as Jews and are proud of their heritage. Yet, whenever you ask them about the words in the Jewish prayers, they generally shrug, saying they don't believe there's a God who listens to them. "God is something people made up to feel better about dying. Or to scare their children into behaving," they tell you.

You begin to write about a young woman who works in a nursing home. One of the patients is a Holocaust survivor whose family was murdered at Auschwitz. He is bitter, isolated, and vacillates between anger at God and rejecting God's existence. He rails against the visiting rabbi, accusing him of perpetuating a hoax.

The main character attempts at first to speak with the patient about the mysterious nature of God's will, but eventually she is convinced that he is correct – that God does not exist. She becomes depressed and angry, and her personal life crumbles when she decides that everyone around her is deluded. She's about to leave her job and take to the road to look for meaning, when a stranger's kind and selfless act explains the purpose of God-belief.

Perception is published by a Simon and Schuster imprint and attracts attention from reviewers, college professors and book clubs. The novel is praised for its thoughtful questioning of traditional religious assumptions, and it wins several literary awards. In your next book, *The Other*, you craft a modern rendering of the life of Elisha ben-Abuya, the atheist rabbi of the Talmud.

You have taken your place among the most influential writers of the era.

Chapter Eight

I Want to Be a Sportscaster

Sports as a serious pursuit was virtually unknown in the Jewish world before our arrival in America. Back in the days of the Maccabees, Hellenistic culture offered athletic competition like foot-races, wrestling, and discus-throwing in honor of the Greek gods. And there were several prominent Jewish boxers in England before the twentieth century, like Daniel Mendoza and Barney Aaron.

Jewish athletes first appear in significant numbers after the big 1883-1920 East European immigration. The new arrivals saw that America seemed to love sports, and the Jews badly wanted to be true Americans. For many, the success of slugging third baseman Hank Greenberg, a legend beloved across ethnic lines, seemed to prove that Jews could be as American as anyone else.

You'll find the complete history of Jewish athletes at the National Jewish Sports Hall of Fame in Commack, New York. In this chapter, the sports journalists take the spotlight. Depending on your choices, you may meet Marty Glickman, Myron Cope, Shirley Povitch, Warner Wolf, Al Michaels, Len Berman, Mel Allen, Johnny Most, Howard Cosell, Bert Sugar and Bill Mazer. ESPN will hire at least a dozen on-air Jewish sportscasters. Also important in American sports history are the Harlem Globetrotters' Abe Saperstein and Red Klotz, and the Major League Baseball's Sandy Koufax, Art Shamsky, Hank Greenberg and Jay Horwitz.

You must be the biggest sports fan in Cleveland, Ohio. You follow baseball, football, basketball and hockey, both college and professional. Your parents feel that driving you to practices and games is their major job. Always, your birthday and Hanukkah wishes are for Municipal Stadium tickets. You're the first to grab the newspaper every morning to see the sports pages.

In 1965, when you're fifteen, your Jewish and sports-fan identities merge. Sandy Koufax, the Los Angeles Dodgers' best pitcher, refuses to pitch the first game of the World Series. You know that Koufax is not the first Jewish baseball player to refuse to play on the year's holiest day – Hank Greenberg did the same – but never during the World Series! Your school buzzes with conversation about a holiday most kids never heard of before.

When it's time to go to college, you choose Case Western Reserve University here in Cleveland to major in English and communications. You enjoy going to the university's football and basketball games and compile statistics for the team. You also begin writing sports columns for the campus newspaper, the *Observer*, reporting not only on football and basketball but also track and wrestling.

In your senior year, with the 1972 Munich Summer Olympics approaching, you want to write a column about the last Olympics held in Germany: the 1936 Berlin Games. You know that Marty Glickman, the current broadcaster for the New York Giants football team, was a track star on the 1936 team. How great would it be to interview Glickman about the upcoming Games?

You phone the Giants' public-relations office, tell the secretary that you write for the Observer, and request to interview the Giants' broadcaster in Cleveland before the upcoming Browns-Giants game. Checking with the boss, she says you can talk with Glickman an hour before kickoff. But bad weather delays Glickman's arrival. He offers an alternative date: in New York during your spring break. You had planned to visit your grandparents in Florida then, and go to some baseball spring training camps.

If you visit your grandparents during spring break, turn to page 141.

If you go to New York to interview Marty Glickman, turn to page 142.

Your grandparents live in Sarasota, Florida, and it will be a nice warm week with them after a cold Cleveland winter. With your graduation from Case Western only two months away, they ask about your future plans – and are happy to learn you have a line on an entry-level position with a Washington, D.C. TV station.

Near Sarasota is Payne Park, spring training home of the Chicago White Sox. Spring training has an intimate and informal atmosphere. The games are broadcast on local radio from an open-air booth next to where the fans sit, and you arrive early to sit near legendary White Sox broadcaster Bob Elson. He arrives with a tall, middle-aged man with thinning hair who greets nearby fans with a friendly smile as people keep staring at him. Your grandfather whispers, "You're looking at the first Jewish Hall-of-Famer."

You look at the tall man again. Grandpa's right: he's Hank Greenberg, slugging first baseman for the Detroit Tigers in the 1930s and 1940s. Four-time All-Star, and twice American League MVP.

Greenberg used to be the Sox' vice president and general manager. When the game begins, a Sox player hits a foul ball in your direction. You field it smoothly, to applause. "Nice catch!" cries Greenberg. Politely, you ask him to autograph the ball. As he does, he wants to know more about you. You tell him about your work at college and your efforts to land a job after graduation.

"Pittsburgh is a great sports town," Greenberg says. "I spent my last season as a player with the Pirates. If you're looking for a spot closer to home, I know the WTAE sports director." He writes a name and phone number on your program. "Call him and tell him 'Hankus Pankus' said he should give you a close look."

You consider this second option. Pittsburgh is much closer to Cleveland than Washington, but you've spent a long time selling yourself to the Washington station.

If you want to work at ABC's Pittsburgh affiliate WTAE-AM, turn to page 143.

If you apply to WTOP-TV in Washington, D.C., turn to page 144.

Marty Glickman has a round, affable face and a bushy moustache, and he motions for you to sit next to him in the broadcast booth. He tells you to ask him any questions you want.

At the Berlin Olympics in 1936, American sprinters Sam Stoller and Marty Glickman were suddenly pulled from the 4 x 100 meter relay the day before they were to compete, replaced by Ralph Metcalfe and Jesse Owens. Apparently the U.S. team didn't want to offend the Chancellor of the Olympics' host country – Adolf Hitler. Stoller and Glickman were Jewish.

"Marty, you weren't just pulled from the relay event; you were replaced by Jesse Owens, one of the greatest athletes of all time. Why wasn't that a fair decision by the track and field coaches?"

"A number of reasons," he answers. "Stoller and I had been practicing passing the baton for two weeks. A smooth baton pass is essential in the relay. Jesse hadn't practiced that at all. He told the coach he didn't want to replace me, he'd already won three gold medals. Coach said, 'You'll do as you're told.' Jesse felt terrible about it; he knew we were unbeatable in the relay. To this day, I feel anti-Semitism robbed me of my Olympic medal."

After some more questions, you have enough information for your column. But Glickman makes no move to end the interview, so you take a chance. You know of Glickman's long history of broadcasting professional football, basketball, and hockey games, among other sports, and so you ask him for career advice.

He has two suggestions. Since you told him you maintained the statistics for the Case Western basketball team for several seasons, he tells you that the Boston Celtics need a new statistician. Alternatively, he knows of an assistant producer opening with ABC Sports. He offers to put in a good word for you at either job.

If you accept a job offer maintaining basketball statistics at WBZ-TV, Boston, turn to page 145.

If you want to be an ABC Sports assistant producer, turn to page 146.

It's a two-hour drive to Pittsburgh, a city dominated by the steel industry. It's the home of the football Steelers, the hockey Penguins, the baseball Pirates, and many college teams. Pittsburghers are known for their distinctive lingo and staccato speech patterns. And this becomes quite clear to you when you meet Myron Cope.

In two years, Cope's raspy delivery has become the voice of the Pittsburgh Steelers. Team executives liked his local accent and uncontained enthusiasm, and hired him for color analysis, although his nasal voice can, as he says, "cut through concrete."

"Pleased to meet you! Welcome to the team," Myron greets you. "So you're going to be my spotter? Can you pick out a tackler? Good. I hear you're from Cleveland. Don't tell me you're a Brownie fan!" Your silence your confession. "Aw – well, we like you anyway!" It's impossible to resist this guy.

You spend several years at WTAE, researching player back-stories and summarizing data, and you're constantly floored by Myron's outrageous on-air remarks. The Pittsburgh fans love his highly original vocabulary and wacky stunts.

The Steelers make the playoffs in 1975, and a tough game against Baltimore looms in late December. Team execs want a gimmick to rev up the Three Rivers Stadium crowd. Myron is thinking about this one day in his office, when you come in to borrow a staple remover.

He rummages through his top desk drawer, discovering long-lost objects. "Here ya go, here's a gragger," he says, tossing it to you. "Drives 'em crazy on Purim." You wave it over your head, and he suddenly falls silent, staring at the gragger.

During his next radio broadcast, Myron tells the Steelers fans to bring a towel to the stadium. "Black, yellow, gold dish towels," he suggests. "Terrible Towels! Wave them for the Steelers!"

Countless fans will soon be waving Terrible Towels for their team.

If you stay with the Steelers broadcast for a while, turn to page 147.

If you'd rather cover various sports on local television, turn to page 148.

WTOP, an affiliate of CBS, carries the Washington Redskins games on Channel 9. The sports anchor on their nightly news is Warner Wolf, who also does play-by play for broadcasts of both college and professional sports.

You have begun to notice that sports announcers often work multiple assignments for different teams, and they travel a lot. You are too polite to ask why, but you figure it out. These guys don't get paid very much. It's a hectic and difficult career, not giving back a lot besides fame and attention. Shirley Povitch, the sports editor at the Washington Post, who has covered thousands of events, confesses to you that the travel is grueling and it's a challenge to maintain balance. But he is abundantly calm and sane, so you figure that a disciplined journalist can remain human.

So, inevitably, there are scheduling conflicts for any sports announcer, and you decide to make yourself available as a backup when needed. You find an assignment covering a local high school game, and the station generously sends a camera crew with you to record your announcing skills. The news producer likes what he sees, and calls you frequently to fill in for various broadcasters during busy times.

You build a good reputation in local television as a concise, informed commentator who prepares well and conducts intelligent interviews. Your knowledge of baseball is especially notable, and several years after joining WTOP, you're hired by ABC. It has just picked up TV rights for Monday Night Baseball, and you will be working as an on-field reporter. In the postseason, your interviews on the sidelines during the National League championship series support the announcers in the booth, Warner Wolf and Al Michaels.

If you think you have a talent for seeing the big picture – all the elements of a sports broadcast – and might be a good producer, turn to page 149.

If your heart really belongs to baseball, and you want to focus on it all day, every day, turn to page 150.

In Boston, you sit courtside at the scorer's table and record all the details of Celtics games: points, fouls, turnovers, and assists. You also calculate players' shooting percentages and assists, and write up report at the end of each game. It is there at courtside that you meet the team's longtime, legendary radio announcer.

Unpretentious, scruffy Johnny Most is known for his love for the Celtics and his scorn for their opponents. Considering his vicious verbal abuse, even during road games, it's amazing that he's never been assaulted outside other teams' arenas. But Boston's fans love his loyalty, and though his personal life tends to be solitary, in his perch 'high above courtside' he has a million friends.

In a coffee shop after a Sunday afternoon game, Most discusses with you the importance of sports, generally. You suggest that, as much fun as sports provide, in the last analysis, they're just games.

"Sure, they're just games," Most answers. He was an Air Force gunner who flew combat missions during World War II, so he has perspective on these matters. "But think about the function of sports, here or in any country. There are people who can't even interact with their own family without conflict. There are guys who don't know how to express love. But that's no good. Everyone needs personal connections. Sports gives you that. Even if he has trouble telling his dad "I love you," every fan can pour out his love for his favorite player. They find other guys who root for their team – they have a family, no matter how lonely real life is. Sports is glue. It brings people together who don't know how to do it on their own."

Johnny is right. If it weren't for sports, many fathers and sons would never communicate with each other at all. In a way, sportscasters are like family therapists who never meet their clients. You realize that sports creates community.

If you decide to spend the evening watching a Harlem Globetrotters game, turn to page 151.

If a guy who's launching an all-sports cable channel wants you to take a train to Hartford, Connecticut, to interview tonight, go to page 152.

ABC may have the best sports programming of the three networks. Every Saturday you can remember, you've watched *Wide World of Sports*, an anthology created by Edgar Scherick and hosted by Jim McKay. *Wide World's* production staff is preparing for the 1972 Summer Olympics in Munich – and your roommate's brother, a cameraman, will be on an ABC production truck.

You phone the guy to ask whether he knows about any production openings, and learn that the network's research department is expanding for the Olympics. You get a sports producer's name.

You update your résumé and send it, with photocopies of your best sports writing, to an assistant producer at ABC Sports. And apparently your experience and knowledge of events like judo, squash and handball are in short supply; after an interview in the New York office, you're hired to get background information on the athletes and coaches. Basically, your job at the Olympics will be to make on-air commentators look smart.

This is going to be enjoyable. Your greatest talent is your ability to remember things, both important and trivial, and, since sports is your passion, you are an encyclopedia of information.

In early August, you arrive at the Olympic Village and spend several weeks before the opening ceremonies familiarizing yourself with the facilities and speaking to as many athletes as possible. You are in great demand among the anchors and writers as they prepare broadcasts, since they require details immediately.

It's fun talking to the youngest Olympian, a Jamaican swimmer named Belinda Phillips, who is not yet fourteen, and to Otl Aicher, who designed the Olympic mascot, Waldi the daschund. Aicher was arrested in 1937 for refusing to join Hitler Youth.

But your Olympic enthusiasm is utterly destroyed on September 6 when Palestinian terrorists massacre eleven members of the Israeli team whom they had taken hostage. You leave Munich as soon as you can, hoping to find a new job that will soothe your soul.

If you want to bring sports fans close to the action, turn to page 153.

If you find it rewarding to interact a lot with fans, turn to page 154.

A new Steelers season begins on September 19, 1977. Pittsburgh is riding high after two consecutive Super Bowl wins, and the fans are tailgating in the Three Rivers Stadium parking lot long before kickoff. The excitement of a national telecast is palpable. You meet Myron at the radio booth, and he greets you boisterously.

"Hey, kid!" he exclaims. "You want to meet Mr. Monday Night?"

Definitely! So you two go over to the ABC network booth. A long-nosed, middle-aged man wearing a canary-yellow jacket and a toupee is looking at a statistics briefing. You wait for Howard Cosell to look up.

When he does, he cuts off Myron's introduction and addresses you in a nasal Brooklynese twang, punching out each word. "So you're *about* to *enter* the *toy department* of *life.* Welcome to sports broadcasting. I wish you the *best* of *success.* If you ask my advice, let me *just* say *this.* Do your *homework.* Always be *sure* of yourself. Tell it like it *is* and don't spare anyone's *feelings. Softball questions* accomplish *nothing,* and serve only to *corrode* the *fiber* of the *already crumbling structure* that is entertainment media. This is not international diplomacy. This is only sports. But, nonetheless, we come here to report *reality.* Do *not* respect a man, *until and unless* he is *forthcoming* with the *truth.* You are *not here* to be an athlete's *friend.* If you do *not* live *constantly* on the *precipice* of *peril,* you are wasting your *time.* Now. Have you anything you'd like to *ask.* I'm yours for *one minute.*"

"Mr. Cosell, how do you respond to the frequent charge that you're an arrogant, obnoxious showoff?" you demand.

He laughs. *"That's* what I'm *talking* about!" he cries approvingly. "In *answer* to your query, I can only say, of *course* I am. It is now fifteen minutes to air, so may I suggest that you *locate* your *binoculars* and get to work."

You know you'll never be like Howard Cosell. But you can be honest and direct. You can point out the greed of many club owners, the racial prejudice of some managers, the exploitation of student athletes, and the pandering to fans' lowest instincts.

So you do, for your entire career. And you get respect. ✡

After spending a while in Pittsburgh, identifying players on the field for Myron and interviewing players and coaches for audio cut-ins, you begin thinking about getting some anchoring experience, or a job at an actual microphone in a broadcast booth.

One evening, you're recording a high-school hockey game as a favor to a family friend. With the VHS camera on your shoulder, you track her son back and forth across the rink, trying to keep him in the frame. You turn off the camera after the second period, but turn it back on to capture the silly antics of the Zamboni operator. The crowd is howling with laughter.

"Hey!" your friend exclaims. "Send that video to Len Berman!"

Although you're far from New York, you know about Berman's feature "Spanning The World," on NBC television. It's a spoof of ABC's introduction to *The Wide World of Sports,* a montage of unusual and ridiculous moments in athletic competition. But why send the videotape – you have an excuse to visit the studio now.

At your next opportunity, you fly to New York and show up at the NBC studio, saying you have a delivery for the sports editor. You ask the secretary if you could give the tape to Len Berman. She buzzes his phone and points you toward his office.

Berman is pleasant and affable, accepts the video, and when he hears that you work with Myron Cope, invites you to sit down and talk. You tell him Pittsburgh stories and ask for career advice.

"Well, here's what I'd tell you. Don't sound like a snob. Don't assume that everyone knows famous sports figures; identify them, like "Knicks coach" and "Jets linebacker." Speak plainly and avoid pretentious clichés. Oh, also, call this producer in Boston – his sports anchor is about to take a medical leave. Say I sent you."

You thank him warmly and follow the lead he gave you. A few weeks later, you're asked to fill in at the sports desk – just reading copy, since you aren't familiar with the Boston teams in action. You dress sharp, read clearly and expressively, and radiate assurance. You end the segment with "Thanks for listening," and after the broadcast, you're offered a long-term assignment covering local sports on the noon news program. Congratulations! ✡

Reporting from the sidelines during broadcasts is a mixed bag. It's great being on camera on national television, but it's difficult to get interesting, relevant information out of exhausted athletes and distracted coaches. You are often frustrated by missed cues and bland scripts. And you're not likely to supplant any of the hosts, Jim Lampley, Keith Jackson or Al Michaels.

Michaels senses your discontent. He sits down to talk with you. "I think you have a good feel for the overall shape of the broadcasts," he says. "You like detail, and know how the audience hears and sees the program. Those are valuable talents. Maybe you'd be a good producer. Why don't you talk to the senior producer about it?"

That's what you do, and are assigned to spend a few weeks with different ABC Sports people. You learn the patterns of the daily feeds from assignment editors, the most effective writing skills from the associate producers, and the various skills of the sportscasters. You listen to the advice and gripes of the production-truck crews. Finally, you are asked to coordinate an entire game-day broadcast – closely shadowed by several executives.

You do the job well, and are soon producing three programs a week. For nearly a decade you're at this exhausting, exciting job, when a staff shakeup sends you looking for another place to work.

One spring afternoon you're at Shea Stadium in Flushing, Queens, with a tabloid sportswriter friend. "Hey!" he says during warm-ups. "You want to meet Jay Horwitz? Sure you do. Let's go!"

Jay Horwitz, VP for media affairs, is a Mets institution. A lovable teddy bear of a guy, he shakes your hand warmly. "Great to meet you! You a Mets fan?" Suddenly you feel like one. "So you were a sports producer at ABC. Are you working now? WOR needs producers. Here, I'll introduce you to Bill Webb, the director."

More handshakes and an exchange of contact information. After the game, you're asked to an impromptu interview with the executive producer. He likes you, and after more interviews, WOR hires you as an associate producer. For the rest of your working life, you give Mets television viewers the best seat in the house. ✿

When you were in high school in Cleveland, baseball games were carried on WJW television, and for just one year they had a commentator named Mel Allen. He was an experienced sportscaster by then, having begun his career as the public-address announcer at his college football games in Alabama. He broadcast the 1938 World Series on radio, and had been a runner-up for the job of broadcasting for the Yankees. He got a lucky break when the announcer they hired lost his job: he mispronounced the commercial sponsor, Ivory Soap. (He called it Ovary Soap. Twice.)

So Mel Israel changed his name legally to Mel Allen, and became the Voice of the Yankees, except during the war when he worked for Armed Forces Radio. He called the historic Game 7 of the 1960 World Series, which the Pittsburgh Pirates won when Bill Mazeroski hit a walkoff home run. He was the most beloved sportscaster the Yankees ever had, and no one ever understood why he was fired in 1964.

He worked in Milwaukee and Cleveland for a few years until the Yankees relented in 1976 and called him back to do pre- and post-game shows. Now he's been hired by Major League Baseball Productions to host a new syndicated highlights program called *This Week In Baseball*. And this is really great for *you*, because during the off-season, you work at the official Archives of Major League Baseball. You know the collection cold, so you seek out the new show's producer and ask if you can be the program's historian.

You just solved a problem the producer didn't know he had, and when the first planning meeting takes place, you're on hand to suggest which bits of background film can be used to illustrate the changes baseball is experiencing, like new rules, new records, controversial calls, and improvements in equipment. Mel and you get to be friends, and he shares with you mountains of sports lore.

For the program following Len Barker's perfect game for the Cleveland Indians, you bring out the footage of Vin Scully calling the last out of Sandy Koufax's 1965 perfect game for the Dodgers. Mel watches the celebrations with a wide grin on his face. "Come on, say it, Mel!" you plead.

Mel laughs, and indulges you. *"How a-bout that?!"* ✡

The Globetrotters are in town and they're hilarious. Johnny and you are perched at mid-court by the Washington Generals when Johnny asks you, "Want to meet a coach who's lost 8,000 games?"

Rarely do you receive such an intriguing invitation, so you say yes. While the teams are warming up, a short fellow with thinning hair, wearing a gray suit and tie, seats himself in front of you. "Hey, Red!" calls Johnny, and the man turns around.

When you're introduced to him, Red grins and puts out his hand. Red Klotz is the founder and coach of the Washington Senators, the perennial losers to the Globetrotters. "This team was originally called the Philadelphia Sphas," Red says. "Know what that name meant?" No, you don't.

"South Philadelphia Hebrew Association!" he exclaims. "Then Abe Saperstein, may his memory be a blessing, asked me in '53 to put together a team to play the Globetrotters. He'd done his part for the NBA and wanted to tour strictly as entertainment."

"What do you mean, 'done his part'?" you ask.

Red turns his chair a little to explain it to you. "See, the Globetrotters were a black team," he says. "Abe started as their manager. At that time the Basketball Association of America – that turned into the NBA – why, they were all white. They didn't take black players seriously at all, until the Globetrotters beat them. I know, because I played for the Baltimore Bullets at the time. So finally the teams are so impressed that they started signing our players. The Globetrotters integrated basketball," Red concludes.

The teams are announced, "Sweet Georgia Brown" is whistled, and the comedy begins. The referees and several Globetrotters are wired for sound, and the mockery of the Generals and their coach punctuates the theatrics. There's as much posturing and dancing as shooting, and the players feel free to invade the audience and drink their sodas. Red gets dragged into the antics, and eventually, the inevitable bucket of water splashes the fans.

What a great way to remember that it's just a game, you think, as you exit the arena with all the other exhausted, happy fans. ✿

Sometimes, history is made by a totally crazy idea.

In 1979, television is a limited medium. Programming is on the air from early morning until midnight, or a little later. No network broadcasts 24 hours a day. Cable television, based on subscribers paying to watch, is very new, and many people think it will never succeed. But a father and son named Rasmusssen decide that a cable network with *round-the-clock sport programs* is exactly what America wants. It's insane. People laugh. But you don't laugh. You shriek with excitement. And you arrive promptly at the tiny Connecticut studio, which is still being built, to apply for a job.

The skeleton team, just a few dreamers busy getting financing and program rights, is impressed by your experience with the Celtics and invite you to help them form the new company, which they're calling the Entertainment and Sports Programming Network, or ESPN.

You have zero experience with studio production, but one of ESPN's founding sportscasters, Chris Berman, sends you to his former employer, WVIT-TV in nearby Hartford, where you'll be allowed to shadow the news director and learn the ropes. When you're not doing that, you attend planning meetings. A hundred sixty-eight hours a week is a lot of time to fill. It's a logistical challenge to plan coverage of volleyball, kick-boxing, bicycle races, Munster hurling and the Slo-Pitch Softball World Series.

The operation launches on September 7, 1979, and its first broadcast is *SportsCenter,* scheduled opposite the three networks' evening news. The gamble begins to pay off. An audience builds, and a contract for NCAA games is signed. Major league sports agreements are signed with the Whalers and Capitols. Offices in five cities are eventually added; you find yourself directing in the studio and on the field. And ESPN adds radio programming.

As years go by, new stars arrive at ESPN. You work with many of them: Dick Schaap, Charlie Steiner, Dick Stockton, Steve Levy, Mike Greenberg. With the new millennium, sportscasting opens to more women: ESPN adds Dana Jacobson, Bonnie Bernstein, Linda Cohn and Suzy Kolber. The network is a roaring success.

Some days, you can't believe they pay you to have so much fun. ✿

The horrifying violence at the Olympics has shaken you to the core, and you feel a strong aversion to any kind of violence. You avoid reading about the war in Vietnam and racial tension in the streets of America. You want to be insulated in the safe, pure world of sports. And so you decide to immerse yourself in the most beautiful, most balletic kind of athletic competition. You devote yourself to boxing.

You loved the "sweet science" as a young kid taking lessons in a Cleveland gym. The boxers you knew there were disciplined and focused. They work to develop a whole spectrum of skills: speed, strength, agility, and balance. They learn the tactics of fighting and continue to develop them throughout their careers. And they respect their opponents, their trainers, and their fans.

Your press credentials had gotten you in to see some welterweight and light flyweight bouts at the Olympics, which were called by Howard Cosell with all the passion that you yourself feel for the sport. Now you start reading *Boxing Illustrated* and discover that the lyricism of boxing commentary isn't confined to Cosell. The magazine's editor Bert Sugar also describes it poetically.

You study boxing intently, by reading analyses of fights, and also by attending as many as you can. You learn to recognize how strategic boxers wear down opponents by controlling a fight's pace, and how stronger, less agile fighters use combinations to score knockouts. The more you learn, the more you appreciate fighters' courage, emotional strength, and commitment. You also value the sport's quality of equal opportunity: there are weight classes for everyone who wants to train. No one is excluded.

You feel that boxing journalism already has its brilliant practitioners, and you'd like to try to become a ringside announcer. Starting at local competitions, you eventually begin approaching promoters, and get a few chances to describe fights of low-ranked boxers. You are well prepared, knowledgeable, and clear, and promoters like you. Soon your reputation attracts the attention of fight associations in Detroit and Miami, and you become a regular sight behind a microphone at ringsides, painting word pictures of the fight for fans everywhere. It's a wonderful career. ✿

You have noticed that sports enthusiasts have opinions. They love to dissect statistics about athletes and games, and argue that this player is better than that one. The debates occur in bars, at barbecues, between innings – anywhere there's two or more fans.

In 1964, sportscaster Bill Mazer gave fans a huge audience. He began taking phone calls from listeners on New York's WNBC-AM radio. He listens to callers politely, corrects them respectfully, and revels in the lore of athletic competition. Listeners love him. Soon other stations copy the call-in format.

You meet him in a WNEW-TV studio. In front of you is a human encyclopedia, who recalls statistics about obscure Soviet weightlifters as well as last year's American League MVP. His memory was honed in yeshiva. You ask him what's so special about radio.

"A radio host can be what the best TV guy can't: a personal connection between the fan and the game," Mazer explains. "On TV, the visuals interfere. On radio, you're the listener's eyes. It's very personal. Also, radio doesn't care if you're old or unattractive!"

The host of a call-in program, of course, needs to be an expert on stats, history, records, quotes, and all sorts of current sports news. "So, you think you can handle it?" 'Amazin' Mazer' asks you.

You confess that you're pretty good. "Okay, do this. Write your résumé and make a demo tape. Put your phone on speaker and get your friends to call and argue with you. Send copies to radio stations with sports programming. Something good will happen."

Taking his advice, you mail tapes to sports directors at dozens of midsize markets across the country. Soon an AM station in Fresno, California, phones to ask you to pilot a sports talk show. You fly there, set up in the studio, and take your first call.

"Who lost a horse race by standing in the stirrups too soon?"

Easy! "Willie Shoemaker, aboard Gallant Man, the 1957 Kentucky Derby. Bill Hartack won on Iron Liege. Thanks for calling!"

Chapter Nine

I Want to Be a Scientist

In the nineteenth century, until the 1930s, if you wanted to be a scientist, you had to study German. Germany was the center of scientific research, and the textbooks were of course in German.

But Nazism arose in Germany, and many German scientists were Jewish. Some fled, never to return, including Nils Bohr, Erwin Chargaff, and Albert Einstein. In fact, 1,150 Jewish scientists left Germany for the United States, and conducted research and made discoveries that ushered in the modern age. Many others stayed, thinking that fascism would be a brief phase. We will never know what they could have accomplished.

In this chapter, you might encounter physicists Albert Einstein, Leo Szilard, Victor Weisskopf and Martin Kamen; computer scientists Herbert Simon, Allen Newell, and Marvin Minsky; biochemists Erwin Chargaff and Gertrude Elion; microbiologists Selman Waksman, Albert Schatz, Esther Lederberg and Wolf Vishniac; chemists Sam Ruben and Giuliana Cavaglieri Tesoro; evolutionary biologists Tilly Edinger and Stephen Jay Gould; NASA aeronautics engineer Abe Silverstein, and astronomer Carl Sagan.

And after the reality of atomic weapons ended World War II in 1945, a contingent of Jewish anti-war and pro-environment activists stepped forward, including Norman Cousins, Barry Commoner, Bella Abzug and Lenore Marshall. Some of the Jewish organizations that were formed to protect the planet in the following years are COEJL, the Coalition on the Environment and Jewish Life, Hazon, and the Green Zionist Alliance.

I would like to thank Tamar Ezekiel Granor and Riley Risteen for their advice and assistance.

One of your earliest memories is the 1933 Tournament of Roses parade in Pasadena. You were eight years old, and your parents had driven you and your sisters from your home in Boyle Heights to see the grand spectacle. The crowds, the excitement, and the beautiful floats all make an indelible impression on your young mind. You are an alert observer, so you also notice that an older gentleman in a long gray coat and black homburg hat is attracting as much attention as the huge flowery sculptures.

"Who is that?" you ask your mother, pointing.

"That's Professor Einstein!" she shouts over the noise of the crowd. "He's the greatest scientific genius alive. Wave to him!"

You wave at Einstein as he greets thousands of well-wishers, smiling benevolently under his bushy moustache. And you wonder that a scientist can provoke so much adoration.

Since your childhood, your strongest interest has been nature, and exploring how it acts by observing, asking questions, figuring out its rules, and testing your theories. You have measured the growth of flowers in different locations in the garden, recorded your observations of temperature and barometric pressure, and studied melting ice cubes in various liquids.

When you get to high school, you spend many free periods pestering the science teachers to explain how the lab equipment is used. You ask them how to collect data about insect populations and plant growth in order to see and predict patterns. Your teachers are impressed by your interest and discipline, and suggest that you audit classes at the University of California at Los Angeles, near Beverly Hills. You take one evening class every semester for credit, in physics, chemistry, and biology, feeling proud that you can understand the material as well as the college students.

If a friend's illness and medical treatment provokes your interest in biochemistry and pharmacology, turn to page 157.

If a natural disaster directs your attention to physics and geology, turn to page 158.

During sophomore year in high school, your best friend falls ill and is diagnosed with a *Streptococcus pyogenes* infection. He had been bitten by a dog, and bacteria infected the site. Your friend is no longer feverish or vomiting, but the red, swollen rash, looking like an orange peel, is still painful.

You visit him in the hospital, and are sitting by his bedside when his doctor comes in to check his vitals. When you ask the doctor about the infection and the treatment, he says,

"It is really quite a serious infection. But we're using a new treatment developed by Bayer Laboratories in Germany; it's called Prontosil and it's a sulfanomide drug. It was used a few years ago to treat President Roosevelt's son. This could be more effective than immunotherapy. So far it's working well against a number of *Streptococcus* strains, which is fantastic news."

"Does Prontosil destroy all types of harmful bacteria?" you ask.

"No, just a few. Bacteria are complex, and for the ones that cause disease, we need lots of ways to attack them. I read about some promising research being done; is this something that interests you?"

It is. Most people don't think about the life-or-death power of many bacteria until illness strikes. You are fascinated by the tiny creatures, and want to learn how they resist destruction and evolve into more efficient organisms.

If you decide to study genetics and evolution, turn to page 159.

If you're more interested in how chemical compounds affect the behavior of living organisms, turn to page 160.

It is late Friday afternoon. The date is March 10, 1933. You are setting the dinner table for Shabbat, putting candles in the silver candlesticks and covering the hallah with its embroidered cloth. Your older sister is coiling the cord of the vacuum cleaner and putting it away, and your younger sister is in her room picking up her toys. Your mom is in the kitchen, and your dad will be home from work any moment.

The chandelier above the dining room table begins to swing. The plates on the shelves rattle. A glass lamp crashes to the floor and shatters. It feels like the floor is rolling. You drop to your knees as your mother runs to hold you, screaming your sisters' names.

The earthquake seems endless, but finally the house is still. Dad runs in. Everyone is safe, but there are wide cracks in the walls.

That's what happened in your Los Angeles home. The big picture is that a 47-mile-long fault between the North American and Pacific tectonic plates has ruptured. Deep below the earth's surface, tremendous energy is released, sending seismic waves in every direction. The quake centered on Long Beach, twenty miles to the south, and registered a devastating magnitude of 6.3.

As far as transfers of energy are concerned, this one is pretty dramatic. It has collapsed buildings, including your school, which luckily was empty. But over a hundred people were killed. You're frightened, but also very curious: why did this happen?

As southern California endures the aftershocks and rebuilds, you read every book about earthquakes you can find. Three years later, you join the physics club in junior high school. The club conducts experiments and invites scientists to come teach about their work. In your junior year, the club visits the Lawrence Berkeley National Laboratory to see the newly-invented cyclotron, an accelerator which moves particle beams at nearly light speed.

If you decide to study the building blocks of the universe at the University of California at Berkeley, turn to page 161.

If you want to study aerospace and rocket engineering, turn to page 162.

Your first day of introductory biology at Columbia University in New York reveals that if you are going to understand living cells, you're going to have to learn about their molecular components. The molecules most interesting to you are those which carry genetic instructions through generations. So in the spring semester, you enroll in a biochemistry class taught by assistant professor Erwin Chargaff.

Professor Chargaff speaks with a soft Viennese accent, having left Europe to escape the Nazis. In his lectures you learn about the four molecular building blocks of life: lipids, proteins, carbohydrates and nucleic acids. He teaches about current experiments proving that it is a nucleic acid in cells, DNA, that contains genes. The structure of those genes, however, is still a mystery.

You stay at Columbia to work toward your Ph.D., and with a team of students in Professor Chargaff's laboratory, use chromatography to measure the four nucleobases of DNA. Attaching DNA to a cellulose matrix, you apply DNA-binding proteins to the sheet. You record the data. The process is endless, as the measurements have to be repeated thousands of times.

Different living species have varying amounts of each nucleobase; but after years of arduous lab work, the team determines that every organism always has an equal amount of adenine and thymine, and an equal amount of guanine and cytosine. This is a hint that those bases are connected in pairs. Within two years, Francis Crick and James D. Watson have used Chargaff's discovery to theorize the double-helix structure of DNA.

If you want to study how genetics drives the evolution of life, turn to page 163.

If you're interested in detecting microscopic life forms on other planets, turn to page 164.

When it's time for college, you choose Rutgers University in New Jersey, which has a distinguished department of biochemistry and microbiology. There you meet a young graduate student named Albert Schatz, who is enrolled at the university's College of Agriculture. Schatz is studying the properties of microbes that live in leaf and barn compost, supervised by Professor Selman Waksman.

While the Second World War is being fought, less famous battles are taking place in science laboratories. Diseases like cholera and typhoid fever kill more people than war does, and the search for cures, vaccines and treatments occupies many brilliant minds.

Professor Waksman is looking for compounds in microorganisms which kill several types of bacteria. He calls these compounds "antibiotics" and, when he isolates them, he sends them to be tested on guinea pigs at the Mayo Clinic. Albert Schatz is concentrating on finding an antibiotic to control the tubercule bacillus. This bacterium causes tuberculosis, a horrible infectious disease of the lungs that kills millions of people every year. Even penicillin isn't effective against tuberculosis.

You're in the lab, copying data into notebooks, when Schatz comes in, carrying a pot of soil from the college farm. "I'm looking for *Streptomyces griseus*," he announces, and starts preparing glass slides for the microscope. He's concentrating so intensely that he doesn't hear your questions.

You set up petri dishes with cultures of *Escherichia coli* for some preliminary tests of the threadlike microbes Schatz has extracted from the soil. Just as you hoped, *S. griseus* knocks *E. coli* dead, and now comes the great test. Schatz introduces the *S. griseus* extract into the tubercule culture. The hours of waiting are agony, but when the lids of the petri dishes are lifted, the triumphant answer is plain to see. The tubercules are destroyed. Albert Schatz calls his discovery "streptomycin," and Professor Waksman rushes it to the Mayo Clinic for tests and clinical trials.

If you want to work on developing anti-cancer drugs, turn to page 165.

If you want to study how bacteria develop antibiotic resistance, turn to page 166.

When you arrive at the University of California at Berkeley as a freshman, you get a part-time job in the Berkeley Radiation Laboratory. There, a chemist named Sam Ruben and a nuclear physicist named Martin Kamen are investigating how the carbon in CO_2 acts in the photosynthesis process.

They are employing the Berkeley cyclotron, the first of its kind, also called the 'atom-smasher.' A short-lived radioactive isotope of carbon, called carbon-11, is being used as a tracer. Carbon-11, however, doesn't last long enough to be useful in studying photosynthesis. But then they discover another isotope, carbon-14, which can be produced artificially in the cyclotron.

When they publish their findings, the two scientists predict that carbon-14 will have many uses in science and industry. But Sam Ruben won't live to see the significance of his work. In 1943, while researching chemical weapons for the American war effort, he accidentally inhales the toxic gas phosgene, and dies.

You follow the work being done on carbon-14, which occurs naturally in plants and is ingested by the animals that eat them. When an animal or plant dies, the carbon-14 inside it begins the process of radioactive decay. Half of the carbon-14 is gone in 5,730 years.

This means that the age of anything organic – since all organic matter contains carbon-14 -- can be calculated by measuring how much of the isotope remains.

You spend a number of years testing artifacts from museums and archeological digs, and even ancient burial sites. Your work is deeply appreciated by scholars around the world. However, you have a restless mind and seek new challenges.

If you want to work with chemists to make consumer products safer, turn to page 167.

If you are more interested in exploring how much computers can do, turn to page 168.

Because of your high grades and scores, you are accepted to Cal-Tech and take classes in mechanical engineering, astronomy and physics. In your senior year you learn that the National Advisory Committee on Aviation, NACA, is creating an Aircraft Engine Research Laboratory. You have completed two internships in engine design, and apply for a job on the aircraft testing team. You move to Cleveland where the lab is being built.

At the facility, you meet Abe Silverstein, who has just arrived from the aeronautical laboratory in Langley, Virginia, to oversee the Altitude Wind Tunnel. During the war, Silverstein has been redesigning military aircraft to reduce drag. This increases the speed of the craft and improves fuel efficiency.

You, Silverstein, and dozens of other engineers are standing on the tarmac when the nation's first jet airplane, the Bell YP-59A Airacomet, is rolled into the Lab. This gorgeous silver bird is going to transform aviation, and your team gets right to work on baffles and a cooling system.

At the war's end, the next task is to design and build a supersonic wind tunnel. Based on models that your team spends months calculating, drawing, and assembling, this tunnel is crucial in testing the ability of aircraft to travel faster than sound.

The next few years of your career is spent working with Silverstein on perfecting cryogenic fuels for aircraft. He is convinced that liquid hydrogen will work far better than hydrocarbon fuels. Hydrogen-fueled aircraft are never built, however – that innovation will be used only in the space program.

If you decide to leave aerospace engineering to learn about the outer universe, turn to page 169.

If you wish to work to develop America's nuclear defense systems, turn to page 170.

The mechanics of genetic inheritance are fascinating, but your mind frequently turns to the traits controlled by the DNA blueprint. All the plants and animals on earth, in their infinite variation, evolved into their present forms via mutations of their genes; but the circumstances that favored those mutations are a big part of the story. Their effects can be found in the fossil record.

You accept a position at Harvard University in 1951, teaching undergraduate genetics and organic chemistry. At the university's Museum of Comparative Zoology, you attend a lecture one afternoon by Dr. Tilly Edinger. She studies the brains of the extinct ancestors of horses, which left imprints on fossilized skulls, and has introduced a new theory that evolution occurs in a branching pattern – one species yielding two or more new ones.

This is an interesting alternative to the accepted idea that species change gradually, in a linear fashion. You ask Dr. Edinger to show you the fossil evidence, and she points out the differences between the cranial imprints. The scientist is mostly deaf, but communicates clearly in elegant English, which she learned in her native Germany before fleeing the Nazis in 1939.

You work with her on composing possible models of the genetic paths of equine evolution. Within a few years, you are publishing your own papers on paleontological genetics, sharing success with your distinguished friend. But, tragically, Dr. Edinger loses her life crossing a street in 1967; she could not hear the car's approach.

Despondently, you avoid the museum for several months. You return only when you're pressured to attend a luncheon welcoming a new geologist from Columbia, Stephen Jay Gould. You are cheered to learn that he loves science fiction, music and baseball.

Gould has come to Harvard to study evidence for his new theory about the nature of evolution. He thinks that natural selection doesn't operate as a slow, gradual process, but in shorter bursts. Some criticize his thesis as "evolution by jerks," and he cheerfully rejoins by calling the alternative "evolution by creeps."

You are delighted at Gould's success in attracting non-scientists to the study of paleontology, and proud to work alongside him. ✡

Your work in molecular biology leads to an invitation to join an advisory board to the National Academy of Sciences in 1958. A member of the Space Science Board asks your group to discuss ways to search for microscopic life on other planets.

The conversation gets very interesting when a Stanford University microbiologist named Wolf Vishniac remarks that a pure, uncontaminated culture medium remains clear until living bacteria are introduced; then it turns cloudy. He says he'd like to create a chamber which could culture bacteria, and then be sent to extraterrestrial surfaces and monitored remotely.

You suggest that a light sensor in the chamber could measure the changes in the amount of light passing through the culture; the light would decrease as more cloudiness filters it out. You offer to help design a light sensor that can resist the extremes of the Martian atmosphere, since you have experience modifying the viewing mechanism of an electron microscope.

A thrill of excitement passes through the scientists and one of Vishniac's friends volunteers an idea: "This chamber of yours would act as a trap for microorganisms – it'll be a Wolf Trap!"

Although the Wolf Trap experiment gets too expensive and is dropped from the Viking missions to Mars, Wolf Vishniac continues his work in the field of 'exobiology,' the term coined by his fellow molecular biologist and space enthusiast, Joshua Lederberg. Because he considers the Antarctic region as the place most resembling Mars, Vishniac conducts missions to find and examine the microbiotica of its soils, using a modified Wolf Trap.

During the southern hemisphere's summer in 1973, Wolf Vishniac is killed falling from an Antarctic cliff while collecting samples. The entire scientific community is shocked and grieved. His friend, cosmologist Carl Sagan, proposes that a large crater on Mars be named "Vishniac" in his memory, and it is done.

You dedicate the rest of your career to the search for extraterrestrial life, and hope that your work honors your brave colleague. ✿

When cells grow abnormally in an organism, and those cells invade other areas of its body, the organism has cancer. If those cells can be stopped from replicating, the disease is defeated.

The radioactive element radium is used to target and destroy cancer cells, and doctors have also begun to treat cancer with chemotherapy, a powerful but brutal method. These treatments unfortunately destroy healthy cells, also. So some scientists are trying to interfere with the cancer cells' growth by modifying their DNA.

You study the replication of leukemia cells in academic settings, and later, develop screening techniques at the Clinical Trials Cooperative Group of the National Cancer Institute. You continue working in government until 1966, when a generous offer from a pharmaceutical company is too good to pass up.

At the Burroughs Wellcome research facility in Tuckahoe, New York, some amazing drugs have been developed. Gertrude Elion, who until a few years ago had to work in a supermarket quality control lab because she's a woman, has engineered pyrmethamine to treat malaria, and Purinethol for autoimmune diseases.

You assist Miss Elion in isolating a cancer-fighting compound called Imuran. You are conducting tests when she suggests that Imuran might block the immune system. "The greatest danger in organ transplantation is the rejection of foreign tissue," she explains. "Imuran blocks that immune response. Possibly it can help patients through the initial phase. Let's test for it!"

Imuran works brilliantly, and will save many thousands of lives. You also are part of the assessment process of acyclovir, a synthetic compound superhero against the herpes virus.

In the 1980s, an unknown disease appears that attacks the human immune system, spreading quickly and killing its victims. Miss Elion has retired, but returns to the lab to help her colleagues modify her drug, AZT, to boost patients' immune systems. It's a vital step in the battle against AIDS, a merciless global plague that strikes tens of millions. You realize that developing antiretroviral medicines will be your mission for the rest of your life. ✡

You have spent countless hours staring at small glass plates. These little round Petri dishes, containing agar solution or other gelatins where bacteria like to grow, are dosed with swab samples from human subjects, or, actually, any surface at all. Then they're left in a dark, warm place so that any bacteria colonies you introduced can grow large enough to see.

The process of culturing bacteria for observation is simple enough. But looking for ways to kill harmful bacteria, seeing exactly how antibiotic substances function is complicated and frustrating. Quantifying the bacteria's reactions is close to impossible.

You are laboriously tracing the destructive patterns of a bacteriophage, or bacteria-eating virus, in hundreds of Petri dishes at the University of Wisconsin in 1951. The plaques formed by dead bacteria seem too random to count and record.

A research assistant remarks that, in a nearby lab, a microbiologist experimenting with *Escheria coli* cultures has identified a bacteriophage she calls Lambda. It replicates with the host bacteria's genome, and so may be useful in cloning recombinant DNA. You go find Dr. Lederberg and, in the course of your conversation, mention your difficulty seeing and recording plaque patterns.

"We're working on that, too!" Esther Lederberg says. "Look, it's possible to duplicate a colony on one plate onto other plates. If your second plate has a substance not on the original plate, and the second colony doesn't grow, you've identified its sensitivity."

"But how do you copy a colony of bacteria?" you wonder.

"It's like a mimeograph machine," she answers. "Here, look at this round block. It's covered in velvet, and you place the original Petri dish over it so the velvet fibers draw off the colonies with capillary action. Then you take it off and place your second dish on the block, where it absorbs the culture, and makes you a copy."

"Where would I obtain this velvet?" you ask, planning to place an order with a specialty laboratory-supply house.

"From a fabric store!" answers Dr. Lederberg, and gets back to her work. ✡

The middle of the twentieth century brings an explosion of scientific advancements in chemistry, engineering, and medicine. These include the invention and manufacture of consumer goods using new materials. Fiberglass, nylon, plastics, and polyurethane are used to make cheaper products. Synthetic fibers, including organic polymers, become the clothing fabrics worn by hundreds of millions of people.

Earlier in your career, you had imagined that you would probably spend your life in university or government laboratories. However, private industry has plenty of work for scientists, and it pays very well. Manufacturers who develop and patent new processes, machines, chemicals and medicines can potentially make fortunes, and they're willing to invest.

So you take a job at a large textile company in Massachusetts, J.P. Stevens, refining the process of making synthetic fabrics. Carbon disulfide, derived from coal oil, is made into threads by being forced at high temperatures through spinnerets. The fabric this produces is tough, durable, and cheap. But there's a problem: most of these fabrics are highly flammable, and if people are going to wear them safely, and use them to make mattresses and upholstery, this needs to be fixed.

The new assistant director of organic research at the company is Giuliana Cavaglieri Tesoro. At the age of seventeen, she had left Fascist Italy, where racial laws did not permit Jews into universities. On arriving in the U.S., she proceeded to skip college, enter Yale University's graduate program in organic chemistry, and receive her Ph.D. at 21.

Now she is working on a process to prevent static accumulation in J. P. Stevens' fibers, and at the same time is tackling the problem of flame resistance. You help her prepare acid derivatives and suggest various amine compounds for reactivity process. The testing procedure involves laundering, flaming, laundering, and flaming again, a hundred times. Finally, fabric resists fire.

Without a doubt, Tesoro's invention will save thousands of lives. "Better Things for Better Living Though Chemistry," as they say at Dupont! ✿

Deciding you need to widen your skills to improve your chances of making a livable salary, you go back to Berkeley to take computer courses. In a large, highly air-conditioned room, a massive IBM 704 mainframe computer is surrounded by tables with keypunch machines, where students create stacks of cards in FORTRAN for the mainframe to read. You quickly master several computer languages and create a library book-retrieval program.

A computer can read and execute commands with lightning speed, and calculate millions of math problems as well. A professor of industrial management at Carnegie Tech, Herbert Simon, has a theory that, since complex human behaviors are the result of simple, programmable units, then computers can be programmed to reason, learn, solve problems and plan.

In 1956 at Dartmouth College, Professor Simon, his colleague Allen Newell, Marvin Minsky of MIT, and several other scholars from various fields, meet to discuss the future of "artificial intelligence" – the process of a computer assessing a situation, summoning relevant data, and devising an action to accomplish a task. The group has successfully programmed strategies that enable computers to beat humans at checkers. You are part of a team that 'teaches' a computer to respond to questions in English.

There is a great deal of excitement about AI for a while, and lots of grant money, but problems persist. Not enough data has been coded to enable computers to use all their potential power. After spending many years overseeing a medical database project, you program a dense integrated circuit to diagnose metabolic diseases. This expert system is successfully tested and your company markets it to hospitals worldwide.

Your skills in chess, which you play for fun, suddenly become useful in the 1980s. You join a development team at IBM that's building a second-generation chess-playing computer, "Deep Blue." It will eventually defeat chess champion Garry Kasparov.

After that, you take a job at Intel, and, taking advantage of the increasing processing power of personal computers, you design educational software for engineering students. For you, every day seems like living in the future. ✿

Playing with rockets – that is, aerospace engineering – is great, of course, but more and more your attention wanders toward the ultimate goal of those rockets: the planets. For several years, you spend all your free time with the local astronomy club, becoming an expert in telescopes and even designing new measurement devices. Eventually, you give in to your instincts, and apply to the Ph.D. program in Cornell University's astronomy department.

You are comparing ways to assess electromagnetic radiation in space in the late 1960s when a young professor you had met at NASA arrives at Cornell. He is Carl Sagan, and his special ability is tying together different branches of science to advance space exploration. Robotic space probes are his passion.

Sagan is pleased to meet you, and asks about your radio telescope. He wants collaborators to help him demonstrate that radiation can turn simple chemicals into amino acids, and when he says that, you realize he's searching for possible life on other planets.

He invites you to the 1969 symposium of the American Association for the Advancement of Science, where he presents his view that alien visitors to earth almost certainly never existed. "But you *do* think there's extraterrestrial life," you challenge him.

"If there's one *advanced* civilization that can handle interstellar travel, then there are probably a million of them," Sagan answers. "If any of them are cruising around, looking at other planets, why would they choose Earth? They'd be looking at lots of planets. In fact, they'd have to launch thousands of craft regularly, and that would require a huge chunk of the universe's resources. No. It's not happening. It's a distraction. Let's not waste our time."

Instead, you and other scientists help Sagan design an interstellar radio message to the Hercules Global star cluster. Sent from the Cornell observatory in Puerto Rico in binary code, the Arecibo message describes human beings, their DNA, and a map of the solar system. It will arrive at its destination in 25,000 years.

Working with a brilliant mind like Carl Sagan, you understand why millions of non-scientists love him; his wonder and excitement about the universe touches one and all. ✡

In his 1905 publication of the Special Theory of Relativity, Professor Albert Einstein wrote that a large amount of energy could be released from a small amount of matter. Forty years later, this was demonstrated by an event that would change the course of world history. Scientists detonated the first artificial nuclear explosion near Alamogordo, New Mexico, with the radiance of a thousand suns. The nuclear age had begun.

Neither Einstein nor any of the other physicists, had ever wanted such a massively destructive bomb to be used. But Germany had split the uranium atom at the end of 1938, and the logical next step was the engineering of a horrifying weapon. Leo Szilard had described the nuclear chain reaction in 1933, and there was every reason to believe that Germany could do the same, and gain unlimited world power. To contain the Nazis, the U.S. had to build its own atomic bomb.

You had been just a few years out of college when the Germans surrendered in 1945. A few months later, the war with Japan ended when the U.S. dropped two thermonuclear bombs on Hiroshima and Nagasaki. Although you were happy the war was over, you were appalled to read about the civilian casualties: hundreds of thousands of Japanese people died agonizing deaths on those two days in August.

The war's end should also have been the end of nuclear weapons. But a new conflict begins – the cold war, a struggle between the U.S. and the Soviet Union, two nations terrified of each other. Both were blessed with brilliant scientists, and both proceeded to build up their nuclear arsenals frantically until each was able to destroy the planet many times over. The nuclear arms race frightens everyone, from the Joint Chiefs of Staff in Washington to schoolchildren hiding under their desks during preparation drills.

Eight scientists who had been involved in some way in the production of the atomic bomb, formed the Emergency Committee of Atomic Scientists in 1946. Some of them, like Albert Einstein, Leo Szilard and Victor Weisskopf, had fled Nazi Europe, and were passionately devoted to preventing another kind of holocaust. This committee launched a hundred others.

Many of the organizations trying to raise awareness of the dangers of the arms race are religious. You identify strongly with them as a Jew, and look around for an organization that expresses your values, that you can join and support in defense of a safe world.

Norman Cousins and Lenore Marshall start the Committee for Sane Nuclear Policy, or SANE, in 1957, and peace activist Bella Abzug co-founds Women Strike For Peace in 1961 against the continued testing of nuclear weapons. And a biologist named Barry Commoner, who conducted a study of baby teeth that proved the presence of strontium-90 from nuclear test fallout, influences President Nixon to form a new federal department, the Environmental Protection Agency.

You spend a lot of your time and energy lecturing and campaigning for organizations like these. Finally, near the end of your working career, you accept an invitation from Al Gore and Carl Sagan to meet with Jewish organizations' representatives, rabbis and Jewish senators in Washington.

This historic meeting creates Jewish leadership in the environmental crisis for the American Jewish community in the protection of the planet. It's called COEJL, the Coalition on the Environment and Jewish Life. You and many others will push for education, new laws and action for sustainability -- for Jewish reasons.

You spend your retirement years in the company of powerful Jewish environmentalists: Ellen Bernstein, who invented the modern Tu B'Shvat seder, the Green Zionist Alliance, and Hazon. Jewish holidays take on new meanings when your colleagues re-visit old traditions. You spend many afternoons brainstorming with them.

And one of your most satisfying moments is when you explain to a synagogue-school assembly that the miracle of Hanukkah isn't that one cruse of oil lasted eight days – but that Jews of today can learn to conserve the earth's resources far, far into the future.

Chapter Ten

I Want to Be a Musician

The Jewish musical tradition goes back to the Biblical period. King David is said to have played the lyre, and may have written the Psalms, of which only the lyrics remain. Music was carried to Jewish diaspora, picking up accents of many countries. Sephardic melodies have a Moorish sound, while East European Jews added Slavic flavors to their dances, love songs, and religious music.

A popular assumption about Jewish immigrants to America is that "they all played instruments." Not true, but grounded in a certain reality. Musical literacy is treasured in the Jewish community. The joke about the massive influx of Russian Jews after the Cold War was, "How do you know which of them are pianists? They're the ones coming off the plane NOT carrying violins."

The portable, versatile violin is indeed associated with American Jews (and with other cultures in other places). American-born and immigrant Jewish violinists include Yehudi Menuhin, Jascha Heifetz, Itzhak Perlman, Isaac Stern, Nathan Milstein, Mischa Elman and Joshua Bell, and violist Pinchas Zukerman.

During the twentieth century, Jewish teachers and performers dominated U.S. orchestras, conservatories, and festivals. Jewish composers figure prominently in our classical and popular music: George Gershwin, Leonard Bernstein, Louis Gottschalk, Kurt Weill, Arnold Schoenberg, Aaron Copland, Jerome Kern, Stephen Sondheim, Richard Rodgers, Yip Harburg, Marvin Hamlisch, Frederick Loewe, Paul Simon, Carole King, Bob Dylan, Janis Ian, Benny Goodman, Glenn Miller, Stan Getz, Neil Sedaka, Neil Diamond, Irving Berlin, Lou Reed, and Paula Abdul come to mind. In this chapter, you may also encounter Billy Joel, Phil Ochs, Danny Kaye, Madeleine Kahn, Joey Ramone, Steve Goodman, Carly Simon, Randy Newman, David Bromberg and Bette Midler.

My appreciation to my friends, violist Maria Lambros Kannen and Rabbi Larry Pinsker, for their help and advice.

It's 1961, and you're in the living room of your family's row-house in the Portage Park section of northwest Chicago. Sitting at the Sohmer upright piano, you're playing the Hanon exercises that your teacher assigned. You're wishing the half-hour of scales were finished and you could get to the Clementi sonatina that's already printed on next Sunday's recital program.

Your piano lessons started six years ago, when you were four. There's always been music in your house; your dad plays piano and your mother plays flute, and they said you could have lessons only if you agree to do all your homework before practicing.

When you were six, your family went down to Orchestra Hall on South Michigan Avenue to hear Isaac Stern perform with the Chicago Symphony Orchestra. Stern is your father's favorite violinist, and you've heard his recordings many times. But hearing him playing the Mendelssohn concerto with such warmth and joy in live performance, you felt your heart singing with the soloist. You had a powerful yearning to play the violin.

Your parents were pleased, and rent a half-size violin. They ask the music teacher at the local high school for a recommendation, and are sent to the Chicago Musical College. A faculty member who also teaches children agrees to take you on. The first lesson was about how to hold the instrument, and you played some pizzicato games on the violin's neck. Practicing hours every day, you progressed rapidly. The violin seems to love your hands.

In 1964, your family and some neighbors take a train to Detroit to see a new musical, *Fiddler on the Roof*. The lyrics are by the son of your old family dentist, Dr. Harnick, and everyone is excited: it's the first musical with a Jewish theme, for one thing, but also, the songs are terrific. Afterwards you can't stop singing "If I Were A Rich Man" and "To Life." Words set to music reaches people in a very special way, and singing with other people is as joyful as playing instruments together.

If you decide to train to be a singer, turn to page 175.

If you want to focus mainly on violin, turn to page 176.

If you want to advance your piano skills, turn to page 177.

Your parents know that the right teacher will help you develop a strong technique from the beginning, but a poor teacher will let you sustain bad habits that you'll have to break. They go straight to the Chicago Lyric Opera to look for a coach for you, and find an under-employed tenor with good teaching skills.

You begin your lessons standing up straight, taking your vocal chords from bottom to top with a siren-type exercise to warm up. Then you're strengthening your tongue and lips with drills you're glad your friends don't see. When everything's limber, your teacher has you start to sing scales – and you're impressed that you can sing higher and stronger pitches than you ever have.

Since you also want to continue taking piano, and to take guitar too because it's fun and relatively easy, you don't have time for your high school chorus. You take the bus downtown for lessons and to hear various recitals. On family vacations, you often attend concerts – Beverly Sills at La Scala in Milan, and Barbra Streisand in "Funny Girl" in London's West End.

You love not just classical song forms, but organic American styles. Of the millions of southern black people who migrated to northern cities, many arrived in Chicago, bringing with them the blues: you go to Maxwell Street to hear future Bluebird and Chess Records artists every chance you get.

The musical theater repertoire is very compelling to you. Great shows have been composed by Leonard Bernstein, Stephen Sondheim, Rodgers and Hammerstein, and many others. "Climb Ev'ry Mountain" and "Maria" are showcases for a strong voice. But you're also intrigued by solo performers who accompany themselves on guitar, singing traditional songs and those they have written themselves, in more intimate club settings. You like the personal stamp that folk musicians and singer-songwriters put on their performances.

If you see yourself in the competitive, exciting atmosphere of the musical stage, turn to page 178.

If you would rather explore the more personal folk club scene, turn to page 179.

Music lessons aren't cheap. Your parents say that you can continue with both piano and violin, but if you want to go to music camp, you're going to have to drop one. You drop piano.

The summer you finish tenth grade, you take your violin and a footlocker full of clothes to the Interlochen Center for the Arts in Michigan. As your parents drive away, you watch them for only a moment and then turn to survey this magical place – a gorgeous country camp where everything is designed to make you a better musician. The kids in the chamber music program love the same things you love, and you're relaxed and excited immediately.

From morning till night, Interlochen gives you complete immersion in music. You're assigned to another violinist, a cellist and a violist, and your twice-daily rehearsals are closely supervised by a well-known conservatory teacher. She corrects your bowing problems, and advises different shifting to improve your accuracy and intonation. You don't always understand right away, but you trust her, and your playing improves -- you can master more challenging pieces.

Performances at camp are both thrilling and nerve-wracking. This is not the audience you're used to. These are real musicians. Walking onto the stage requires courage. The risk to your ego, though, is worth it, and you conquer your fear to gain the confidence of experience.

Music camp is great for you. You now have a second family, and many of your new friends will be taking the same path as you.

A year later, it's time to think about what conservatory to choose. You will have to identify the right teacher, and go where he or she teaches. Like every aspiring musician, you have deficiencies, and you'll need a teacher who can recognize and work on them.

If you are organized, analytical and disciplined, and want a teacher who can help you play more freely and expressively, turn to page 180.

If you are a passionate and imaginative performer, and need support for your technique, turn to page 181.

Your parents think your piano teacher is too committed to a pre-set learning program to accommodate your particular talents, and they go shopping for someone else.

The Music Institute of Chicago has an extensive program for young people, and after taking sample lessons with three different instructors, you select one who appears to understand where you need discipline and where you should be allowed to use your imagination.

By eleventh grade, you are playing a pretty sophisticated reper-toire. Your recent recital included the Schumann Novellette opus 99, and the Bach Fugue in D. Your teacher was concerned that the piano you have at home cannot provide the versatility you need, and so you have been practicing at MIC on a Steinway several hours every day after school.

You soon realize that you want a better piano at home. You take a job as an accompanist at a ballet school, and get paid to play at re-hearsals of musicals at community theaters. This is all heady stuff for a kid not even in college yet, and you are very pleased to be able to buy your own Baldwin, with your savings and the sale of the old piano. You revel in the deep, beautiful sound it gives you.

It's time to figure out where to continue your studies after high school. You visit the Curtis Institute in Philadelphia and the Juil-liard School in New York, and take a lesson at each. At Curtis, the teacher expresses the opinion that you have lost the music you want to express, and are relying completely on technique – your playing is more engineering than art. At Juilliard, you are told that you don't play freely: you have too much unnecessary ten-sion in your arms and shoulders, and the resulting fatigue is draining your expressiveness.

You audition for admission to both conservatories, and are ac-cepted at both.

If you decide to attend Curtis, turn to page 182.

If you choose Juilliard, turn to page 183.

You attend Oberlin Conservatory in Ohio, taking a lot of vocal performance classes, but majoring in theater. You want the rigorous training, but you're not interested in taking German, Italian and French in order to perform opera and lieder. You audition for all of the musical-theater productions, learn the songs from the classic shows, and get a Young Artists residency in New York during your senior year.

At the Imperial Theater, you receive a weekly stipend to be an understudy for several roles in their current production, *Two By Two*. It's a musical about Noah, and the score's composer is Richard Rodgers. Your absolute favorite performer since childhood, the hilarious Danny Kaye, plays the lead.

"Welcome to the ark!" Danny exclaims. "Let me introduce you to the zoo. Here's Maddy – Maddy, come meet our Young Artist." Madeleine Kahn, in makeup and feeling whimsical, extends her hand. "Dahling," she drawls, "it's a pleasure, I'm sure. But I must warm up now. Please move to the fallout shelter," and she floats away. What a character she is!

You watch every performance from the wings, studying the preparations of the professionals. After Danny breaks his leg and has to perform on crutches – which costs the show some integrity – you learn a lot about working in sub-par conditions. You get several opportunities to go onstage when members of the cast can't, and have the unique thrill of singing before a Broadway audience.

When you get your bachelor's degree, you think about where you should go. For the talented and lucky singer, there's work in New York, performing live in front of audiences, and in commercials. But there's also the entertainment industry centered in southern California, which needs a lot of talent voiceovers, backup, theme songs, maybe even Disneyland shows.

To look for opportunities in Hollywood, turn to page 184.

To stay in New York and pursue a stage career, turn to page 185.

It's 1969, and you've applied only to colleges in New York. That's the center of the folk music revival, and you want to be as close as possible to Greenwich Village, where the nightclubs and cabarets gave so many singers their start. You enroll at New York University, for music and political science, and, after a mind-expanding experience at the Woodstock summer music festival, you bring your guitar to your shared apartment near Washington Square.

In the Village cafes, it's not uncommon to see songwriters like Janis Ian, Carly Simon, or Phil Ochs having dinner, talking with friends, and sometimes scribbling on scraps of paper. You are a regular at Max Gordon's Village Vanguard, a basement music club where you hear jazz masters like Miles Davis and Stan Getz, as well as the 'folkies' who fill out the schedule. A Holocaust refugee named Bill Graham has just transformed a Yiddish theater on Second Avenue into a rock venue, the Fillmore East, and when you're in the mood you take in a concert there. Some of the blues musicians you knew in Chicago, like Sonny Terry, are performing in smaller places like the Gaslight Café, and it's there that you first hear David Bromberg and Arlo Guthrie.

At an open-mic night at Gerde's Folk City on West Fourth Street, you get up on the stage. First you play Woody Guthrie's "1913 Massacre" about the deaths of striking miners and their families, which Bob Dylan performed at Carnegie Hall. Then you segue into your own song, "My Lai Village," which you wrote after reading about the atrocity in Vietnam that has just come to light.

They woke me from my dream, my deep dream of peace, my loving dream
And I won't sleep again, till justice rolls down like a mighty stream.

The audience jumps to their feet, applauding, and won't let you leave the microphone till you sing it again. Flushed with triumph, you start down the steps and are collared by a talent agent, who wants to know if you've written other songs like that.

If want like drums and electric guitars in your music, turn to page 186.

If you prefer to sing your songs with acoustic accompaniment, in the folk-rock style, turn to page 187.

You find the school you need in Boston, at the New England Conservatory, where musical imagination is cherished and nurtured. As one of the few violinists taking classes in contemporary improvisation, you find lots of opportunities to jam with student jazz ensembles. You frequently perform the works of student composers; it's a unique honor to be a partner with the composer, and present music that has never been heard before.

When the weather is good and you have a few free hours, you sometimes improvise a little concert space on Boyleston Street, where the tourists are, and perform with your friends – behind an open cello case. Busking is kind of fun, and a lot better money than waiting tables. Also it feels nice when strangers thank you for your music. One Sunday afternoon, after you've played the Prokofiev Sonata #2 in D and some jazzy Gershwin preludes, you and your roommate find enough money in the case to cover most of the month's rent.

You never miss an alumni recital at Jordan Hall. Because you can't decide what sort of career offers the best chance at success, you often talk with the alumni afterwards. They offer you some interesting guidance.

"If your nerves can stand it, you could freelance," you are told. "There are pickup ensembles working all the time, playing movie scores or Broadway shows. You could be playing baroque one day, and pops the next. It's fun if you don't mind hustling for work. Or you can start a new group, maybe niche music that nobody else is playing. If you like to travel, why not join a chamber ensemble? Successful quartets can be on the road more than 200 days a year."

This is a really tough decision. You have to look inside yourself to find what you really love.

If you want to freelance and meet lots of new people, turn to page 188.

If you want to create something entirely new by starting a band, turn to page 189.

After many visits and sample lessons, you find that the school you want is the Eastman School of Music, at the University of Rochester. The string department is dedicated to training students in excellent technique, and you work with Donald Weilerstein who knows how to solve students' technical problems. Isolating each of your issues, he tells you to practice certain passages of etudes and concerti that will correct the problem.

Even when you don't understand why you have to work on skills, you trust your teachers. They've seen what helps students create the richest sounds and the most agile shifts. And they themselves are brilliant musicians.

Your goal is to prepare for the high-pressure process of music competitions. Only the best students will win, and the rewards are considerable. Winners may get several years of prestigious recital dates and major media reviews, or coveted orchestra jobs. Even better, those talented few will have management contracts with ICM or Columbia Artists – a certain road to success.

Informing the faculty that you're aiming for the most important international competitions – the Paganini Competition in Genoa, the Tchaikovsky Competition in Moscow – you set an exhausting practice schedule of six to eight hours a day, working on extremely difficult pieces and taking every opportunity to perform. Some days, you're too tired to eat dinner. But your fellow students support you, and your teachers coach you daily.

The work pays off as you finally achieve the deep, rich tone you want, and an elasticity of execution. You begin auditions, and finally are admitted to the 1976 Queen Elisabeth Competition in Brussels, Belgium. A few days before your departure for Belgium, you receive a call: Itzhak Perlman cannot perform with the New York Philharmonic due to illness, and the orchestra needs someone to play the Brahms Violin Concerto. You know and love it very well.

If you decline the invitation because it will distract your preparation for the competition, turn to page 190.

If you accept the chance for such a high-profile concert, turn to page 191.

The Curtis Institute in Philadelphia is one of the nation's most prestigious conservatories.   Its alumni include Peter Serkin, Eugene Istomin and Leonard Bernstein, and the admissions committee must have heard something very special in your audition. You hope that their faith in you is well-founded.

Till now, you have mostly played music of the classical period, Mozart, Clementi and Haydn; you like their orderly, reliable forms. The prominence of chords, which emphasizes the tonal structure of the music, appeals to your systematic nature.

But the piano teachers at Curtis encourage you to explore the emotional Romantic period with its more complicated harmonic progressions and its violations of classical rules.   They assign pieces by Liszt, Chopin, and late Beethoven. You have to leave your safe places and open yourself to the music's passion. They suggest that you sing the music, and even dance to it.

You take a few young students to help cover your living expenses, and find in some of them the same love of music that first brought you to the piano. Each presents a sort of puzzle: what gifts do they have naturally, and what do they need to understand and experience in order to embrace the works they're learning to play?

When a student finally hears the subtlety of a Schumann bagatelle, or masters a difficult arpeggio at last, you feel an overwhelming sense of triumph and joy. And you think you understand something new about yourself when a ten-year-old girl looks up from the sheet music and says to you, "You know, you're a really good teacher."

If you think that your most important contribution to the arts will be nurturing piano skills in young people, turn to page 192.

If you still love performing a lot, and want a career accompanying soloists and students, turn to page 193.

Your joy in playing piano is the center of your existence. You feel there is no decision to be made about your future; there is no life without music. Everything outside of practicing, rehearsing and performing is just less fun.

This is what the faculty at Juilliard sensed in you when you auditioned. It's not something that can be taught or acquired. Your sense of wonder and celebration is something they perceive only in the most brilliant musicians.

However, you have a number of problems. Your hand position is flawed – it causes tightness and limits your freedom of motion. You tend to lose track of tempo, which affects your accuracy and compromises your tone. And sometimes you seem not to listen to your own playing, which makes your dynamics ill-planned and not as effective as they should be.

Five years with the conservatory's experienced piano teachers take care of the worst of your habits. At last, the music you play is as beautiful and expressive as the music you hear in your head when you look at a score. You graduate Juilliard with honors.

More than just technical skill, you have experienced the real, almost physical power of music to impart comfort, strength, and peace to listeners. It's even more potent to people singing or playing instruments. You're talking with a cousin about this when she says: "Lots of people don't experience this at all, at least not consciously. How many people do you think listen to music to calm themselves, or for inspiration? It just doesn't occur to most folks. What can you do for *them?*"

You give some serious thought to music's greater mission – and your role in it.

If you decide to become a synagogue music director, turn to page 194.

If you want to bring music to people who never hear it, turn to page 195.

Arriving in Los Angeles, you rent a tiny apartment and join the American Federation of Television and Radio Artists, a performers' union. You ask around and locate a talent agent who's just starting out in the business and charging only 5% of clients' fees.

She finds you a gig dubbing a song for a pitch-deaf actor in a sitcom, and then a job singing with a band on a cruise ship; this is exhausting, and pays badly, but at least you get to see Hawaii.

This goes on for a couple of years, and then your agent calls to send you to an audition for a short film musical being made by three film students, called "Junior High School." It will have a few dance numbers, but they mainly need ensemble singers.

You show up on the set – a local private school that's empty during the summer – and see that this will be a really low-budget production. The singers sit in a biology classroom, being called out one by one to sing for the directors in the cafeteria. You write your name on a clipboard and take a seat near a cute, exotic-looking teenager, Paula.

Paula is friendly and energetic. She tells you she grew up nearby, and wants to be a choreographer, and also sings her own songs. You ask about her family, and she tells you her dad is a Syrian Jew raised in Brazil, and her mom's family is Ashkenazic. She has lots of questions about your music conservatory training.

You both get parts in the movie, and it's not high art, but lots of fun. She and you stay in touch through her college years while you're singing in clubs. You are so proud when she calls to say she's choreographing for the Jacksons. She wants you to coach her so she can make a singing demo – and you'll sing backup on her debut album. You have a blast rehearsing "Opposites Attract" and "Straight Up" with her. *Forever Your Girl* reaches #1 on Billboard 200, and makes Paula Abdul a star – and gets you the connections you need for more studio recording jobs, and some solo work in Las Vegas.

Being a session musician makes very good money. Even better, it lets you work with some of the most exciting rock bands of the era. ✡

With your Young Artists residency over, and your conservatory degree in hand, you join the throngs at every Broadway "cattle call." You've prepared a ballad, "All The Things You Are," and the up-tempo "It's De-Lovely." Whichever the director requests.

You get a few callbacks, but no parts for a year. Then you see in *Variety* that Tony-winner Stephen Sondheim has a new show called *A Little Night Music.* It's pretty challenging musically: complicated meters, huge range, and frequent modulations. All the songs are in waltz time. You are well trained. You've got this.

You stand in the glaring light of the stage; out there in the dark are the director, Hal Prince, and Sondheim the composer. "We'd like to hear a love song. Something tender," a voice says.

Your two audition songs disappear completely from your mind. Drawing a deep breath to stave away panic, you softly repeat the words, "love song" – and then one jumps into your mind. It's even in waltz time. You say to the pianist, "Tumbalalaika, in D."

The older Jewish woman at the piano smiles. You turn to the dim figures in the second row and sing the Yiddish riddle song. It's about a boy who cannot decide between two girls, testing them with impossible questions. To show off your range, you take the last verse up an octave. Your phrasing conveys the heartbreak of a lover who will not be chosen.

Silence at the end of your song, and a subtle throat-clearing. Someone out there in the dark has been very moved. "Thank you. Please sing something happy now."

Relaxed now, you finally remember "It's De-Lovely," and belt it out with verve and humor. It connects. "That was de-lovely, thank you," Prince says. "See Elizabeth at the back of the hall."

You get a part in the company! Rehearsals begin two weeks later, and, on opening night, you step onstage in elegant Edwardian costume in the opening number, "Night Waltz." It's an honor to be in a cast supporting Glynis Johns and Hermione Gingold. The show is a hit, winning a Tony for best musical and the Drama Critics Circle award. And your career ratchets up a notch – the first step to a wonderful life on the Broadway stage. ✿

The agent is interested in representing you – finding you gigs in venues where you'll be heard by record company scouts and booking agents. You meet him on a park bench a few days later.

There, among the pigeons and the chess games, you sing him your ballad about a man who languishes in jail, falsely accused of murder, another song mocking President Nixon, and a funny love song to a pizza. The agent says he can get some club owners to listen to you, and asks what your goals are. "I'd like to get together with a drummer and a bassist," you answer, "and give these songs a heavy beat and an electric sound."

"Interesting," he says. "Give me your phone number." He departs for his office and you go back to class.

A month later, you have a band – a bohemian drummer, an unemployed poet for lead guitar, and a bass player who recently left a commune in Big Sur, California. You write the songs, sing and play rhythm guitar, and your first gig is your own college graduation party. You write "Sheepskin Rag" for the occasion.

Eventually, Fred Weintraub asks you to open for Randy Newman at his Bleecker Street coffeehouse, the Bitter End. A few months later you open for Lou Reed and the Velvet Underground.

After the show, the audience drifts away, and you're sitting in the back with your drummer and Billy Joel, who's on tour and needs to kick back and listen to someone else for a change. Billy is in a thoughtful mood; he's been depressed that his first big hit, "Piano Man," was cut down for radio play, compromising its integrity. He feels like writing a song about the sad realities of commercial success. "I won't be here in another year, if I don't stay on the charts," he mumbles, and starts to hum.

Punk music has just arrived at CBGB, Hilly Kristal's new club in the East Village. Tonight's concert has ended, and a young guy in a black leather jacket drifts into the Bitter End. He is Joey Ramone, and he feels good; it was an excellent show. Billy buys him a beer, and you drink to the Ramones' success and to the recent resignation of President Nixon. You pick up your guitar and begin to strum Robby Krieger's "Light My Fire," and soon everyone's riffing. The night doesn't end till dawn. What a life. ✿

Greenwich Village is the place to hear American folk music. The "folk revival" began there in the 1940s, introducing new audiences to the old songs that helped create country and western music, jazz, and rock. TV and radio popularized folk music, and folk festivals were born in Newport, Philadelphia, and other places. The hootenanny became popular with crowds who liked singing along with Peter, Paul and Mary, and the Weavers.

Charlie Rothschild, who books talent at Gerde's Folk City, invites you back for a solo gig. This is huge: the walls there are covered with pictures of musicians whose careers were launched there: Rambin' Jack Elliot, Bob Dylan, Melissa Manchester, Phoebe Snow. Paul Simon and Bette Midler have performed there.

With your set-list taped to the side of your guitar, your bass player and mandolinist next to you, you start your set. First, "Little Boxes," an homage to Malvina Reynolds, and Phil Ochs' "Draft Dodger Rag," you transition to your own songs, using familiar folk chord progressions and picking styles. The audience's eyes are shining in the semi-darkness as you play "Won't See Me No More." They applaud warmly, and you launch into "Astor Place," "Mother Jones," and "Not a Minute Too Soon."

Sometime during the evening, the audience becomes your fans. They love your deft rhymes, your poetry, and the surprises in your lyrics – but most of all, your fluid, warm voice that caresses the words and stays in the ears of the listener. At the end of the concert, they stand and clap and demand two encores. The very last person to leave is Bruce Kaplan, president of the brand-new Flying Fish record label. He wants you to sign.

Your calendar fills up with gigs, and you spend many hours with your guitar and stacks of manuscript paper, writing new songs. But you get home to Chicago often. One night at the Old Town School of Folk Music, you're in the third row listening to your idol, Steve Goodman, play his "City of New Orleans."

"Guess who's here!" Steve exclaims, and beckons you to the stage. Grinning, you join him, and harmonize "You Never Even Call Me By My Name." That's it. You know you've arrived. ✿

The day you graduate from the conservatory, you join the American Federation of Musicians. Union members are entitled to certain minimum fees wherever they work, and protect each other by demanding, collectively, decent working conditions. Your dues are an investment in your career, and support your colleagues.

Then you make a demo tape that includes Leonard Bernstein's "One Hand, One Heart" from West Side Story, and Mendelssohn's Wedding March; these will get you wedding gigs. A few church hymns might attract music directors putting together holiday programs, and your own pop-song transcriptions are a route to studio recording jobs. You send tapes, wrapped in your contact information, to every possible employer you see in the telephone book. You pin your business card to hundreds of bulletin boards.

A few restaurants hire you to stroll through their dining rooms, playing popular favorites; you really hate this. On the night you swear is your last, a customer asks if you're interested in recording a film score. You are! It turns out to be an animated student film, but it's a credit, and you add it to your résumé.

A wedding planner hires you for an elegant ceremony in a hotel. It's pleasant and pays well, but its true value is the exposure it gets you. One of the guests is a Hollywood executive TV director.

"You play beautifully. Would you be interested in being on my call list?" he asks. "There's a TV pilot that's about to start shooting, and they're going to need string players for the soundtrack." Your business card is in his hand before he finishes the sentence.

Live performances, though, are your real preference. While waiting for the call from Hollywood, you take a walking tour around Boston's many theaters, collecting programs and noting the names of the violinists in the pit orchestras. Some are friends of friends, and you contact them to let them know you're available to sub.

Subbing leads to a contract. You now have a steady, two-hour-a-day job playing wonderful theater music, and your contract lets you accept gigs with touring shows whenever you like. With lots of free time, you can premiere new works, compose, or teach. A life of music, every day – this is your dream come true. ✿

During a visit back home, a childhood friend urges you to go with her to an unusual concert in a synagogue in Skokie. "It's Dave Tarras," she says. "You want to hear him. He plays klezmer."

You ask what klezmer is. "It's Jewish jazz," she explains. "Dance music from Eastern Europe. Lots of improvisation. You'll like it."

So the two of you arrive in the shul's sanctuary and applaud politely when the band goes up on the bima. Dave Tarras is nearly eighty; he plays the clarinet, and his band includes a drummer, pianist, two fiddlers and a tenor saxophone. They begin to play.

The tune is "Chassene Tants," a wedding dance -- high, fast, and light, with a heavy backbeat. Your foot begins tapping the floor in time. Something is happening to you. You're transported to a shtetl in the Ukraine; but you're also here in synagogue, hearing the prayer modes you know so well. Somehow, you seem to be *remembering* klezmer music, not hearing it for the first time.

Tune after tune: a scissors-dance, a tango-like terkisher, a slow waltz. They're intoxicating. At the end of the concert, you're breathless and euphoric. After asking when and where the band's next date is -- because you'll be following them there -- you return home in a pleasant daze, write a list of the instruments in the Tarras band, and start phoning every Jewish musician you know.

It takes a while to get a klezmer ensemble in place. Meanwhile, with a sheaf of blank manuscript paper, you visit a dozen Jewish retirement homes, asking each resident, *"Bist du a klezmer?'*

Many respond, humming tunes and sometimes singing in Yiddish, while you write down everything. Afterward, you track down active klezmorim and collect at least a hundred more songs, each one a jewel. You make copies, and rehearsals begin.

Someone knows an announcer at a local public radio station, and you're invited to perform on air. A lot of people hear it, call the station, and the station refers them to you. Invitations follow, and the pianist becomes your band's manager. You play Hadassah conventions, weddings, summer camps, bar mitsvas, and festivals. Within a few years, other klez bands have formed; you've helped to launch an international klezmer revival! ✡

The first round of the Queen Elisabeth Violin Competition is held at the ornate Grand Hall of the Royal Brussels Conservatory. It's enormous – and intimidating. You wait in a green room for your turn to audition. When your name is called, you walk onto the stage, lift your violin, and play a Paganini caprice, and then the Meditation from Thaïs. You feel good about your performance.

One of the judges thanks you and you return backstage to put the instrument back in its case. You have hours to wait before the decision. A cellist you met yesterday takes you out for coffee.

But the answer is not the one you want. You won't be advancing to the next round; your playing was excellent, but other candidates were better. Your new friend, the cellist, tries to console you. "What about starting a quartet?" he asks.

That's a nice thought. You loved playing chamber music, back when you had the time. "Is that what you want to do?" you ask.

"Yes," he says, "that's been my wish for years. I know a brilliant violist from my conservatory. Let's find another violin."

You feel comforted and optimistic. Returning to the U.S., you meet with the violist and arrange to audition a fourth musician. In three months, the right violinist is found, and she joins you.

The others agree to be based in Chicago, and you set up a rehearsal schedule and start working on repertoire. The four of you become as close as colleagues can be. You travel together and eat together. While you're playing, even your breathing seems to be synchronized. When you disagree about interpretation, you work it out. When a performance crashes and burns, you laugh and start again. And when it comes together beautifully, you rejoice in unison.

The pleasure of performing music you love – Beethoven, Borodin, Haydn, Shostakovich – eclipses the struggles of a life on the road. During your tours of the great concert venues of the world, you meet famous pianists, clarinetists and singers. A few avant-garde composers ask you to premiere their works. And what you treasure most is bringing music to audiences in remote places who rarely experience a live performance. It's your gift to them. ✿

You accept the assignment and hurry to New York. The Philharmonic's conductor, Pierre Boulez, schedules extra hours of rehearsals in the next two days. The orchestra members cannot be compelled to put in overtime, and Boulez tells you a pianist will play the orchestral part for some of the rehearsals.

Walking into Avery Fisher Hall from the rear entrance, you approach the stage. The conductor is engaged in close conversation with the pianist, who faces away from you. But there's no mistaking that distinguished white mane. Your accompanist for today's rehearsal is Leonard Bernstein.

Far from being intimidated, you feel encouraged. With support like this, you're bound to perform well. Bernstein shakes your hand warmly and says it's his pleasure to work with you; Boulez is charming and somehow makes you feel completely at home.

You have mastered the quick rhythm changes in the concerto, and its multiple stopping, where you're playing two or more strings at once, producing several pitches. The challenge is understanding and internalizing the conductor's sense of the music, and much time is spent explaining, gesturing and singing passages. Finally, the afternoon of the performance, you feel the concerto the same way Boulez has described it. You're ready.

From backstage, you hear the Hall manager explain to the audience that Mr. Perlman is unfortunately indisposed, and that the Philharmonic is pleased to welcome a new artist to its stage. You can't quite hear their reaction, but tell yourself it's enthusiasm. You and Pierre Boulez walk onto the stage, to applause.

The orchestra softly introduces the first theme of the allegro, and then the second; your powerful entrance is at measure 90. You feel good; you and your violin are one, and you're enveloped in love of the music. Your joy seems to fill the auditorium.

As the third movement ends, the audience erupts in cheers of "Bravo!" and congratulatory applause. The conductor is beaming, and the concertmaster, too, who hopes he's about to fill a vacancy in the string section. The New York Times music critic sings your praise next morning. Congratulations on a great career launch! ✡

By the time you graduate from Curtis, you have a plan. You are going to return to Chicago and start a school in the South Side. You want to plant music seeds wherever students are hungry to learn.

A struggling strip mall seems like an affordable location to set up shop, and you negotiate the rental of 3,000 square feet of space with the owner. A lawyer friend helps you incorporate, and you borrow the money to buy three baby grand pianos from a college music department that's upgrading. Visiting the local public schools to scout the music teachers, you identify voice, violin, and wind instructors who are both talented and popular, and make them offers. Soon, you have a staff of four, including yourself, and an administrator.

You distribute flyers in supermarkets, summer camps, pediatricians' offices and day-care centers. A local newspaper, feeling you have an interesting project going, runs a feature story about your music school, and you manage to get interviewed on radio. Parents begin calling to sign up their kids for clarinet, violin, piano, and voice. When fall comes, most of the practice rooms are occupied every afternoon and all day Saturday. Word of mouth builds your school like no paid advertising ever could.

Although some students are casual dilettantes, others are devoted, and put in an hour or more of practice every day. In a few of them, you or one of the other teachers sees a spark – they will be nurtured with close coaching, and given more ambitious assignments. With decades of practicing your art, both solo and in ensemble, you know which children have both a musical ear and an unswerving focus. You call in their parents for conferences, telling them that their son or daughter has an undeniable gift that must be supported and cultivated. Many make great sacrifices to buy the instruments, provide the transportation, and pay the considerable tuition charged by the children's programs at the best conservatories.

And as you sit in the front row, listening to your students' recitals, you're filled with wonder at the beauty that flows through them to illuminate your life, theirs, and the world. ✿

You are a practical person. You know that soon, you'll need to make a living. But you also want fulfillment as an artist. After two decades in the music world, you conclude that the most indispensible type of musician is the accompanist.

After all, nearly every vocal recital requires piano accompaniment, as do sonatas for most other instruments. Ballet students need a pianist; so do choral rehearsals and musical auditions. Even conducting students learn by conducting a pianist. This seems like a good path. You take many classes in accompaniment, and are coached closely.

Supporting a melodic line is the main task of the accompanist, but this is misleadingly simple. At the piano, you maintain the appropriate tempo for the soloist, set up key changes, and create the mood of a piece. You cultivate the ability to judge your dynamics so that you neither overwhelm nor abandon the soloist. Sometimes you have to transpose keys on sight, reduce an orchestral score, and even adjust to a diva's mistakes. This is not an easy job.

But you focus everything on your specialty, absorbing criticism and using it, listening to other musicians prepare for recitals. You constantly learn new repertoire in many genres. You get used to being completely ignored by audiences.

And it pays off, as you begin to receive requests from both students and established artists. Sometimes you accompany tenor Jan Peerce and flautist Paula Robison; you even get to perform with Benny Goodman, the big-band leader, when he premieres a sonata for clarinet and piano by Poulenc.

Not everyone recognizes that you make great solo performances possible. But that doesn't matter. The person in the spotlight knows. As the word spreads that a new, competent accompanist is in town, your phone starts ringing and you can be choosy about your assignments. It's a very good living. And the respect you earn among musicians is almost as satisfying as the musical collaborations you present to your audiences. ✿

A few months after graduating Curtis, you go to Rosh Hashana services with your parents back in Chicago. It's one of the holiest days of the year, of course, and you do your share of self-reflection, but like everyone else in the sanctuary, you're focused much of the time on the cantor. It's his time to shine.

His rich, warm baritone lifts the hopes of the congregation for a better year. "*Aleinu*," he sings, "it is upon us" to acknowledge the divine power that inspires us to make a better world. A keyboardist at an electric organ plays some chords.

At the kiddush after the service, the synagogue president drifts over to wish you a happy new year and congratulate you on your degree. "What are you planning to do?" she asks. "You know, we've budgeted for a music director. Is that something that interests you? Think you might want to apply?"

As a matter of fact, you have just spent hours thinking about what instruments could support the prayers effectively and where the cantor should sing a cappella. The music today missed a lot of opportunities to interpret the ancient words on the spiritual level. "I think I'd be very interested, yes," you answer.

After the holidays, you meet with the ritual committee and cantor to discuss the position. "Let's say we could assemble a string quartet for Yom Kippur," the cantor says. "Would you arrange an introduction to Kol Nidrei, to show us how you work?"

Your arrangement introduces the well-known theme of the prayer, repeating its initial notes to create anticipation for the entrance of the voice. The cantor naturally loves it. So do the others.

In short order, you are hired to direct the music at your old shul, a job that requires all the skills of a complete musical education. You assemble a volunteer choir, some of whose members don't read music and must learn material by rote. You compose or select material that fits their abilities. You accompany services on piano, and also plan and rehearse special programs.

Your career transcends musical performance; you give a voice to the souls of the congregants. You were born for this unique challenge. To the members of the synagogue, you are a blessing. ✡

One day, you're helping a friend assemble some donated furniture at a shelter for victims of domestic abuse. It takes most of the afternoon, time enough to absorb the atmosphere of the house. There are cooking and sleeping facilities, but not much comfort or warmth. No art or music. This is only a physical shelter.

You ask the director of the facility if she'd accept a piano, if you could find one. She has room and agrees, so you call a few newspaper ads, inquiring whether anyone would give a piano to the shelter and get a tax deduction. A month later, you've brought in a nice Baldwin upright and it's been tuned. You sit on the bench and begin to play Gottschalk's "Golliwog's Cakewalk."

Several round-eyed children sidle up to the piano and watch your hands move on the keys. A young mom, whose smile you haven't seen till now, begins bouncing her baby joyously in time to the music. When the piece ends, there's an instant chorus of "Don't stop!" And you play a mazurka by de Falla, a Bach two-part invention, and Beethoven's "Für Elise."

All the shelter's residents by now are in the room, and after the first shy question from a five-year-old – "Can I touch the piano?" – there's a flood of excited conversation. The women tell of their first memories of being moved by music, and the kids discuss which compositions they like best. You take several children onto your lap and show them a C major scale, then a C major chord. They're amazed to see what music looks like.

You show them the D and G chords, and a little girl named Molly giggles with delight. "Listen to this," you say to her, and sing "Good Golly, Miss Molly" playing just those chords.

The group is buzzing enthusiastically now, and they won't let you leave until you commit to come back very soon. You drive away wondering where you can get the kids some guitars.

Clearly, something's changed in that house. Though you haven't solved their very real problems – the reasons they're in a shelter – somehow their spirits have been elevated. They almost seem more optimistic, if that's the right word.

Thinking for the first time about the *absence* of music, it occurs to you that prisons, too, provide no connection to what is beautiful and immortal, other than prayer services and possibly some books. Those are places where it's difficult to build up the strength and hope successfully to re-enter society. You know that music can help relieve despair and bring a sense of peace.

Your investigation of the relevant government agencies reveals that there is no music program in any jail or prison, municipal, state, or federal. Some hospitals have regular visits by musicians, but that's because patients are seen as more deserving than convicts – as if prisoners' welfare doesn't affect society.

But learning and making music is much more important than most people know. It requires discipline, and builds a habit of mutual respect. It acknowledges personal history and culture. And it means that one's voice will be heard. All these factors change a person's self-image and the prison environment, and they filter outward to families and community.

It takes months of persistence to get to see a warden at the Cook County Jail, and all your eloquence to convince him to give the idea a chance. He thinks it's a waste of time, but you promise that your program will be organized through the prison ministry, which has programs already in place. You will be allowed to try.

The prisoners you and your partners meet are interested and grateful. Many come from cultures that value music; some are experienced instrumentalists. For others, you offer a new means of self-expression. You're allowed to leave a few instruments in the prison library, with instructional audiotapes. It takes time, but music begins to change lives in this severe, cold place.

You have only begun. Grant money lets you hire an administrator to engage musicians, arrange logistics and set up schedules. You're in demand for interviews and lectures; many people have never thought about what music can achieve in under-served communities.

But you always reserve some time to share your art personally: the piano is your true connection. Thank you.

Chapter Eleven

I Want to Organize the Workers

There were several reasons why so many Jewish Americans had leadership positions in the urban labor movement.

For one thing, capitalism in this country was growing rapidly and was nearly unrestricted by laws. Huge fortunes were being made in industry – made possible by the work of poor immigrants.

For another, after devastating riots against Jewish communities in Eastern Europe began in the 1880s, over two million Jews from Romania, Austro-Hungary and Russian immigrated to the United States, generally settling in crowded city districts.

And, last, a large number of these Jewish immigrants had been part of the Labor Bund movement in the old countries, which worked toward legal equality for Jews, gender equality for women, and a socialist approach to society: the democratization of workplaces, with workers sharing the profits.

So, this combination of circumstances was fertile ground for the formation of unions in the U.S. Some of the leaders you'll meet in this chapter are Joseph Barondess, Samuel Gompers, Daniel De Leon, Pauline Newman, Clara Lemlich, Meyer London, Rose Schneiderman, and Lillian Wald. They and other organizers helped to form the United Hebrew Trades, the American Federation of Labor, the Socialist Labor Party, the International Ladies Garment Workers Union, Workmen's Circle, the Hebrew Free Loan Society, the Women's Trade Union League, the American Civil Liberties Union, and the Henry Street Settlement.

Today, we are still benefitting from their work. Their memories will be a blessing forever.

It is March of 1886.   You are fifteen years old, and have just stepped off the ship from Hamburg, Germany.   You stand with thousands of other immigrants in the Great Hall at Ellis Island, New York.   It was a ten-day crossing, but you feel a million miles from your home city of Dniepepetrovsk, Ukraine.

After proving your health and financial security – you have ten dollars in your pocket – you walk the crowded, noisy streets of the Lower East Side to find the Orchard Street tenement building where your cousin lives.   Someone tells you in Yiddish that he'll return from work at eight.   You set your old leather suitcase down on the front stoop and sit down to wait, and look around.

The smells of boiled cabbage and fish are familiar; the spicy Hungarian and Polish cooking isn't.   You hear Irish, Yiddish, German and Italian accents.   People are loud and pushy.   And exhausted.

Finally your cousin arrives, hugs you hard, and peppers you with questions about the voyage.   You follow him up the dark stairway to his dingy room, where two men are working at sewing machines, cloth piled high on the floor next to them.   "I share the room with these fellows; we each pay $1.25 a month," he says. "I'll cover your rent till you get work."   The other men barely look up; they are obviously intent on sewing as fast as they can.

He shows you where the outhouses are behind the building, and asks the balesboosteh for some soup left over from supper.   Your father is a tailor back in the Ukraine, and you can sew; your cousin says he'll bring you to the cloak factory where he works tomorrow, to ask for a job.   This sounds good.   You want to earn money to send your family, so they can come here too.

"Nu, I haven't seen you for such a long time," your cousin says. "What are you hoping for your future?   Do you want to work your way up into management?   Or do you want to see the whole capitalist system overthrown, and the workers take over?"

If you accept the American system as it is, turn to page 199.

If you think that the workers should own the factories, turn to page 200.

You arrive at the cloak factory where your cousin works, which occupies an entire floor of a building near Broadway. Men, women, and even young teenagers are seated at rows of tables, bent over sewing machines. As you follow your cousin past them to find the foreman, you look at their faces: pale, with dark circles beneath their tired eyes. It is seven-thirty in the morning, and they will keep sewing, sewing, sewing till long past dark, with no breaks and no fresh air.

The foreman looks you over, asks a few questions about your knowledge of the machines; satisfied, he says you can start tomorrow. You are to arrive at seven in the morning and leave at ten at night – no weekends off. Four dollars a week.

Without much choice, you agree. Arriving on time, you are assigned a place at a machine and told to sew hems on the pile of cloaks next to your feet. As fast as you sew, the cloaks arrive even faster. Your back begins to hurt from hunching over the work, and you inhale wool fibers constantly. During a brief lunch break, you swallow some bread and apples as fast as you can before the foreman barks at you to get back to work. After fifteen hours, the workers are allowed to go home, to drop bone-weary into bed.

This daily existence continues, except for a few holidays. When you're sick and must stay home, you earn nothing. After a year you haven't saved enough to buy $30 steamship tickets for your family; and you wonder, why should you bring them to this?

As you leave work one evening, a young man is outside the door, handing flyers to anyone who will take them. "The capitalists live in luxury!" he's shouting in Yiddish. "They rob us of our labor and leave us nothing! How are they any better than the Tsar? Our only strength is in our numbers. Join the trade union!"

You read the flyer he handed you. It invites you to a meeting in a synagogue on Hester Street two nights later. The next morning, you discuss the meeting, quietly, with other workers.

If you decide to go with a few others to the meeting, turn to page 201.

If the stories you've heard about police shooting and beating union strikers are too scary, and you don't want to unionize, turn to page 202.

After several failed attempts at revolution against the Russian government, millions of Jews emigrated to America. Many were skilled in the clothing trade, one of the few occupations permitted to them in Russia. Some felt that factories and farms should be democratically owned and controlled. They were socialists.

You agree with them: the workers' situation in America is close to slavery, and capitalists will never voluntarily treat their employees humanely. They will pay poverty wages, give no benefits, and they won't maintain safe workplaces. When you go to the sweatshop with your cousin, you look for other workers who have the spirit and determination to organize. And you find them.

But the shop foreman takes you aside to warn you that unions are not allowed in this factory. "You want better wages? Go somewhere else!" he shouts. "There are plenty of people outside who want your job. I don't wanna hear no more union talk!"

A few weeks later, a section of the factory ceiling comes loose and falls on a young woman, causing a serious head injury. She can no longer work, and her elderly parents will be forced to seek charity. The sweatshop owner, who never makes repairs to anything in the shop except the sewing machines, is unsympathetic. "It's bad luck," he says, and orders everyone back to work.

The workers are outraged. "It's *your* bad luck!" they shout at him bitterly, and stand up and walk out. You lead the exodus.

Outside the factory, the workers look around, surprised by their own courage. You draw a deep breath, and then announce to passers-by, "This capitalist stands in the blood of workers!" Then you say it again, louder. The others join you. It becomes a chant.

A policeman arrives to tell you that you're disturbing the peace. He orders you to disperse. Then, a man nearby begins to sing, in a powerful baritone, "Arise, you prisoners of starvation; arise, you wretched of the earth," and some of the workers sing along.

If you tell the policeman that you have the right to speak, go to page 203.

If you look beyond this local dispute to try to build a massive labor movement, go to page 204.

Arriving at the Bialystoker Synagogue at 9:00, you find a seat at the back of the sanctuary; the room is already crowded. A few of your cloak-maker friends are there. Most people are speaking Yiddish; but some are speaking Russian or German.

Mr. Joseph Barondess ascends the bima and introduces himself. "I would like to welcome the workers of the cloakmaker shops," he announces dramatically. "I greet you in the name of the United Hebrew Trades. We are from many occupations, fighting in solidarity for decent conditions, a living wage, so we can live as human beings, not animals!" A cheer rises from the crowd.

"Does your employer forbid a union in your shop? But he does not have that right! We are in America now. You can associate with whomever you wish. And when your workers form a local, you will become one of the United Hebrew Trades. Tailors, cap-makers, cigar-makers, and workers of every kind will be beside you in the struggle! When you strike, all will strike with you! In solidarity, there is power!"

Excitement flutters through the workers, and you join those surging forward to sign up for the union and receive membership cards. The next morning, nervously hopeful, you return to work, mentally listing the changes you want to see in the factory.

Over the next several months, you meet frequently with the shop stewards of other factories, drawing up a list of demands to present to the owners. You begin with the condition that the shops may only employ union members, and must pay union wages.

The owners do not agree, and a strike is called. The strikers picket the factories, not allowing 'scabs' to cross the line and work for starvation wages. The union members outlast the factories, and finally a settlement is reached; you go back to work for more money. Finally, you can save money to send your family, and open your own bank account.

If you're tired of working for wages, and decide to use your savings to become a clothing subcontractor, turn to page 205.

If you have seen so much misery in the tenements that you want to force landlords to be more responsible to their renters, turn to page 206.

You remain at work when, a few months later, many of your fellow employees walk out. They've joined the Cloakmakers Union and demand higher wages and an all-union shop.

It's a nerve-wracking experience to cross their picket line the next morning. Hundreds of strikers are holding signs in English and Yiddish saying "Workers Need a Living Wage" and "We Demand a Safe Workplace." You squeeze quickly between two strikers, and the air fills with their shouts: "Scab, scab, scab!"

You're shaken as you walk up the stairs to the factory floor. Your own friends were screaming at you. By crossing their line, you are no longer one of them. The foreman pats you on the shoulder and assures you that your loyalty won't be forgotten. It's strange to sit at your sewing machine with only four or five other workers in the big room.

The foreman and the owner pace irritably, stopping only to peek at the picket line. They have orders to fill, and you can't possibly produce all the garments they need for their customers. They will soon lose their contracts. Within a week, they give in. They hire back the union members on their terms.

But the union will not tolerate workers who aren't members – people who enjoy the benefits of the strike without risking anything or paying dues. You are offered a choice: join the union or go find other work.

If you regret that you didn't stand with the strikers, and feel that getting a union wage is worth paying union dues, turn to page 207.

If you leave to find other work, turn to page 208.

"This is America!" you yell at the policeman, and begin to quote the First Amendment to the Constitution: "Congress shall make to law abridging the right of the people peaceably to assemble ..." He swings his nightstick at your head and everything goes black.

You awaken in a charity hospital. A portly, well-dressed man with a moustache is sitting beside your bed. You stare at him.

"Young friend, it appears that you've incurred the wrath of the authorities," he tells you. "I commend your courage. The workers must take what is rightfully theirs, even at such a cost. My name is Samuel Gompers," he adds.

"What ... who ... ?" you stammer, unable to understand.

"I'm with the American Federation of Labor, a union of unions," Gompers explains. "I live in Chicago, but I'm visiting New York to meet with labor leaders here. I heard about your run-in with the authorities, so I dropped by to wish you well. Tell me what happened? And how do you feel?" he inquires kindly.

You sit up, sending a flash of pain through your forehead. "A cop failed to understand that all wealth is the product of labor. So he used the tactic of the ignorant. He hit me," you tell him.

He laughs. "I like you, you're tough! Are you tough and smart?"

"Smart and tough people have told me so," you answer.

Gompers becomes very serious. "Listen, the shirtwaist workers are struggling to organize, and other garment workers as well. There are some local unions, but they need to federate. A few talented leaders are doing their best. Can you help?"

The AFL provides a stipend better than what you earn at the factory, and you agree to organize in the clothing industry. During the last decade of the century, you hold meetings, make speeches, walk picket lines, and build up the membership of several locals.

If you decide that economic assistance is the way to help immigrants 'find their feet' in the new country, turn to page 209.

If politics is the best way for you to be useful to workers, go to page 210.

The workers disperse, unhappily, but you remain to talk to the baritone who had led the singing of the Internationale, the socialist anthem. "What is your trade?" you ask him in Yiddish.

"Can't you tell? I'm so hurt," he jokes, "I'm a singer. I'm in the chorus union." Chorus union? You think he's still joking.

"But it's true!" he insists. "Wherever there are workers, there are unions, or there should be. There's vest makers, actors, pressers, trunk makers, bookbinders – Italian, Polish, Irish, lots of people. But many unions are mostly Jewish, especially clothing workers. So the Socialist Labor Party is organizing the United Hebrew Trades, to give us a louder voice. The union makes us strong!"

Factories continue to expand in all the trades. They operate with coal power, like railroad trains, steel production, and steamships. Millions immigrating from abroad find employment in steel-making and other urban trades, and coal-belt counties attract workers to the mines. These people are constantly endangered by dangerous and unhealthy conditions, long hours, and few benefits. Black lung disease, lead poisoning, and byssinosis shorten lives, and industry and government offer little help.

Your chorister friend brings you to a speech by socialist Daniel De Leon, a Sephardic Jew from Curaçao who believes that industrial unions will lead the class struggle in a Marxist revolution against capitalism. He argues that low wages are essential to capitalism, and that all workers must take the first step against it by organizing. De Leon is supported by many discontented workers who dream of an idealistic, economically equal society.

You agree with him in theory, but are very concerned that unions don't treat female workers as the equals of men. Though women strikers are beaten and arrested just like men, they often do not receive the strike benefits or leadership roles that men receive.

If you campaign within the new International Ladies Garment Workers Union to accept women workers as labor leaders, turn to page 211.

If you think it's more realistic to form a new union of women workers, turn to page 212.

Moving to a larger apartment, you invest in two sewing machines, hire a cutter and two operators, and obtain orders for a quantity of cotton shirts for a factory that will provide the finishing. You purchase the cloth from a textile wholesaler, provide thread, patterns and equipment, and launch your operation.

After a month, you examine your accounts. To turn a good profit, you see you'll have to lower your workers' wages, or else produce more shirts than you do now. Pondering the question the next morning, you watch your workers come in and start work. You grow impatient for them to return quickly from their lunch break. They sense your discontent, and become quiet, worried.

One operator is fifteen years old – a bright kid, but not too quick at the sewing machine. You consider replacing him with another employee, when it occurs to you that you were exactly his age – and just as desperate – when you arrived here and started work.

What have I become? you ask yourself, and the answer is unbearable. You use your neighbors the same way the cloak factory owner once used you. You are no better. Suddenly, you stand up.

"Stop!" you call out, and the workers look at you, alarmed.

"*Tayere chaverim,*" you say, "dear friends. I must make a change. I can no longer make my living from your misery. There is money to be made in this business, certainly, enough to give us all a decent life. This is what I propose. When these machines are paid off, and we can accumulate an operating fund for supplies, let's form a company and share the profits. We'll work together, and everyone will have a hand in his own destiny. God did not put me on earth to stand on the necks of others. Do you agree?"

It takes some long moments for the workers to understand what you're saying. They look at each other to see whether they heard you correctly. A smile spreads around the room. Then, embraces.

Together, you work even harder than before, but with dignity and hope. The business grows, and within a generation, it's a fashion cooperative known throughout the garment industry. When you finally retire after many years, it occurs to you: maybe you're a bit of a socialist after all. ✡

The security of working in a union shop is a fine thing, and you stay at the factory for fifteen years. There are occasional disputes, and sometimes your local must strike in solidarity with other workers; but generally life is good, as management comes to accept the reality of organized labor. You spend many evenings speaking with non-union workers, explaining the advantages of affiliation and calming their fears.

Union membership lets you to save a little money and, eventually, marry and start a family. Having children makes you even more aware of the unhealthy conditions of tenement life. Lack of sanitation brings smallpox, cholera and tuberculosis. People live in dark apartments without windows, bathrooms, even running water. So it's a rude surprise in 1907 when landlords, acting together, announce a rent hike: a two-room apartment is now $20 a month, up from $15, with no building improvements.

Soon after, there's a knock at your door. Two young ladies introduce themselves and ask you to support a 'rent strike' they're organizing all over lower Manhattan. "What an idea!" you agree. "How many tenants will strike? And who's organizing this?"

"We're hoping 10,000 tenants will hold back rent," they answer. "We demand that rents be lowered. And it's Pauline Newman who started it. She's wonderful!"

It's not long before you encounter Miss Newman herself, giving a speech at a social club. She's tough, assured, and effective. Though the rent strike is only partly successful, it gives tenants a sense of their collective power. Tenement activism is energized. The next year, Newman runs for secretary of state as a socialist, campaigning for women's right to vote. And after organizing a women's general strike in the garment industry, she begins working for the International Ladies' Garment Workers Union.

After the catastrophic Triangle Shirtwaist Factory fire in 1911, which kills 146 employees, New York State establishes a Factory Investigation Commission. You apply to be a FIC inspector, and find yourself working alongside Pauline Newman. This is not just a job – it's a sacred calling, and you're proud to do it. ✿

You ask your fellow workers for their forgiveness; your fear had stopped you from walking out with them. You're grateful for the chance to join the Cloakmakers Union, and pledge to support it.

In 1900, two thousand garment workers, mostly Jewish immigrants, join their locals together to form the International Ladies' Garment Workers' Union, which will affiliate with Samuel Gompers' American Federation of Labor. This includes your local, and you volunteer to serve on the district council.

But the fight has only begun. Management still has the upper hand in disputes, and supervisors can be abusive, factories lack ventilation, and workers can be fired whenever foremen wish. Locals frequently strike, but few changes are made. Picketers are still beaten and jailed. Stronger measures are needed.

At an ILGWU joint board session, late in 1909, you propose that a mass membership meeting be called. "The workers themselves must determine the course we take," you declare. The meeting is held on November 22, at the Cooper Union. A young woman from Local 25 comes to the speakers' platform, moving slowly; some of her ribs were recently broken by factory gangsters.

"I am Clara Lemlich. I wish to hear no more talk. We must decide whether to strike. I move that we go out on general strike!"

A strike vote is taken, and 20,000 shirtwaist workers walk off the job – an action that lasts six weeks. This time, the strikers win. Management signs contracts at dozens of shops, and the settlement includes higher wages, shorter hours, and somewhat better working conditions in many factories.

Lemlich's charisma inspires you. Following her suggestion, you join the fight for women's voting rights, because, as she says, until the legislatures represent women, women will have no rights.

Decades of strike actions have taught you the power of the picket line. You join National Women's Party members outside the White House in Washington, protesting President Wilson's failure to support the cause. It takes years, but finally Wilson changes his mind. To your joy, American women get the vote in 1920. ✡

Discouraged, and sick of the noisy, dirty city, you decide to take yourself into the country for a new life, maybe on a farm, working on the land and breathing fresh air. You sell what you own, and take the Hudson River Railroad north into Patterson, New York, in Dutchess County.

You tramp down country roads, enjoying the birds' songs and the beautiful rolling hills. It's almost spring, and the air is beginning to warm. Near the town of Beekman, you see a farmer in a meadow, loading rocks and stumps into a cart. You ask if he needs any help. He does, since he'd like to plant this field but it isn't yet cleared.

The work is hard, but satisfying. You sleep in the farmhouse and eat with the farmer's family. You learn to plow, and the field is ready for corn by April; then you tend the strawberry fields and lettuce all summer until harvest time. It's a pleasant life, and it stretches into a winter of repairing fences and clearing debris. The months turn into years. You make friends, plant your own roots, and spend your time reading books and carving wood.

One day, you hear people speaking Yiddish in the local lumber-yard. Surprised, you approach and greet them. It turns out that they're members of a new fraternal organization called the Workmen's Circle, and they are here to buy land for a vacation bungalow colony for their members. You certainly understand why city workers need a few summer weeks in the cool rural beauty that has become your home. You offer to help build the camp, and they gratefully accept.

It's on the shore of Sylvan Lake that you re-connect with your Jewish roots. Circle Lodge is a refuge for good, hardworking people committed to supporting each other, and all workers. They have set up health plans, education programs, burial bene-fits, and a pension fund so that workers can retire in comfort.

You spend half your time maintaining the Lodge facilities, and half doing farm work. Eventually, you are persuaded to return to New York City during the winter, to organize English and citizen-ship classes for new immigrants. This is the solidarity that you have always needed: the kind that comforts the soul. ✿

Not every union has the financial resources to rescue its members from disaster when illness or eviction strikes. There isn't any government assistance program to assist citizens who cannot work, nor any business loans for those seeking to pursue the American dream of self-sufficiency.

In fulfillment of the Torah command to lend money to the poor and charge no interest, a group of community leaders have started the Hebrew Free Loan Society. With a fund of $95, they begin to make loans as small as fifty cents. You know several people who could use some help paying for medical care, and for supplies to start businesses.

Since you believe enthusiastically in the mission of this Society, and you know how to keep financial records, you ask the Society's financial secretary if you can assist them. Mr. Markel tells you it's an enormous task to keep track of all the applicants as the program grows; would you like to take charge of the records for the Richmond section of Brooklyn?

The Society rents a storefront there, and soon you're spending three evenings a week interviewing borrowers, filling out forms, and writing reports for the main office. Sometimes, beneficiaries visit you long after the loans are repaid, to convey their gratitude and tell their stories. You're astonished at the power of even the smallest amounts of money. Children have received medicine and musicians have obtained instruments because of the Society. You even know of a peddler who was enabled to buy a cart-horse.

It's a life well spent, bringing the dreams of new Americans to within their reach. ✿

Gompers meets you for lunch after a morning in court. "The fur workers will have to pay a small fine for the recent strike action," he tells you. "But not much. And no jail time. What a lawyer we have. Ah! Here he comes now. Listen," he leans close to you and whispers. "Meyer London is going to run for Congress. If he asks for help, we're all saying yes. Because he never accepts one nickel for the work he does for unions. The man is a living saint."

A young man comes to your table, shakes hands with everyone, including the waiter, and sits. He listens attentively to the latest news of the cigar makers' union -- Gompers is their vice-president -- and they're soon arguing over immigration. London wants to let more people in, and Gompers wants fewer.

"So is this part of your campaign platform?" Gompers asks.

"Yes," London answers. "Also I'll propose a minimum wage for every American worker. I believe the government should institute unemployment insurance. And since the Constitutional rights of the children of slaves are not adequately protected, there must be strong laws passed against lynching. Also, employers must be compelled to give maternity leave to new mothers."

At this, everyone at the table laughs. "But I am quite serious," London continues. "If the workers are expected to carry the prosperity of the nation on their backs, then they must be supported and respected as every human deserves."

This is a candidate you could support with all your heart. "I want to help you run your campaign," you say. "I can organize rallies, I can write letters, I can give out handbills. Please allow me."

London smiles. "I am deeply grateful. It will be a tough fight for a socialist like me; but I do seem to have some popular support."

He loses three elections, but finally, in 1914, Meyer London goes to Washington. You go with him as his chief staffer, writing many speeches for him, including advocating higher taxes on the wealthy. After his tragic death in 1926, you carry on his work. You serve on the New York City Council, and later, on the National Labor Relations Board. The welfare of America's workers will always be your highest priority. ✡

Your role as a delegate of the cloakmakers' local to the ILGWU brings you to meetings with other delegates. Chatting with the Cloth Hat, Cap and Millinery Workers rep one day in 1903, he says to you, "Some lady from a non-union factory asked us for a charter. I don't understand the point of it. These women won't work for long; they'll leave to get married, and then what?"

There are so many things wrong with this opinion that you can hardly frame a response, and then you realize that you may know this lady. "Is her name Rose? Short, with bright red hair?"

"Yes, that's her. I told her to come back with twenty-five names."

"Oy, what a mistake you made," you warn the cap delegate. "She's a firecracker. She'll run right over you and keep going."

You are so right. Less than a year later, Rose Schneiderman is on the ILGWU's executive board. She is a leader of the gigantic shirtwaist workers' strike in 1909, and a vice-president of the Women's Trade Union League. You meet her in a night class at Hunter College, and ask what's going on in the shirtwaist trade.

"In the shirtwaist trade it's *shrekhlekh*," she says. "Factories without fire escapes. Foremen locking exit doors so the girls can't step outside to breathe for a moment. This will not end well."

It ends tragically in 1911, when a ninth-floor factory littered with flammable scraps catches fire. The workers are trapped; 146 die. "You are not excused!" she tells you, as she tells everyone. "Bring the message to the lawmakers. Picket the owners. Write to the newspapers. Organize rallies. We are humans, not property!"

You bring your local's entire membership to the office of state senator Robert Wagner, demanding safe working conditions for the million manufacturing employees in New York. He creates an investigating commission and asks the district attorney to prosecute the factory owners. But they are acquitted at trial.

Protective laws are passed, but it's not enough. Feeling that the government needs more encouragement to protect citizens' rights, you become a founding member, with Rose, of the American Civil Liberties Union – a friend to the voiceless and the oppressed. ✡

In all this massive popular movement to get legal and economic rights for the nation's oppressed workers, women have few leadership roles – and not because they don't want them. There seems to be a view that women are less important as workers because they're primarily wives and mothers.

In 1903, you have bronchitis, and seek treatment at the Henry Street Settlement, where a team of nurses treats everyone regardless of ability to pay. There you meet its director, Lillian Wald, and discuss the role of women in organized labor.

"Working women have supporters they don't know about yet," Miss Wald remarks. "I'm speaking of *wealthy* women. You should never underestimate the power of sisterhood."

It's an astonishing thought. Society ladies, in their pearls and furs, campaigning for sweaty tenement dwellers? But Nurse Wald sits down with social reformer Jane Addams and several female AFL members, probably over tea, and forms the Women's Trade Union League. When you hear of it, you contact Rose Schneiderman.

"I already know," she tells you. "And I'm joining. You come along too. This is an immense step forward."

Of course, Rose takes a leadership role and soon becomes a vice-president of the WTUL New York branch. Their demonstrations get respect and attention that others don't. Police don't beat well-dressed society women, and clothing manufacturers tend to settle with the unions when boycotted by their rich customers. WTUL members benefit from large contributions to their strike funds, and lawmakers open their doors to donors when they visit to demand justice for workers. These are victories.

But right now you're sitting in your tiny kitchen, watching your children play. In other places, other people's kids are working in textile mills, glassworks, and coal mines. Hundreds of them are killed, injured, or sickened at work every day. Their bosses know they are cheaper, less likely to complain – and highly replaceable.

It's only the beginning of the struggle.

Chapter Twelve

I Don't Want to Be a Slave

Every spring, Jews all over the world gather their families for the ancient ritual of the Passover seder. Reading from the haggada, we explain the symbols on the dinner table and re-tell the story of the exodus from Egyptian slavery.

*Throughout the seder, we try to follow the instruction of the ancient rabbis, to fulfill these traditions **as if we ourselves came out of Egypt.***

In pursuit of that goal, this chapter places you among the slaves of Pharaoh. It's a difficult, unhappy life. Your choices seem quite limited. How will you feel? Whom will you see? And, when you have a chance to take actions that will affect your situation – what will you do?

You are a young Hebrew in the Egyptian city of Pi Ramses in the year 1255 B.C.E. Like all the Hebrews in Egypt, and some other minorities, you and your parents are slaves.

When he was younger, your father worked in a copper mine near Pi Ramses, and your mother spent most of her life as a field worker. However, they and several others were sold to a nobleman before you were born. Now they are forced to labor in a brickyard, because their master is building a new home for himself.

Neither you nor your parents have ever learned to read or write. The only stories you know were told by your parents, who heard them from their parents. You are curious about the things and people you see, but at the end of the day, you're always too tired to ask questions.

Since you were six years old, you too have had to haul the straw and sand that is mixed with clay to make adobe bricks. Your back hurts almost all the time, and the skin on your hands is dry and cracked. But you rarely cry anymore – it does no good.

One morning, when the rising sun wakes you, your fingers are swollen and red. Some gritty sand has gotten into your cracked skin, and it feels like it's burning. You think that soaking your arms in the waters of the nearby Pelusa branch of the Nile River would make them feel better.

If you dare to slip away to bathe your sore skin, turn to page 215.

If you don't dare to be late to your work, turn to page 216.

The waters cool your burning skin as you sit in the river, hidden by the low-hanging branches of a willow tree. You can hear the far-away voices of men loading vegetables onto a barge. It feels sweet to rest here, and watch a white ibis stalking through the shallow tidal flat.

Suddenly you hear barking, and it seems to be getting nearer. You turn to see a yellow hunting dog running toward you, followed by a supervisor from the brickyard. You stand to run, but he sees you; it's no use. You've been found, and after kicking you hard several times, the man forces you back to work.

"There's no reason to keep living like this," you think to yourself as you haul sand on a woven mat to a mixing puddle. But you don't want to die either. Nearby, you see an older girl stomping straw into the clay. She looks angry.

"What are you thinking about?" you ask her.

"I'm wishing I lived a long time ago, with my ancestors," she says. "They had no masters. They were free to work for themselves."

"How do you know about this?" you ask.

She looks at you intently. "Because my grandparents told me. And they also told me that someday we'll be free, too."

You laugh bitterly; such an idea seems impossible. But then you begin to think: is it possible for slaves to become free?

If you cannot imagine that you could ever be free, turn to page 217.

If your imagination is captured by this idea, turn to page 218.

You hurry to work, but the pain in your hands brings tears to your eyes. You don't see a rock on the path, and you trip over it, falling hard. A searing pain shoots through your leg. It's broken!

Another slave calls your mother, and she rushes to your side. Several people carry you back to your hut, where they place you on the bed of straw where you sleep. An old woman pushes your bone into place and calls for two sticks to make a splint.

You're not going anywhere for a while. It will take over a month for your leg to heal. You'll be alone with your thoughts. Soaking your sore hands in a bowl of water that your brother brought you, you wonder about the future. Is this life all you can ever expect?

One afternoon, while everyone else is still at the brickyard, you hear a rustling next to the hut. As you're wondering what it could be, a short, scared-looking man runs in. His eyes widen when he sees you. He turns to run back out; but you call, "Wait! Who are you?"

You learn that the man is a Hebrew slave named Shva. He has run away from his master, the ruler of a small town, in order to find his wife. She has been sold to someone further north on the Nile Delta. Shva loves her so much that he cannot bear to be without her.

"But," you ask him, "What will you do if you find her? Where can you go? Certainly someone will see you and tell your master where you are. People get rewards for finding a slave and returning him. You'll be beaten for running away."

Shva looks at you sadly. "Are you going to turn me in?" he asks.

If the idea of a reward is so tempting that you decide to contact Shva's master, go to page 219.

If you would never add to Shva's misery by turning him in, go to page 220.

You have heard of an individual slave being given freedom, usu-ally at the end of his or her life, by a kind master – or a master who does not want to feed an old person who can't work very hard. But the idea of a whole group of slaves going free – that's absurd. No master would ever do that. It wouldn't make sense.

Thinking about the girl in the brickyard, you start to laugh at her ... but actually, you're angry. Why should she say something like that, pretending there's something to hope for? It's cruel to give illusions to suffering people. You feel she's mean and irresponsi-ble.

You shake your head, and decide never to listen to people who raise false hopes.

If you decide to remain silent and ignore people who share their dreams of freedom, turn to page 221.

If you decide to try to convince them to give up their hopes, turn to page 223.

You try to think about this logically. The Egyptians will never voluntarily free their slaves. They get too much benefit from their work. Slaves farm, transport and prepare food for rich Egyptians. They construct walls, storehouses, and homes. They mine copper and gold. All without any pay, just the minimal amount of food needed to sustain life.

So, freedom can only come when the Egyptians are forced to give up their slaves. But what force is that powerful? The rulers of the land, the pharaohs, are considered gods ... and who could be more powerful than gods?

That evening, as you crush grain into flour on a stone in front of your hut, you ask your mother, "Are there gods more powerful than the pharaohs?"

She stops scraping scales from a fish. There is a far-away look in her eyes. After a moment, she says, "My mother used to tell me that, long ago, there was one true God who created the world. That God is more powerful than anyone."

You are stunned. "Is this true? What's the name of the God?"

"That God was called Adonai."

"But where is Adonai now, mother?"

She smiles sadly. "I don't know, child. I don't know." Straightening up, she says, "Go bring some oil from the olive press, so I can start baking the bread cakes."

You put down the stone pestle and start toward the olive press. Then your mom adds, "Oh, and get four or five onions from the common garden."

If you go for the oil first, turn to page 222.

If you go for the onions first, turn to page 224.

Your leg is nearly healed, and you're able to limp slowly toward the master's house. Your sandals are made of woven papyrus leaves; they don't give your feet much protection from the rough path.

You're almost there when you see someone you know – a Hebrew slave about your age, who's sitting at a large bowl mixing ashes and animal fats to make soap.

"Hi!" he calls out. "You're on your feet! What are you doing here?"

You tell him about Shva the runaway slave, and add that you want to collect the reward for helping return him to his master.

Your friend suddenly loses his friendly smile. In a low voice he says, "I can't believe it. You're going to turn in your desperate brother. I would never have thought that of you."

"My brother?" you ask, shocked. "He isn't my brother. I've never seen him before."

"All slaves are brothers," shouts your friend. "You live in slavery yourself! You know exactly how he feels! If it were *you* on the run, and Shva saw you, what would you want him to do? Would you want him to betray you?"

Shocked into silence, you turn and begin to walk slowly back toward your hut. Your thoughts are confused. You wonder what your role is, in Shva's attempt to be free.

Suddenly you hear cries. In a field to your left, you see an Egyptian taskmaster viciously beating a field slave with a leather whip. The slave is on the ground, trying to roll away from the slashing blows. You've seen this happen before, but you're still horrified.

If you leave the scene because you feel so helpless, go to page 221.

If you stay to see if you can help after the taskmaster leaves, turn to page 228.

You give Shva some food and tell him to fill his leather pouch with water from the common pool. You look around to see that no one is watching, and point toward the north road. He thanks you and continues his journey to find his wife. You wish him well.

After Shva leaves, you discover that your leg has healed somewhat, and you can walk a little. Because you are bored of sitting alone in your hut for weeks, you decide to take a short walk. Nearby is a wheat field, and maybe you can talk to the field workers if there are no Egyptian supervisors around.

As you approach the field, suddenly you hear a scream, and then sobbing. Moving toward the sound, you also hear the whistling sound of a whip, and you soon see a taskmaster beating a slave who's lying on the ground. The slave is bleeding from the red whip-cuts on his back, legs and neck, and you see the agony in his face.

But the whipping continues. It seems the taskmaster isn't going to stop until his unfortunate victim is dead.

You feel you have to do something. You've seen so much suffering in your young life, and at this moment, it's just too much to take. But you're small, you have an injured leg, and no slave has ever fought back against an Egyptian.

If you decide to try to stop the whipping, turn to page 227.

If you hesitate a few moments more, turn to page 228.

The days drag on. The work never ends. Although you haven't even reached your twelfth birthday, your knee and elbow joints hurt all the time, and you cough constantly from clay dust.

"Maybe life wouldn't be so bad if we had just one day, once in a while, when we didn't have to work," you think. The masters rest whenever they like. Even their servants, the taskmasters, don't have to work every single day.

"One day of rest, that we could look forward to while we work. It would help to heal the body and the spirit. Time to sleep, to talk, to play."

But it's no use. These thoughts only make you more miserable.

One morning a supervisor comes to the brickyard to announce that the building project is almost finished. All slaves age ten and over who are now making bricks, will be sold to the Ka, the supervisor of the royal copper mines at Mughara.   A few will be sent to Thebes, to work in the garden of the Pharaoh, Ramses.

If you are sent to work in the mines, go to page 226.

If you are sent to Thebes, go to page 229.

At the oil press near the slave huts, you see a tall, old man leading an ox in circles around a huge, circular stone. The stone is pushing the oil from olives, and the oil is draining into a tub below it.

You have seen this man before, and you've always been a little afraid of him. His name is Aharon, and other slaves whisper that he's a magic-master. Children say he can strike illness into animals and people, though you don't know anyone who has seen this. But among the adults, Aharon is loved and respected. Husbands and wives who argue go to Aharon for advice, and peace comes to their homes. Likewise, Aharon counsels friends who are angry at each other, and he always helps to heal the friendship.

"Elder Aharon," you say to him, "may I ask you a question?"

Aharon smiles. "Certainly, dear child."

"Is there a God called Adonai?"

He stops the ox and looks at you quietly. "Yes. Adonai lives. Adonai is real." You ask, "Is Adonai stronger than the gods of the Egyptians?"

"Much, much stronger."

You ask, "But, whose God is Adonai?"

Aharon answers, "Adonai is the creator of all the universe. And Adonai is the God of your ancestors, Abraham and Sarah."

This idea is too stunning to comprehend. Slaves have a powerful God? How could this be? Then why are we still slaves?

"We can speak of this later, child," says Aharon. "I must go back to pressing the olives. Go in peace."

You take some oil, and then get some onions from the sandy soil of the slaves' garden, and head home. There you get shocking news: you and several other Hebrews will be sent tomorrow to the royal palace at Thebes. A disease has struck down many gardeners there, and they need more workers in the vegetable beds.

Turn to page 229.

One night you have a disturbing dream. In the dream, you are walking to the river because you feel thirsty. But there's no water in the river. You feel confused. Then you hear a voice saying, *"You have dried up the waters of hope."*

That's all the voice says, but in the dream, you understand the meaning. It means that because you can't imagine freedom, you're killing the dreams of your fellow slaves. Hope, like water, is what's keeping the slaves alive – even if they don't know it themselves. As long as you say there's no possibility of redemption from slavery, you are preventing any possibility of freedom.

If you decide to ignore the dream because you think it's meaningless, turn to page 226.

If you decide to go to a wise old slave and ask him to help you understand, go to page 222.

On your way back from the community garden, you hear the whinnying of a horse. That's an unusual sound around here; slaves have no horses, and nobody rich enough to ride a horse ever comes here. Following the sound, you're surprised to see a nobleman astride a beautiful gray mare. The horse is standing still, shaking her head, and the nobleman is looking toward the slaves' huts.

As you watch the horseman curiously, you suddenly get a bigger shock. There's a golden insignia on the man's breastplate. This is not just a nobleman. This visitor is a prince.

He sees you looking at him, and nudges the horse's ribs to approach you. You are terrified.

If you run away, go to page 225.

If your curiosity overcomes your fear, and you stay where you are, turn to page 231.

You go back to your hut. A dark depression settles upon you. Everywhere you look is fear, pain, and the endless, meaningless work that brings you no benefit – only survival to slave away for the Egyptians for another day, for the rest of your life.

As you walk, slowly and sadly, you hear a man's voice crying and screaming. Across a field, a slave supervisor is beating a worker with a stick. The slave is on the ground, begging for his life, but it's as if the taskmaster doesn't hear. He keeps hitting him, so hard that he could be breaking bones.

You stand as if paralyzed. Then you hear a pounding of horse's hooves! The Egyptian prince is galloping toward the violent scene! The taskmaster looks up in time to receive a powerful whack of the nobleman's staff. He falls dead instantly. There is silence except for the heavy breathing of the royal horse.

Slowly the rider dismounts. He looks toward the unfortunate slave; still lying on the ground, he appears to be unconscious. The nobleman bends over the slave, and asks, "Are you alive?" There is no response.

The slave's digging tool is lying on the ground nearby. Picking it up, the nobleman starts to dig a hole in the sandy earth. In a half-hour's time, the hole is large enough to hide the body of the task-master. He drags the body into it, covers it with sand, and quickly remounts his horse to rush away.

You come out of your hiding place and walk over to the injured slave.

If he is still unconscious, go to page 231.

If he's beginning to awaken, go to page 232.

You are horrified when you learn that you have been sold to a work platoon in the desert – the royal copper mines at Mughara.

Many of the mine workers are prisoners of war or convicted criminals. You are filled with dread as you follow the donkey caravan which brings supplies to Mughara. The mining itself is difficult and dangerous, and the desert surrounding the copper mines assure that no escape is possible.

Your first days are as bad as you imagine – even worse. You fear the other workers and the taskmasters. At least, underground it's a little cooler than up at the surface.

But your life is both unhappy and short. A stone wall crumbles one day and falls, killing everyone working at the back of the mine. You are among them. ✡

You hobble toward the brutal scene. "Stop!" you yell. The task-master turns with fury in his eyes. He walks to you and raises his arm, landing the whip on you repeatedly as the other slave lies dying.

The pain is unbearable. As your blood runs freely into the sandy soil, your last thought is: "Will no one ever stop this cruelty? Is there no power on earth or in heaven to stop the Egyptians?" ✡

Your heart is pounding. Just as you decide to stop this terrible injustice or die trying, you hear running footsteps behind you. Hiding among the shrubs, you turn and see a tall man, wearing a beautiful robe, rush past you toward the taskmaster and the slave.

He reaches the scene, raises his staff and lands it hard on the taskmaster's head. The jeweled head of the stick sinks into his skull, and he falls like a stone.

Everything seems frozen in the sudden silence that follows. You watch the tall man look slowly around him. He cannot see you, as you've stayed hidden. You observe the jeweled cloth of his headdress and his gold arm-rings; this stranger is no slave. He's a nobleman, possibly a very important nobleman.

Where you get the courage to do the next thing, you don't know. You walk slowly toward the tall stranger. He sees you, and looks into your eyes with something that may be fear. You say to him:

"Sir, I thank you for your kindness. Would you like me to help you hide this man's body, or should I bind the slave's wounds?"

He keeps looking at you, but seems to relax a little. He answers:

"Peace be upon you. Please help this unfortunate man. His life is as sacred as any other. I will bury the taskmaster, who has brought even more evil to an evil place."

You are so stunned you nearly fall where you stand. The man is speaking to you in Hebrew – the language of the slaves.

Wordlessly you walk, as if in a trance, to the fallen Hebrew. As you pass the prince, he says to you: "I ask you not to tell anyone what you have just seen."

"I promise to you that I won't," you say to him. He smiles.

You kneel beside the injured man.

If he is unconscious, turn to page 232.

If he is conscious, turn to page 230.

In the gardens of the royal palace at Thebes, you work carrying skins of water to the plantings that are far from the irrigation trenches. It's quiet, lonely work.

One day the royal prince comes to inspect the gardens. This isn't too unusual, but you're totally shocked when he speaks to you. "You are from Pi Ramses, I think the master gardener said,"

You stand there open-mouthed. The Egyptian prince has spoken to you in Hebrew, the slaves' language. Finally you answer, "Uh – ah – yes, my lord, I have just come here from Pi Ramses."

He continues, "Do you know a family ...." He pauses. "I was riding there some time ago," he continues, "I saw an accident – a fight. A man was injured. Might you know if he recovered?"

Now you're confused. Of course you remember what happened. But why is this prince asking about the welfare of a slave?

The unforgettable event was not an everyday fight. A taskmaster had been beating a slave, when suddenly a nobleman appeared and killed the taskmaster. You remember it well – the injured slave was your friend. You stare at the man in front of you. Suddenly you realize who he is.

"Yes, my lord, your servant is now completely well." The prince nods happily, and you ask, "My lord, I am humbled to ask you, but was it not you who killed the taskmaster?"

Suddenly you hear a sound from behind a harvesting wagon. A gardener is staring wide-eyed at the prince. Suddenly he bolts in the direction of the great house.

You turn back to the prince. "Sire, if it was you who did this deed, you must run for your life! One who kills an Egyptian is judged a murderer. You are in terrible danger!"

The prince stares at you. "Yes, of course," he mumbles. Looking wildly around, he sees the royal stable. "P-peace be upon you," he stammers, and begins running to get a horse.

Turn to page 232.

The prince has finished burying the body of the taskmaster he has killed. He prepares to leave, while the injured Hebrew struggles into a sitting position.

"Did you see that?" the slave whispers.

"Yes, I did," you answer.

"What a maniac! A murdering maniac!" he continues.

"Yes, but he's dead now, and buried," you assure him.

"No, no, I mean the prince!" says the Hebrew. "He just blew in and killed the guy!"

You're surprised by the man's attitude. You say, "That prince saved your life! The taskmaster wasn't going to stop beating you – you were a goner!"

The slave seems disgusted. "He was a taskmaster. He was punishing me. That's what they do. He gets in trouble if I don't work hard. I accept that. But this prince dude, what was *that* all about?"

You are astonished.

He continues, "Maybe he'll be back tomorrow and kill us, too; did you think of that? No, you didn't, because you're so dazzled that he's a prince. He's a maniac, that's what he is."

You conclude this man is too stupid to understand anything. You stand up. It's not even worth while fighting him – it won't accomplish a thing.

Turn to page 232.

The horse and rider approach. You find the bravery to look into the man's eyes. He is watching you, too, very intently, as if he wants to ask something. You suddenly remember to bow to him.

"No, rise!" he says quickly. "You must bow to no man."

This is quite a surprising thing to say. But the bigger surprise is: he said it to you in Hebrew. The language of the slaves. All you can do is stare. You're still frozen in a half-bow.

"My lord," you finally manage, "how may I serve you?"

The nobleman dismounts. He is silently pensive. You say, "A visit from such a noble Egyptian is a great honor, my lord."

He answers quietly, "I am not your lord – and I am no Egyptian. I was born among the Hebrew slaves."

This is just completely baffling. A Hebrew – dressed as an Egyptian – riding a horse? He continues: "My family still toils under the whips of the Egyptians. I hear my people's groans in the fields, the brickyards. I must help them, but I don't know how."

Suddenly you remember what Aharon had said. On impulse you say, "A Hebrew elder told me that Adonai was the God of my ancestors Abraham and Sarah. Were they your ancestors, also?"

The prince's keen look sees into your heart. "My mother told me of Abraham and Sarah. And the God of our ancestors – Adonai is real. I have not heard the voice of our God; maybe Adonai is out there in the wilderness. But I know that the power of Adonai can redeem my people from slavery. My prayer is to hear that voice."

This man has said the same thing your mother told you. You say to him, "Peace be upon you. May we meet again in good health."

And the prince mounts his horse again, and rides away.

That night you dream of Adonai, and of freedom. ✡

You realize you have been a witness to something extraordinary. An Egyptian prince has risked his life to defend a Hebrew slave. The thought occurs to you that someone else knows about it, too. What if the injured slave is tempted to tell the authorities about this murdering prince?

And, also extraordinarily, this strange prince speaks Hebrew – a language he certainly never learned in the palace of the Pharaoh. Except for his clothing, he doesn't seem Egyptian at all.

Something is happening – you're not sure what. You sense that this man is very, very important, and that what he did means that some kind of change is coming.

You call out to the departing prince, "You must escape Egypt to save yourself. But I hope that I'll see you again someday. I'll be waiting for you."

And with a light heart and a mind full of questions, you return to your work.

Glossary of Foreign Terms

arpeggio – *the notes of a musical chord played in successon (Italian)*
Ashkenazic – *descended from Jews of the Rhine (Hebrew)*
bagatelle – *a short, light, musical composition (Italian)*
baleboosteh – *lady of the house (Yiddish)*
baytl – *wallet (Yiddish)*
bellisimi abiti – *beautiful clothing (Italian)*
bima – *elevated area in a synagogue sanctuary*
Bist du a klezmer? – *Are you a musician? (Yiddis`h)*
bon ami – *good friend (French)*
bubbie – *grandma (Yiddish)*
caprice--*a lively, free-form musical composition (Italian)*
la causa – *the cause (Spanish)*
diaspora – *Jewish population outside of Israel (Greek)*
drek – *crap (Yiddish)*
dybbuk – *a restless spirit that inhabits a living person (Yiddish)*
Es la primera luna llena del otoño – *It's the first full moon of autumn (Spanish)*
Es la tradición de mi familia – *It's my family's tradition (Spanish)*
fleischig – *of or having to do with meat (Yiddish)*
frish fleysh – *fresh meat (Yiddish)*
gefilte – *filled (Yiddish)*
golem – *a clay being, brought to life with mystical powers (Hebrew)*
goyische – *non-Jewish, literally "of the nations" (Yiddish)*
gragger – *a noisemaker used to drown out Haman's name on Purim*
groyse dank – *great thanks (Yiddish)*
Hadassah – *Jewish women's medical/educational society (Hebrew)*
haggada – *the guide book for the Passover seder (Hebrew)*
hallah – *braided egg bread eaten on Shabbat eve (Hebrew)*
Hanukkah – *festival of lights celebrating the Maccabee war (Hebrew)*
Hoy es viernes – *Today is Friday (Spanish)*
kiddush – *collation after services; prayer sanctifying Shabbat (Hebrew)*
kishkes – *guts (Yiddish)*
klezmer – *improvisational Jewish music of Eastern Europe (Yiddish)*
knip – *pinch (Yiddish)*
Kol Nidrei – *the first prayer of the Yom Kippur services (Hebrew)*
kosher – *permitted to be eaten according to Jewish law (Hebrew)*
koyf zhe beygelekh – *buy bagels (Yiddish)*
la razón – *the reason (Spanish)*

lokshen – *noodles (Yiddish)*
mazurka – *a strongly-accented folk dance in triple meter (Polish)*
meshuggeh – *crazy (Yiddish)*
mitsva – *a Jewish obligation (Hebrew)*
nebbish – *a weak, unimportant person (Yiddish)*
nisht gut – *not good (Yiddish)*
No sé la razón – *I don't know the reason (Spanish)*
oeufs brouilles -- *scrambled eggs (French)*
parve – *food that is neither meat nor milk (Yiddish)*
Por que? – *Why? (Spanish)*
Por que las velas? – *Why are there candles? (Spanish)*
Rosh Hashana – *the Jewish New Year (Hebrew)*
Ryhim Ahoovim – *Beloved friends (Hebrew)*
sabra – *a native-born Israeli (Hebrew)*
schlepping – *dragging (Yiddish)*
schlub – *slob (Yiddish)*
schmaltz – *fat, usually chicken fat. Also, sentimentality (Yiddish)*
seder – *the home table ceremony for Passover (Hebrew)*
Sephardic – *descended from the Jews of Spain (Hebrew)*
Shabbat – *the seventh day of the week, a holy day of rest (Hebrew)*
shmatta – *clothing, literally "rag" (Yiddish)*
shreklekh – *horrible (Yiddish)*
shtetl – *a little town populated by a Jewish community (Yiddish)*
siddur – *the Jewish prayerbook (Hebrew)*
Sof odom moves – *Man's end is death (Ashkenazic-accented Hebrew)*
Talmud – *the ever-expanding volumes of Torah explanation (Hebrew)*
Torah – *the first five books of the Hebrew Bible (Hebrew)*
Tsar – *Russia's ruler before the 1917 Communist revolution (Russian)*
Tsuriss – *trouble (Yiddish)*
Tu B'Shvat – *the festival of trees, now an ecological and Zionist holiday*
treif – *food that's not kosher, not permitted to observant Jews (Hebrew)*
yeshiva – *Jewish school for the study of Torah and Talmud*
yiddische/r – *Jewish (Yiddish)*

Jewish Historical Figures in This Book

Paula Abdul – singer and choreographer
Bella Abzug – activist lawyer and U. S. Congresswoman
Luther Adler – actor
Stella Adler – actor and acting teacher
Martin Agronsky – broadcast journalist
Mel Allen – sportscaster
Woody Allen – comedian, writer and director
Benjamin Altman – clothing retailer
Henry Angel – shop owner
S Ansky – Yiddish playwright
Nathan Appel – businessman
Isaac Asimov – author
Harry Attman – deli entrepreneur
Joseph A. Bank – clothing retailer
Joseph Barondess – labor organizer
Jacob Benjamin – abolitionist
Jack Benny – comedian
Dave Berg – MAD Magazine cartoonist
Gertrude Berg – radio and stage actor
Len Berman – sportscaster
Carl Bernstein – newspaper journalist
Ellen Bernstein – environmental activist
Leonard Bernstein – composer, conductor, pianist and educator
Mel Blanc – cartoon voice actor
Wolf Bluestein – businessman
Judy Blume – children's author
August Bondi – abolitionist
David Bromberg – singer, musician and arranger
Mel Brooks – screenwriter, comedian, actor, director
Art Buchwald – political satirist
Isidore Bush – shop owner
Sid Caesar – comedian
Hattie Carnegie – clothing designer
Morris Carnovsky – Yiddish theater actor
Solomon Carvalho – artist and explorer
Emmanuel Celler – Congressman
Bennet Cerf – author and editor
Erwin Chargaff – biochemist

Leo Cherne – humanitarian
Jerry Cohen – civil rights lawyer
Barry Commoner – environmental activist
Myron Cope – sportscaster
Howard Cosell – sportscaster
Norman Cousins – environmental activist
Jack Dann – science fiction writer
Avram Davidson – science fiction writer
Jacob Davis – tailor
Daniel De Leon – labor organizer
Selma Diamond – television writer
Kirk Douglas – actor
Isadore Dyer – politician
Bob Dylan – songwriter
Tilly Edinger – evolutionary biologist
Albert Einstein – physicist
Alfred Eisenstaedt – photojournalist
Will Elder – MAD Magazine cartoonist
Gertrude Elion – biochemist
Harlan Ellison – science fiction writer
Lee Falk – superhero comic creator
Howard Fast – author
Jules Feiffer – cartoonist
Al Feldstein – MAD Magazine cartoonist
Edward Filene – clothing retailer
Bill Finger – superhero comic creator
Anne Frank – diarist
Victor Frankl – author
Betty Friedan – civil rights activist and lawyer
William Gaines – MAD Magazine editor
Marshall Ganz – civil rights activist
John Garfield – actor
Larry Gelbart – television writer
George Gershwin – songwriter and composer
Stan Getz – jazz composer and musician
Adam Gimbel – clothing retailer
Hermione Gingold – actress and singer
Norman Ginsbury – playwright
Joseph Glaser – activist rabbi
Tom Glazer – songwriter

Marty Glickman – athlete and sportscaster
Samuel Gompers – labor organizer
Benny Goodman – clarinetist and bandleader
Steve Goodman – singer and songwriter
Max Gordon – music impresario
Louis Gottschalk – composer
Stephen Jay Gould – evolutionary biologist
Bill Graham – music impresario
Hank Greenberg – baseball player
Jack Greenberg – civil rights lawyer
Leivick Halpern – Yiddish playwright
Nathan Handwerker – hot dog entrepreneur
Sheldon Harnick – lyricist
Lillian Hellman – playwright
Gertrude Herzfeld – pediatric surgeon
Hochschild-Kohn – clothing retailers
Abbie Hoffman – anti-war activist
Judy Holliday – actor
Jay Horwitz – baseball media-affairs director
Leslie Howard – actor
Hutzler Brothers – clothing retailers
Janis Ian – singer and songwriter
Al Jaffee – MAD Magazine cartoonist
Billy Joel – songwriter, pianist, and singer
Elena Kagan – Supreme Court associate justice
Madeleine Kahn – singer and actor
Lucille Kallen – television writer
Martin Kamen – physicist
Bob Kane – superhero comic creator
Bruce Kaplan – record producer
Kivie Kaplan – civil rights activist and philanthropist
George S. Kaufman – playwright
Danny Kaye – comedian and actor
Jack Kirby – superhero comic creator
Anne Klein – clothing designer
Calvin Klein – clothing designer
Red Klotz – basketball player and coach
Sandy Koufax – baseball pitcher
Paul Krassner – anti-war activist
Robby Krieger – songwriter

Hilly Kristal – punk music impresario
Hedy Lamarr – actress
Rae Landy – Hadassah nurse
Kermit Lansner – magazine editor
Esther Lederberg – microbiologist
Stan Lee – superhero comic creator
Clara Lemlich – labor organizer
Murray Lender – bagel innovator
Primo Levi – author
Morris Loeb – businessman
Meyer London – labor lawyer and Congressman
Bernard Lutz – businessman
Albert Maltz – screenwriter
Stanley Marcus – clothing retailer
Lenore Marshall – environmental activist
Marx Brothers – film comedians
Bill Mazer – sports radio talk-show host and TV sports reporter
Abel Meeropol – songwriter
Sanford Meisner – actor
Al Michaels – sportscaster
Bette Midler – singer
Lewis Milestone – film director
Sally Milgrim – clothing designer
Arthur Miller – playwright
Marvin Minsky – computer scientist
Johnny Most – sportscaster
Allen Newell – computer scientist
Pauline Newman – labor organizer
Randy Newman – singer and songwriter
Phil Ochs – activist songwriter and singer
Clifford Odets – playwright
Miriam Ottenberg – newspaper journalist
Abe Pariser – baker
Mollie Parnis – clothing designer
Jan Peerce – opera singer
S. J. Perelman – humorist
Itzhak Perlman – violinist
Shirley Povitch – sports writer
Hal Prince – Broadway director
Joachim Prinz – activist rabbi

Luise Rainer – actor
Joey Ramone – punk rocker
Lou Reed – songwriter and singer
Carl Reiner – comedian, actor and writer
H.A. and Margaret Rey – children's authors
Malvina Reynolds – songwriter and singer
Abraham Ribicoff – U.S. Senator
Edward G. Robinson – actor
Paula Robison – flautist
Carl Rosen – clothing designer
William Rosenberg – founder of Dunkin' Donuts
Nettie Rosenstein – clothing designer
Ida Rosenthal – clothing designer
Lillian Ross – actor
Leo Rosten – humorist
Charlie Rothschild – folk music agent
Jacob Rothschild – activist rabbi
Sam Ruben – chemist
Jerry Rubin – anti-war activist
Albert Sabin – epidemiologist
Carl Sagan – astronomer
J. D. Salinger – author
Jonas Salk – epidemiologist
Marlene Sanders – broadcast journalist
Abe Saperstein – Harlem Globetrotters founder
Morris Schappes – magazine editor
Albert Schatz – microbiologist
Rose Schneiderman – labor organizer
David Schoenbrun – broadcast journalist
Daniel Schorr – broadcast journalist
Julius Schwartz – superhero comic creator
Maurice Sendak – children's author and illustrator
Art Shamsky – baseball player and manager
Joe Shuster – superhero comic creator
Sylvia Sidney – actor
Jerry Siegel – superhero comic creator
Beverly Sills – opera singer
Abe Silverstein – NASA aeronautics engineer
Shel Silverstein – author, cartoonist and songwriter
Carly Simon – singer and songwriter

Danny Simon – television writer
Herbert Simon – computer scientist
Joe Simon – superhero comic creator
Neil Simon – playwright and television writer
Donald Sobol – children's author
Stephen Sondheim – composer
Henry Sonneborn – clothing retailer
Sol Spiegelberg – businessman
Mark Spitz – Olympic gold-medalist swimmer
Lionel Stander – actor
William Steig – cartoonist
Saul Steinberg – cartoonist
Isaac Stern – violinist
Levi Strauss – entrepreneur
Barbra Streisand – actor, director and singer
Bert Sugar – sports writer
Arthur Ochs Sulzberger – newspaper publisher
Leo Szilard – physicist
Dave Tarras – klezmer musician
Elizabeth Taylor – actor
Sydney Taylor – children's author
William Taylor – activist lawyer
William Tenn – science fiction writer
Giuliana Cavaglieri Tesoro – chemist
Mel Tolkin – television writer
Lionel Trilling – author and critic
Leon Uris – author
Wolf Vishniac – microbiologist
Albert Vorspan – civil rights activist
Selman Waksman – microbiologist
Lillian Wald – public health nurse
Donald Weilerstein – music educator
Theodor Weiner – abolitionist
Fred Weintraub – music impresario
Victor Weisskopf – physicist
Billy Wilder – film director
Warner Wolf – sportscaster
Herman Wouk – author
William Wyler – film director
Charlotte Zolotow – author and book editor

ABOUT THE AUTHOR

Rabbi Shoshana Hantman grew up in the West Mount Airy section of Philadelphia, and was educated at Gratz College and the University of Pennsylvania. She received her ordination from the Reconstructionist Rabbinical College, and a master's degree in education from Temple University. Shoshana has served as both a congregational rabbi and a synagogue education director; in 1992, she founded the independent Halutsim Hebrew School. Rabbi Hantman lives in northern Westchester County, New York, with her husband Richard Weill and their two children. *Choose Your Path* is her second book.

64938497R00151

Made in the USA
Middletown, DE
20 February 2018